Marine Salvage Operations

MARINE SALVAGE OPERATIONS

By

EDWARD M. BRADY

Surveyor, United States Salvage Association, Inc.

CORNELL MARITIME PRESS

CAMBRIDGE   MARYLAND

1960

International Standard Book Number 0-87033-051-9
Library of Congress Catalog Card Number 59-12836
Printed and Bound in the United States of America
Copyright ©1960 by Cornell Maritime Press, Inc.

Second Printing   1966
Third Printing   1969
Fourth Printing   1972
Fifth Printing   1976

DEDICATION

To all men in this most hazardous business.
May they practice salvage with safety and
live to enjoy the fruits of their labors.

CONTENTS

ACKNOWLEDGMENTS

A view in retrospect usually reveals that many persons have been actively involved during the course of writing a book of this nature. It would be appropriate to list those whose efforts contributed to the completion of this work and to express my sincere thanks to them.

First, to the United States Navy, for providing some of the photographs used in this book and for the training received by the author at the United States Naval School, Salvage, Bayonne, N. J., which was the basic start for my intense interest in marine salvage;

To Submersible Operations Corporation, San Diego, California, for the photographs of shallow water diving techniques and the photographs of the equipment which they developed;

To Pacific Towboat and Salvage Company, Long Beach, California, for the photographs they provided;

To the following reviewers whose opinions and comments in the final stages proved most helpful: Mr. Johan J. Schoo, Lloyd's Classification Surveyor, Venezuela and Mr. Joseph K. Tynan, Principal Surveyor-Gulf District, United States Salvage Association, Inc.;

To Mr. Robert MacDonald, San Diego, California, compatriot and friend, in whose Casa much of this book was written;

To Mr. Lewis Holland, Naval Architect, VAZCA Shipyard, Maracaibo, Venezuela, for his efforts in checking some of the formulae and graphs for accuracy;

To Mr. E. P. Pulliam, Pacific Coast Manager, United States Salvage Association, Inc., whose early reading of the rough draft and encouraging comments prompted the successful completion of the manuscript;

To Mr. J. Paul Thompson, President, United States Salvage Association, Inc., whose consideration and interest contributed much to the early completion of this text.

Edward M. Brady
Hotel Chama
Maracaibo, Venezuela

PREFACE

In marine parlance, *salvage* is the act of saving a ship or its cargo. The word *act* is misleading somehow in its simplicity. It does not connote the imagery required to perceive the work often involved in salvage.

Since earliest times, salvage has been an arduous and often frustrating task. Present-day salvage methods are fairly similar to the earliest methods used, because the basic results required are similar —saving a ship and/or its cargo!

With the passage of time, one might be led to expect that salvage would become easier because of the improvement in equipment and the development of specialized techniques. However, this generally has not been the case for, even though equipment has improved, the size of the task has enlarged proportionally. This can be seen in the increase in size of vessels over the years in conjunction with the increasing complexity of their design. The result is that, in time, although we improve methods, as a result of time, we must apply them to a larger problem; one seems to balance the other—a requirement of nature.

In speaking of methods and equipment, it would seem the most important element in salvage has been overlooked—*man*. A pump and a method are only as effective as the man who uses them.

Know your principles, be able to apply them and you will do the best job possible in a given situation.

It is interesting to note a question posed to me in recent years: "What is to be done with various machinery, equipment and cargoes after they are salvaged (particularly after they have been submerged in salt water) so as to preserve and protect their residual value?"

Of course, aside from the actual salvage operation itself, the preservation and saving of material is the most important factor in successful remunerative salvage. The subject of preservation has not been covered in this book because it is not concerned with the immediate problem of ship salvage. In addition, it is a voluminous subject, in itself, concerning a complex and detailed task.

So, with apologies to those who are concerned with preservation, let us proceed to the *business* of marine salvage.

Edward Michael Brady

Marine Salvage Operations

CHAPTER I

TYPES OF SHIP SALVAGE

"Captain, know your ship," is a truism in the maritime world, and the captain who doesn't know his ship is a prime target for catastrophe. It is just as important that the salvor know his ship before he lays out a salvage plan or begins a salvage operation.

Design and construction plans should be studied and all principal information arranged in a ready reference form for checking as the salvage plan takes shape. This information may also be useful as the salvage operation progresses.

A knowledge of Naval Architecture and Marine engineering, ship construction, rigging, underwater cutting and welding, diving, compressed air operations, and numerous mechanical skills is essential for the salvage engineer. We include marine engineering because many of the salvor's problems are problems in Marine engineering and it seems to this writer that salvage engineering has long been a neglected subject.

This work does not delve deeply into the more technical and scientific factors that sometimes occur in ship salvage work, but it does cover the basic techniques, equipment, and problems of general ship salvage.

In most cases large ship salvage is described throughout; however, for small salvage operations, it is only necessary to scale down the size and scope of the required operations and apply the principles described.

Salvage is generally classified in three categories: strandings, sinkings, and rescue (towing).

STRANDINGS

We have heard many and diversified reasons for strandings; however, the *causes* will always remain the same: wind, sea, current, tide, etc. A vessel runs out of water due to an error in navigation or a mechanical failure. The results produced by stranding are surprisingly different, and it may reasonably be said that no two major strandings are alike.

1

Errors in navigation, proximity of land, excessive wind, heavy sea, unknown currents and sets, or mechancial failure are contributing factors to strandings.

When a vessel grounds, the question is generally raised, "How do we get off?" The answer to this is obvious: "Come off the way you went on!" That is, the tow, or pull, off shore should be in the same parallel, but opposite, direction as the vessel went aground.

When a vessel grounds, she usually suffers bottom damage, which may be extensive. Attempts should be made to determine internally the extent, if any, of bottom damage. It is useless to pull a vessel free of the ground, only to find that, upon refloating, a large hole in the bottom is exposed, with the result that the vessel floods uncontrollably and sinks. Inspect internally and externally, if possible. Maintain watertight integrity and isolate suspect compartments, holds, or shaft alleys. A large collision mat should be kept in readiness over the stern or bow, whichever is outshore, so that it may be used to cover any holes as the vessel is freed.

A vessel that has gone aground is subject to riding farther up on the beach, through the action of seas, tides, etc. Of course, the first consideration always is to refloat the vessel; however, after the initial freeing attempts have been made and have failed, the next most important step is to keep the vessel from riding farther up on the shore. This can be done by several methods or by a combination of these methods:

Ballast down. Fill the empty fuel, water, and cargo tanks necessary to maintain a positive ground reaction against the effects of a rising tide or a pounding surf. The amount of extra ballast required may be determined from an estimate of the draft before and after grounding. Overballasting should be avoided, because it may place an excessive strain on the hull, and the vessel is designed to withstand water pressure from without, not within, the hull. Taking aboard more ballast than needed should be avoided, because the excess ballast will increase pumping time during refloating operations.

Anchors. As soon as practicable, weather allowing, set the bow anchors to seaward. This can be best accomplished by the use of the ship's lifeboat or, in the case of heavy anchors, by the use of two lifeboats, with the anchor slung from timbers between the boats. The anchor should be led seaward and away from the set, or current; that is, if the effects of wind and sea have a tendency to set the vessel's stern inshore to starboard, then both anchors should be led away from the set: the port anchor to be led outshore to port and the starboard anchor to be led outshore around the stern toward the port. This will prevent the stern from surging toward the shore, and consequently the vessel may not broach. It is important for a vessel not to broach.

Broaching, provided the vessel is not a total loss as a result, will cause more damage and make salvage operations more difficult for the following reasons:

a. Lying broadside to the beach will present a greater area of the vessel to the forces of wind and sea, tending to drive the vessel harder aground.

b. The ground reaction is usually increased, as a greater area of the vessel's bottom is caused to come into contact with the ground, thereby increasing friction.

SINKINGS

A vessel sinks when it loses positive buoyancy. Some of the causes for sinkings are as follows:

1. Flooding due to material failure of a valve, pipe, hull plate, etc.
2. Striking a submerged object, puncturing planking, plating, etc.
3. Collision with another vessel or floating structure.
4. Heavy weather causing capsizing or springing of hull plates.

Several methods of raising sunken vessels are: pumping, compressed air and lifting.

Pumping requires that the vessel lie in depths not exceeding 35 feet, because it is difficult and expensive to build cofferdams that can withstand water pressure beyond this depth.

Vessels can be refloated using *compressed air*. This is usually the fastest method for small steel vessels, but the operation is very tricky, at best, and requires considerable experience of the planner to be successful.

Lifting requires considerable rigging, and the size of the vessel that can be salved depends upon the capacity of the lifting equipment.

RESCUE (TOWING)

Rescue salvage is, by far, less complicated than salvage of either stranded vessels or sunken vessels. Rescue salvage is simply a matter of taking under tow, or otherwise retrieving, a vessel that has had a breakdown due to mechanical failure, heavy weather, or striking a submerged object.

The following requisites are necessary to attempt successful rescue salvage:

1. Adequate salvage plant; i.e., tug, crew, and equipment to accomplish the job intended.
2. Knowledge of navigation necessary to locate quickly the disabled vessel.
3. Capable seamanship to connect a tow wire expeditiously and maneuver in close proximity to the disabled vessel.
4. Complete towing knowledge and experience.

Rescue towing can involve any vessel from a sailing skiff to a large commercial ocean vessel; consequently, the size of the tow boat required will vary proportionately to the size of the disabled vessel.

As in all commercial salvage ventures, the salvage of sunken vessels requires the consideration of time and expense involved, which, in turn, determines whether or not the venture is worthwhile; for, in commercial salvage, the return, or profit, on the dollar invested is of prime concern. Because of the hazards peculiar to any salvage venture, the return on the investment must be most lucrative, and there should be room for considerable margin for error in the over-all evaluation.

To be considered for salvage at all, the sunken vessel should lie in water not exceeding approximately 150 feet from mean low water to main deck. Vessels lying sunk below this depth should be given serious and careful consideration before salvage attempts are made using present-day methods.

CHAPTER II

PRACTICAL DIVING

Any discussion concerning the use of divers in ship salvage work must cover the pros and cons of the various types of divers, their uses and limitations, and, most important, the safety precautions that must be observed. In order to effectively present the case for and against the use of scuba divers in ship salvage work, a brief discussion of the practices of the salvage diver using a deep sea dress is probably the best approach.

In the past, diving in ship salvage work has been limited to a great extent to the use of divers wearing the deep sea diving dress. The reasons for the extensive use of the deep sea diving rig are primarily its comparative safety, comfort, and all-weather use.

The deep sea diving rig is used for internal salvage work in a submerged wreck in preference to the shallow water diving outfit, because of the hazards that are ever present during the course of underwater work. In any but the best of working conditions, the diver must work in partial and, in many cases, total darkness. Working without light presents to the diver the problem of having to work mostly by feel, and this condition alone requires longer periods of time to do a job submerged than would otherwise be required topside. While working in the bowels of a ship in darkness, a diver is subjected to the dangers of falling, striking protruding and sharp objects, and fouling of air and life lines. Because the shallow water diver is lighter in weight than the deep sea diver, the hazards of falling are not as great. The deep sea diver, however, may experience a bad squeeze, or even death, from a fall into greater depths if the diver does not have time to increase his air supply rapidly enough to compensate for the increase in depth. The shallow water diver may not experience quite so bad a squeeze because he can, more or less, swim in free-suspension. A squeeze, if it does occur to a diver using a shallow water mask, will cause a definite strain to be placed on the eyeballs, for the increased pressure of the depth and the consequent decrease of pressure in the mask will cause the eyeballs to start out of their sockets. A diver using scuba equipment will not experience a similar squeeze because of the supply and demand breathing apparatus; therefore, because of his relatively light weight and complete free-suspension, a scuba diver will not be subjected to the hazards of a fall.

Striking a submerged protruding object in darkness may fracture a face plate, puncture a helmet or suit, or cause bodily injury to a deep sea diver. He may overcome the inherent dangers in fracturing a face plate, tearing the suit, or puncturing the helmet by readjusting his inlet and exhaust valves. By increasing the air supply and closing in or securing the exhaust, he may use the unwelcome opening in his rig as an exhaust. In order to effectively accomplish this, he must re-position his body so that the opening is low down; that is, it should be below the level of his head. A shallow water diver using a face mask may suffer bodily injury or a broken face plate by striking a submerged protruding object. The remedy for bodily injury is the same as topside; namely, repair to hospital. A broken face plate can be temporarily overcome by lowering the head so that the fracture is below the mouth. If this does not work, the diver should duck his mask and ditch his rig and proceed posthaste to the surface, remembering to breathe out slowly as he rises. In order to do this satisfactorily, the diver cannot be too far within the bowels of a submerged wreck. There is trouble enough in making the surface directly from the bottom without first having to try to find a way out of the vessel; so it can readily be seen that the use of a shallow water diver within a wreck on the bottom must, of necessity, be limited so that in case of an emergency he will not be lost.

The fouling of air and life lines can sometimes be cleared simply by the diver retracing his steps and clearing the fouled lines; however, in cases of more complex fouling, which often enough occur, an additional diver, known as the stand-by diver, is sent down to clear the fouled lines. When a life line and air hose are hopelessly entangled, the fouled diver may be extricated by replacing his fouled lines with a stand-by air hose and life line brought from the surface by the stand-by diver. The procedure requires the stand-by diver to descend with an additional air hose and life line and locate the fouled diver. He signals the fouled diver of his intentions and then fits his air hose coupling wrench to the air hose coupling at the air supply valve, closes the exhaust valve and then the air supply valve. Then he quickly backs off the coupling and disconnects the fouled hose and couples up the stand-by air hose. After the stand-by air hose is coupled, he again opens the air supply and exhaust valves of the once-fouled diver. The life line can now be changed. Barring an untimely accident of cross-threading the new coupling, the anxious diver can be brought to the surface, alive. All work of changing the lines is done by the stand-by diver, and the hard-pressed fouled diver *must* remain inactive, with his hands well clear of the air hose coupling. By relaxing and breathing easily, the fouled diver has enough air in his suit to last in excess of three minutes. This length of time should be more than adequate for changing the air hose. To prevent a diver's lines from fouling, it is sometimes necessary for a second diver to descend to the wreck and tend the lines of the first diver as he enters a compartment, hatch, hold, or engine room. When this is resorted to, it is necessary to use two tenders aboard the diving boat or salvage vessel. The second diver relays all signals from the first diver to the tender on the boat.

A shallow water diver using a face mask and air hose can free himself from a fouled air hose and life line by simply ducking the face mask, weights, etc., and swimming to the surface in a free-ascent, remembering to breathe out on the way up. In this connection, the diver should never be so far within a wreck on the bottom that he cannot return to the surface without his mask. The scuba diver does not have the cumbersome life lines and air hoses that cause the deep sea diver and, less often, the shallow water diver to become fouled.

Safety is a prime requisite in any salvage operation or, for that matter, in any operation. Safety in diving deep within a wreck is best provided by the deep sea diving dress. This may be difficult to understand, particularly because of the cumbersomeness of the rig and the restrictions placed on the diver as compared with the freedom of movement afforded by shallow water and scuba diving equipment.

The most important safety feature of the deep sea diving rig is the means of positive communication that it provides between the diver and his tender. Two means of communication are possible: voice contact, via the telephone circuit, and hand signals on the life line and air hose. The telephone circuit provides a combination microphone-speaker in the helmet and a speaker and microphone on the diving boat. The single advantage of voice communication in a diving rig far outweighs most of the advantages gained by using other methods of diving, particularly when the diver is used for internal and external survey work and for work within a wreck. The exchange of questions and answers between the diver and those topside can eliminate many additional exploratory and fact-finding dives. A description of conditions on the scene is far better than a description from memory. Some telephone circuits provide a means for one diver to talk to other divers in his vicinity who are involved in the same task. In addition to the telephone, communicaton can be accomplished by signaling on the lines. The signals are combinations of jerks on the line, which signify prearranged messages. Most signals are standardized in diving work.

The deep sea diving dress can be used in adverse conditions of weather and temperature and still afford a degree of comfort not to be attained in shallow water rigs and scuba equipment when used under the same conditions. The air supplied to a deep sea rig can be preheated so that diving in extremely cold waters may be accomplished for limited times. The duration of the dive will depend upon the degree of cold as well as the depth. Sometimes the air valve will freeze and ice because of the expansion of cold air when passing through the valve. The expansion of the air at the valve will cause an additional decrease in temperature of the inlet air. This can be prevented in an emergency by having the diver open his air supply valve wide and regulating his pressure topside at the compressor. However, this procedure is extremely hazardous because of the increased danger of a squeeze, and it should not be resorted to except in an emergency and when there is no danger of the diver falling. When diving in hot tropical waters, a degree of some comfort may be obtained by the diver ventilating his suit through readjusting his supply and exhaust valves. Sweating will usually occur in hot weather, and, as yet, no nose wiper has been invented to wipe the exasperating perspiration from the end of the nose, which cannot be readily reached by the hands.

Of course, the deep sea dress is cumbersome out of water; but in water the diver can become surprisingly agile. He can swim on the surface of the water by making the suit light. This is accomplished by closing in on the exhaust valve and increasing the air in order to increase the pressure inside the suit over the pressure of the outside water, causing the diver to become buoyant. By reversing the procedure, the diver can become "heavy," which is the equivalent of a minor squeeze. The diver may find it advantageous to make himself heavy while working on the bottom, to prevent his being swept off the bottom while working in strong currents and in order to obtain greater leverage when using heavy pneumatic tools. There are innumerable instances when a diver may find it advantageous to be either "light" or "heavy" during the course of routine underwater work.

SHALLOW WATER DIVING

Diving in waters approximately 100 feet deep may be considered as *shallow water diving* and can be classified into two types: (1) diving with a life line and air hose and (2) diving with a self-contained air supply.

Diving with a life line and air hose requires the use of a face mask, weights, and a lightweight rubber suit (optional). The life line is married to the air hose with small stuff at short intervals (approximately six feet) in such a way that any strain developed by a pull will be taken by the life line. The life line is secured around the waist of the diver by using a spring clip. One end of the air hose is connected to the filter at the pressure tank, and the other end is coupled to the air control valve on the diver's mask.

The shallow water diver using a mask is limited in his movements by the length of the air hose. This rig is handier and faster to use for external surveys than the deep sea rig. When weather and temperature conditions permit, the shallow water diving rig is more practical than the deep sea rig for use in search and survey. Its use within a submerged vessel should be restricted, however, because the air supply available to the diver is limited to that which is contained in the diver's mask, should the air supply from topside fail for some reason. In view of this limited air supply in the event of emergency, the diver must always be in a position or location where he can readily slip the weights, mask, lines, etc., and make a free-ascent immediately to the surface. It can be seen that, if the diver were employed deep within the bowels of a submerged vessel when such an emergency occurred, he would be in a rather delicate position, to say the least, what with trying to find his way out of the wreck, keeping himself from getting entangled, and making a free-ascent.

On the other hand, the deep sea diver can be warned of air failure via his telephones or hand signals on his life line. He can then secure the helmet exhaust and survive for a short period of time on the air in his suit. Sufficient air should remain in the suit to permit the people topside to change over the air hose to a stand-by source of air before the demise of the diver. The new source of air may come from a stand-by compressor, air flasks, or even oxygen bottles. No dive should be made on life line and air hose without a stand-by source of air readily available that is independent of the air supply being used.

The shallow water rig is best suited to underwater search. Sometimes a wreck must be located by divers, or a lost piece of equipment, from a fishing rod to an outboard motor, must be located and recovered. An underwater search requires a systematic coverage of the bay, river, or ocean bottom. The areas searched by the diver must be accurately recorded so that duplication of effort will be averted. The records may be best maintained by taking bearings of known points on land and plotting the resultant position of the diving boat on a navigation chart. Needless to say, the boat should never be unmoored and shifted to a new position of search while the diver is on the bottom.

In order not to duplicate his pattern of search, the diver uses a distance line. The distance line is a known length of line secured either to the bottom of the diver's descending line or to an independent weight. The distance line is marked at intervals along its length, usually simply by tying knots in the line. The diver positions himself at the first knot and proceeds to walk ahead. He will walk in a circle because the line is secured at one end. At the completion of one round trip, the diver moves away from the weight to the next knot and again completes one revolution. He continues progressively from one knot to another until he finds what he is searching for. If he doesn't find it, the descending line or weight is repositioned and the search continued as before. The diver can determine when he has made one complete revolution by observing the direction that his life line and air hose tend, or by placing some large object on the bottom where he commenced his walk. He should arrive at this known object at the completion of one full circle, unless he loses this, too. If this happens, he should promptly abandon his search and try again another day, or let another diver have a whack at it, for apparently it is not his day. In very shallow or clear, tropical water, the slant of the sun's rays through the water will guide in making one circle.

Shallow water divers, with life line and air hose, may be used to good advantage for the following:

Bottom search
External underwater survey
Minor underwater hull repairs to a boat or vessel
Pier and piling repair work
Limited internal underwater survey
Measuring for patches and cofferdams
Fitting and securing small patches
Underwater cutting, using a hydrogen, oxygen, compressed air torch
Placing explosive charges

Shallow water divers, with life line and air hose, should not attempt the following:

Underwater cutting and welding
Internal survey and repair work
Tunneling under a wreck, using hydraulic hose

Shallow water divers breathing air without life line and air hose are called scuba divers (self-contained underwater breathing apparatus).

The scuba diver uses air from one or more portable flasks that are strapped to his back. The flasks are charged with high-pressure air from air compressors. While being employed by a diver, the entire unit is completely independent of any outside source of air supply; consequently, the need for life lines, air hoses, and air compressors is eliminated.

A scuba diving unit consists of the air flasks, mouthpiece breathing apparatus, and air pressure regulator. A flexible rubber hose connects the mouthpiece to the regulator at the air supply.

The cumbersome dress of the deep sea diver is not used, and the scuba diver swims in free-suspension, more or less. He may gain additional required negative buoyancy by the addition of a weighted quick-release belt. The dress of the diver will depend upon the temperature conditions of the water. In warm and tropical waters, the diver will wear little more than swimming suit, canvas or rubber shoes, and a knife on a leather belt. The knife is not carried as a means of protection but, rather, as an all-purpose utility tool; therefore it should be of very heavy construction. The double-edged knife (one edge sharp, the other edge saw-toothed) used so successfully by deep sea divers should prove satisfactory.

When diving in colder waters, the diver may dress in a rubber suit, either insulated (wet) or non-insulated (dry). Most suits function on the principle of providing warmth by retention of body heat. The degree of warmth obtained will depend on the type of suit worn. Some types of suits allow the diver to remain in very cold water for extended durations without extreme discomfort.

The depth of the dive and the capacity of the air flasks are the two limiting factors that determine the duration of any dive. The maximum depth to which a scuba diver descends should be limited to approximately 150 feet, although it is a common practice to dive deeper. Dives to greater depths should not be attempted when compressed air is used.

Scuba divers are best suited for use in underwater search and minor repair work. For underwater search, the diver can swim very rapidly along the bottom and cover a wide area in a short period of time. In this respect, the scuba diver is more useful than any other type of diver. In recent years, experimentation has been carried out in the use of undersea sleds for search and bottom survey work. The sleds basically come under two headings: self-propelled and towed.

The self-propelled type is usually battery powered and, for obvious reasons, is limited in range. The necessity for periodically charging batteries and the possibility of mechanical failure are two of the disadvantages of this type of sled.

The towed sled is connected by a tow wire or line to a surface craft. The diver controls his depth by operating diving vanes. This type of rig is more advantageous than the self-propelled sled because there are fewer mechanical parts subjected to possible failure. The location of the sled, when in use, is always known by those topside. This fact enables a more systematic search pattern, based on bearings taken from points ashore and plotted on a navigation chart aboard the towing vessel. Figure 1 illustrates a sea sled developed and constructed by Submersible Operations Corporation, San Diego, California.

For underwater survey work on a submerged vessel, a scuba diver can be put into operation very rapidly, which sometimes saves hours. Scuba divers usually work in pairs and remain within sight of each other at all times. Slates may be carried for writing under water.

The survey should be carried out as described in Chapter V. All pertinent survey information should be recorded on the slates and should include locations, sizes, dimensions, and other important data. For this purpose, the divers should carry tapes and gauges. In lieu of a tape measure, dimensions may be recorded by tieing knots in a length of string or line.

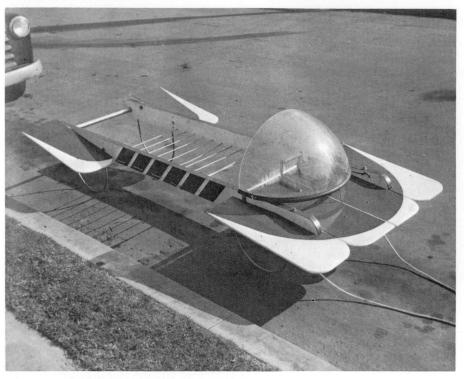

Fig. 1.   Sea sled developed and constructed by Submersible Operations Corp., San Diego, Calif.

The divers should work from a descending line, lowered from a moored or anchored boat. An additional messenger line should be secured to the descending line with snap rings, so that slates, tools, and equipment can be exchanged between the divers and the people in the boat. The snap rings retain the messenger line at the descending line so that the divers can easily locate any equipment. The messenger line eliminates the need for time-consuming ascents and shortens considerably the time required for a thorough survey.

The internal search and survey of scuba divers should be limited. A diver must never place himself in a position where he cannot make the surface in a free-ascent. The extent of information ascertained on an internal survey will depend upon the experience of the diver. Some divers, experienced in both deep sea dress and scuba diving, believe that the use of scuba internally in a submerged vessel is safer. They point out that, among other things, the scuba diver has, in many cases, more than one choice of exit from a wreck, whereas the deep-sea-dressed diver must of necessity exit the way he entered. Freedom of movement and comparative safety from fouled lines are other arguments for scuba; however, it is recommended that unless the diver is experienced he should not test the merits or demerits of either method.

The scuba diver is hampered by the lack of direct communication with the surface. He has no tender; consequently, he must work with a companion diver so that should either diver experience some trouble the other will be close at hand to render assistance.

Direct communication with the surface is important in salvage work because it permits a ready exchange of information and eliminates time-consuming passing of messages via the messenger line. In addition, another important disadvantage of the scuba diver is that his whereabouts is not known at all times by those topside. Sometimes he can be traced by locating his exhaust bubbles, but these are hard to find except under the best of conditions.

One important fact, which is the singular advantage of the scuba diver, is that his diving time is not limited by the conditions of the surface of the sea. When the sea makes up during moderate or heavy weather, diving operations utilizing life line and air hose divers must stop because of the danger in dragging one or more of the diving boat's mooring anchors. The scuba diver, however, is not affected by the surface conditions of the sea, and, once submerged, he will be unaware of even a storm raging topside.

This is important in many salvage operations, because it means that much preliminary rigging and patching, which would normally be delayed until calm weather, can be accomplished by scuba divers. This preliminary and preparatory work, if done during seasonal storms, will allow more time to be spent on the actual salvage operation during limited calm summer days.

In northern latitudes, salvage of sunken vessels is generally limited to a maximum of three summer months. In the past, much of this time was spent by deep sea divers rigging and patching or seeking harbor shelter from local storms.

Whereas deep sea divers are affected by the heaving and pitching of the diving boat, which causes no little distress because of the sudden jerk sustained by the diving hose and air line, the scuba diver is completely free of any effects of surface water conditions.

Figure 2 shows a diver making underwater repairs, using scuba equipment. Note the comparative freedom of the diver from a restraining deep sea suit. Most small, light jobs under water are easier to perform with scuba than with the cumbersome helmeted suit.

Fig. 2. Scuba diver making underwater repairs.

Figure 3 shows a scuba diver conducting an internal survey of a submerged wreck. Note the diver's easy access through a partially obstructed doorway.. The compactness of the rig and the absence of the restricting line and air hose allows the diver to move quickly through the wreck. His almost neutral buoyancy permits access to any height for inspection in a compartment or hold without undue hazard.

EQUIPMENT AND GEAR USED

Basically, the salvage gear required by scuba divers is the same as that required for any other salvage operator, except that the amount of equipment required will depend upon the size and scope of the salvage to be undertaken.

Most surface tools may be used under water and should be washed in fresh water, dried, and lightly oiled after each use.

Underwater pneumatic tools are available that can perform many and diversified functions; among these tools are the pneumatic saw, drill, and hammer.

Fig. 3. Scuba diver conducting internal survey of submerged wreck. (Photo courtesy Subop Corp., San Diego, Calif.)

The gear should include small purchase tackles (handy-billy), chain falls, come-alongs, and wire and fiber ropes of varying lengths. Generally speaking, in recent years, more research and development on new equipment for use in salvage operations have been done by small salvage organizations and groups, who use primarily scuba equipment, than by the large commercial salvage firms, who until recently relied entirely on deep sea divers dressed in the pressure suit.

Fig. 4.   Watertight pressure containers for cameras and equipment, developed
by Mr. Lamar Borin, President, Subop Corp., San Diego, Calif.

Television cameras for use in underwater search and survey have
gained wider and increased acceptance in many fields of salvage.

Underwater searching can be hastened by towing a submerged
camera in a pattern that will cover the entire area thoroughly. The
camera is enclosed in a watertight pressure container. The advantage

of using a television camera, rather than a diver on a sea sled, is that the topography and objects under surveillance are better analyzed topside by one or more observers. A diver need not be sent down until there is some particular information required that is not readily discernible on the television screen. Another important advantage is that the camera may be used for prolonged periods of time, whereas a diver is limited in his stay below, either for physiological reasons or because of cold water.

The television camera can also be used for underwater survey work on a sunken or stranded vessel. A diver is used to direct the camera around the periphery of the underwater body of the vessel so that supervisory personnel, topside, may observe directly the nature and extent of any damage, in order to determine the type of salvage and method of repairs required.

Underwater photography can prove invaluable in ship salvage work, as well as in innumerable other types of marine underwater work.

There is no substitute for photographs or for personal observation of any scene. A description will rarely exceed the value of either of the foregoing.

In a physical observation, memory plays an important part, but a photograph is a permanent factual record of existing conditions and can be referred to innumerable times in order to develop different information.

Figure 4 shows several types of watertight pressure containers for cameras and equipment, which were developed by Mr. Lamar Borin of Submersible Operations Corporation, San Diego, California.

DIVING BOATS

Boats used for diving purposes range from skiffs to tugs and yachts—in fact, any boat that will hold the diver and his gear.

The scuba diver can work from any size or type of boat because his diving gear is comparatively compact and readily portable; however, the shallow water and deep sea diver must work from boats that are large enough to hold the required air compressors, hoses, and diving dresses.

Small boats can be converted for use as combination diving and salvage work boats. The size of the boat converted will depend upon the type of work for which it is intended.

Small landing craft, which are made available through government sales from time to time, are well suited for conversion to diving boats and can be used successfully on small salvage jobs. In addition, these boats lend themselves very well for use in making minor repairs, both above and below the waterline.

Figures 5 and 6 are illustrations of types of conversion possible with surplus government craft. There are numerous ways to convert a small craft for diving purposes, but, regardless of the particular choice of design, the following equipment should be installed aboard:

1. An air compressor of sufficient capacity for the use intended. The air compressor should be of approximately 100-cubic-feet-per-minute capacity. Lacking this, two smaller compressors may be used. The capacity of the compressors should be sufficient to sustain two divers at a maximum depth at which work is anticipated.

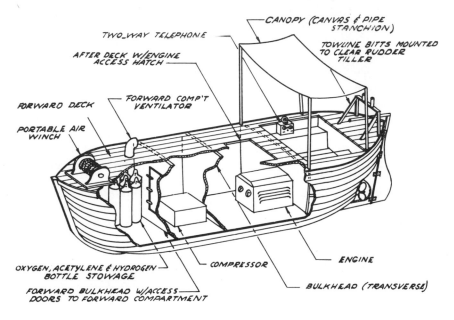

Fig. 5.   Lifeboat or motor launch converted to diving boat.

Even if the boat is intended for use by scuba divers, air compressors should be installed aboard because there are numerous instances where air will be used for minor salvage work.

2. Sufficient 50-foot lengths of air hose, in satisfactory condition, for two divers to descend to the maximum depth at which work is to be accomplished. The hoses should be married to a combination life line and telephone cable for use with the deep sea diving dress or to a Manila rope line for use with the shallow water diving mask.

3. Air line filters to remove any oil that may be carried over from the compressor. There should be one filter connected to the hose of each diver.

4. A portable air-driven winch, which can be mounted and bolted at one of several locations about the deck. The air winch is an invaluable time- and labor-saving piece of equipment.

5. Oxygen-acetylene-hydrogen bottles mounted in cradles and the necessary cutting torches. The number of bottles carried will vary, depending upon the type and scope of salvage work attempted; however, it is suggested that a minimum number of three each be carried aboard for emergency and preliminary survey work.

6. At least three anchors: stock or Danforth. Mooring lines and short lengths of chain for securing the diving boat to the three anchors. The size of the anchors carried will vary according to the size of the boat. For diving operations using a diver dressed in a deep sea rig, the anchors should be a minimum of approximately 150 pounds each. The lines should be approximately three times the depth of the water in which the anchors are laid.

7. A stand-by source of air, either from air flasks, oxygen bottles, or from a small portable compressor. Because portable air compressors are usually powered by single-cylinder gasoline engines, which are sometimes difficult to start, it is recommended that air flasks or oxygen bottles be used as the source of stand-by air. The stand-by air is never used except in case of an emergency; consequently, its source must be positive and its availability dependable. At all times during diving operations, the stand-by air or oxygen should be connected to the diver's air manifold, so that pressure may be supplied to the diver simply by opening a valve. If a connection is to be fouled by cross-threading, it is better that it happen while the diver is aboard the boat; therefore, an experienced diver will always inspect the source and connections of his stand-by air before starting a dive.

8. A portable diving ladder, which can be rigged over the side of the boat for use by a diver dressed in a deep sea rig to facilitate his access to the deck of the boat. The ladder should extend far enough into the water to afford an easy foothold for the diver. The shallow water diver and scuba diver will not need a ladder to board the boat because of their comparatively light rigs, which can be removed and passed into the boat while the diver is in the water. If the diver cannot then climb into the boat unassisted, he is in no fit condition to dive.

9. Tools and equipment for small repair jobs topside or under water. These should include hammers, wrenches, saws, sledge hammers, drills, chisels, wire cutters, tin snips, come-alongs, spikes, nails, wood plugs, canvas, etc. Several sheets of plywood should also be carried, in addition to lengths of lumber of various sizes.

In designing and outfitting a small boat for diving and salvage work, the following points should be kept in mind:

1. The boat should be decked over, even with or just below the gunwale, to provide a convenient platform from which to work or dress the diver.

2. The air compressor should be located approximately amidship or just forward of the main propulsion engine, in order to provide a more even weight distribution.

3. The oxygen-acetylene-hydrogen bottles should be located below the deck, forward, in a well-ventilated compartment. The deck above this compartment can be fitted with portable hatches to facilitate access to the bottle stowage.

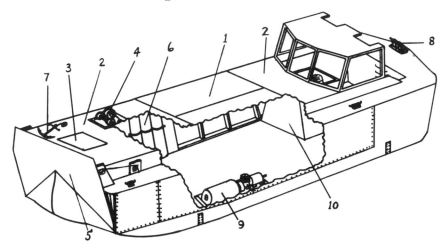

Fig. 6. Landing craft conversion to diving boat. 1. Portable deck hatches; 2. Decking installed; 3. Forward hatch; 4. Portable air winch; 5. Bow ramp secured; 6. Oxygen-hydrogen-acetylene bottle stowage; 7. Anchor stowage; 8. Stern towing bitts; 9. Air compressor; 10. Engine.

4. The air winch should be portable and the deck drilled and fitted with three or four winch foundations at convenient locations. This will permit the winch to be shifted to one of several locations about the boat in order to obtain a better fairlead.

5. There should be a compartment in a watertight bow compartment for the mooring lines, chains, and anchors. Access to this compartment should be through a small, watertight, flush deck manhole.

6. There should be a stowage compartment between the air compressor and the gas bottle stowage. The compartment may be used for the stowage of spare parts, tools, supplies, and equipment. Access to this compartment should be through sliding doors installed in a transverse bulkhead. This will facilitate admittance to the compartment when the deck is cluttered with diving and salvage gear.

7. The gunwale can be fitted with four double pipe brackets, as shown in Fig. 7.

A portable set of double bitts may be inserted in the pipe brackets, which are best installed, one each, on the port and starboard bows and quarters. In this way, the double bitts may be installed in any one of the brackets to obtain the needed fairlead.

8. The compressor should be mounted in an open cockpit to insure an adequate source of fresh air at the compressor intake.

9. The diver's air manifold should be permanently mounted amidship in the compressor cockpit with suitable piping and connections for stand-by air and oxygen.

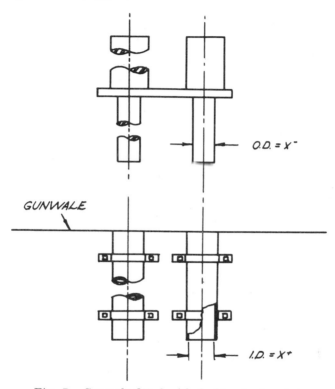

Fig. 7.   Gunwale fitted with double pipe brackets.

10. Permanent and portable fenders should be installed to protect the hull of the boat. On boats built of steel construction, suitable protection can be had by welding one continuous length of split pipe, approximately 4 inches in diameter, completely around the periphery of the hull, midway between the waterline and the sheer guard. The split-pipe fender protects the hull plating from indents and fractures. The fender can be renewed in small sections when necessary.

On wood boats, suitable fenders are used, made of hemp or Manila. Truck tires or lengths of old cargo oil hose may be installed as adequate fenders.

SAFETY PRECAUTIONS

The following are safety precautions that should be observed by all divers:

1. Do not attempt to dive without first knowing how, or without the presence of an experienced diver.

2. A diver should not attempt a task under water unless he is capable of accomplishing it topside.

3. At least one other person should know of a diver's location at all times. This requires that scuba divers operate in pairs.

4. Have available Tables of Optimum Exposure Times for different depths, and consult the table before, during, and after dives. Maintain a diving log on all divers.

5. Determine whether explosive gases are within, or in the vicinity of, a wreck.

6. Do not weld or burn in a poorly ventilated compartment.

7. Do not enter a submerged wreck that is "lively" on the bottom.

8. Use a descending line for all dives.

9. Do not dive without a stand-by source of air.

10. Scuba and shallow water divers should never be in a location or position where they cannot reach the surface by a free-ascent.

11. Do not dive deeper than 150 feet on compressed air.

12. For diving, using the deep sea dress and shallow water rig, moor the diving boat on at least a three-point moor.

13. Never heave on a line leading to a submerged wreck until it is ascertained that all divers are clear.

14. A tender should *always* know the location of his diver.

15. Do not conduct diving operations at night or during foul weather.

16. Check the air compressor fuel supply before and during diving operations.

17. Do not allow engine exhaust fumes to enter the diving air compressor inlet. It is sometimes necessary to direct the engine exhaust fumes to leeward by using a length of pipe or rubber hose.

18. Do not secure a taut, heavy line between the diving boat and a submerged wreck. A sudden settling of the wreck may swamp the diving boat.

19. Do not dive beneath a wreck that is "lively."

20. Determine the extent of bottom damage before refloating a vessel. When in doubt as to condition of the bottom, have collision mats hanging in readiness off the outshore end of the vessel.

CHAPTER III

NAVAL ARCHITECTURE

A basic knowledge of naval architecture and ship construction is necessary for solving salvage problems; that is, it is necessary to understand the qualities of construction and stability of a vessel in order to adequately comprehend and realize the complexities of any salvage operation. An understanding of the complexities involved and an ability to evaluate correctly the problems posed are necessary in order to evolve an effective salvage plan.

This chapter on naval architecture will encompass a basic study of the fundamental hull structure of a vessel and of naval architecture as related to buoyancy and stability, with particular attention paid to the effects of changing and shifting of weights aboard a vessel, and their relation to problems of buoyancy and stability.

It is not the scope of this writing to go into the more complex problems of naval architecture and ship design, and it will touch only on those subjects which will be of use to the potential salvage man. Of course, the study of naval architecture and problems of buoyancy and stability and the application of this knowledge to ship salvage work should be tempered with good judgment and common sense. Theory is no substitute for practical experience; it should be used to augment practical experience.

SHIP CONSTRUCTION

HULL MATERIALS

The term, ship construction, as commonly used refers to the hull structure and its component parts. In this chapter the basic shapes and plates, castings, forgings and other units that make up hull sections will be discussed and illustrated.

The following is a general review of the principal materials used in hull construction.

The most important qualities of the steel used in ship construction are strength, toughness, and elasticity. It is most important to adhere to the uniformity of quality of material throughout hull construction.

Most material used in ship construction is known as medium steel, which is made by the open hearth process and has a tensile strength of approximately 60,000 pounds per square inch and a sheer strength of approximately 50,000 pounds per square inch.

Castings. The following structures are usually steel castings: stem, stern frame, rudder frame, propeller struts, machinery foundations, hull fittings, anchors, pipe flanges, and various small fittings.

Forgings. Forgings are used for special purposes where great strength is required. They supplant the regular shapes required and are used for the special large solid castings needed in hull construction, the forging of which is more or less complicated. Because of the fact that steel castings possessing sufficient strength for most purposes can now be obtained, very few large forgings are used in the hulls of ships. Forgings are used principally for machinery parts, such as crank shafts, propeller shafts, connecting rods, and rudder posts.

Cast Iron. Cast iron is used in certain minor parts where strength is not essential. It is rarely used in the hull proper.

Wrought Iron. Because it is less corrosive than steel, wrought iron is used for anchors, chains, some piping, etc., where the strength of steel is not required.

Nonferrous Metals

Zinc is used to prevent galvanic action in way of propellers, rudders, oxter plates, sea suctions, and any openings in the hull plating under water. The zinc must be attached on the external hull adjacent to the structure it is to protect, and it must be properly bonded with a metal-to-metal contact to be most effective.

Copper is used for steam piping systems for pressure cooking vessels, steam tables, coffee urns, kettles, etc.

Manganese bronze is used in propeller blades and hubs. It has a tensile strength of 65,000 pounds per square inch and contains approximately 58% copper, 40% zinc, 1% manganese, and small amounts of tin, iron, lead, and aluminum.

Phosphor bronze is used in stem, stern, and rudder frames. It is also used in shaft struts. It has a tensile strength of 30,000–35,000 pounds per square inch and contains approximately 90% copper, $9\frac{1}{2}$% tin, and $\frac{1}{2}$% phosphorus.

Naval brass is used for small castings where great strength is not required, such as in small valves, light brackets, etc.

In addition to the foregoing materials, a vessel is fitted out with most all of the materials found in shoreside construction; i.e., wood, linoleum, wool, glass, tile, brick, asbestos, rubber, etc.

HULL CONSTRUCTION

Ship construction varies considerably from one vessel to another. The differences of construction may encompass one or all of the following: internal arrangements, machinery locations, hull structure. Because of the many variations, this work will be a cross-sectional study and may be applied in principle to most vessels. Accordingly, this book will cover only the most important materials and structures and include only a basic knowledge. Any one of these subjects has been covered in great detail in many other publications, so that a review is all that is necessary in this work.

Keel. The keel is commonly known as the backbone of the ship. It is the most important structional member in the hull and the main strength member in the ship. The hulls of most vessels are in the form of a box shape, which is known as the hull girder. The main structural members of the hull girder are the keel, garboard strakes, bilge strakes, sheer strakes, deck stringer plates, gunwale bar, and the main deck centerline plates. The keel in large ship construction seldom extends below the hull plating, as it does in small boats and yachts. Present-day keels are usually constructed of three plates; i.e., the flat, or dished, keel, sometimes called the bottom plate; the center vertical keelson; and, on top of this, the inner bottom plate or rider plate. There are many other types of keels, but it is not necessary, in this study, to encompass their construction (*see* Fig. 8).

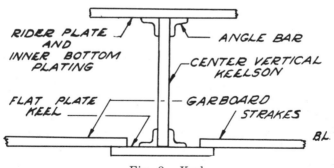

Fig. 8.   Keel.

Shapes. Shapes are used for stiffening different structural members, and they are designed for different structural uses. Figure 9 is an illustration of the various shapes used in shipbuilding.

Shapes are used for a ship's framing and in connecting plates, hull plating, other shapes, and for stiffening and reinforcing. The frames of a vessel are the internal structural members that shape the hull plating and determine the lines of a vessel. The framing is secured at the bottom to the keel and extends outward and vertically upward and is attached to the deck beams at the upper end, in way of the sheer strake and the deck stringer plate. The gunwale bar is attached to the periphery of the main deck at the outboard edge of the deck stringer plate and the top inboard edge of the sheer strake.

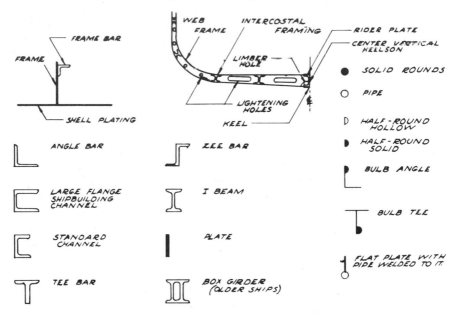

Fig. 9.   Ship construction shapes.

Plating. The hull plating, commonly called the shell plating, is attached to the framing and forms a watertight skin from the stem to the stern and from the keel to the deck stringer plate. The plating is attached to the frames in longitudinal strakes of varying widths. The first strake adjacent to the keel is the garboard. Strakes are then attached successively outward and upward and are identified by letters, beginning with "A," which is the garboard. The letter "I" is not used to identify a strake and is always omitted (*see* Fig. 10).

The plates within a strake are numbered from bow to stern, commencing with #1 plate, which is always adjacent to the stem. The strake fitted along the turn of the bilge is known as the bilge strake. Plates are sheets of uniform thickness ranging from about ⅛ inch to over 1 inch. Plates are used for inner bottoms,. bulkheads, decks, floors, and for the formation of hull girders. Plates under ⅛ inch are usually called "sheets." There are four general types of plating: a. Flush plating is as the name implies; b. In and out joggled plating; c. In and out plating; d. Clinker plating. Figure 11 illustrates these various types of plating.

By far, the most common plating used today is the flush welded type of plating; all the other types are not usually seen today, as they were used mostly for riveted ships.

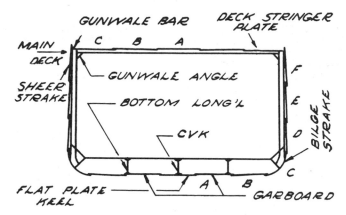

Fig. 10.   Lettering of strakes.

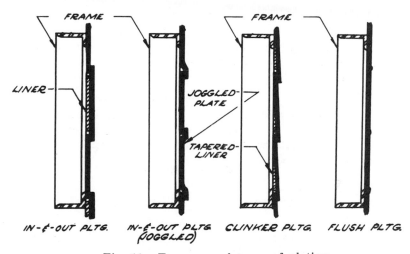

Fig. 11.   Four general types of plating.

Gunwale Bar. The gunwale bar is one of the most important members of the hull girder. The sheer strake and the main deck stringer plating are connected by means of a gunwale bar or angle. Figure 12 illustrates two common methods of attachment.

Framing. The hull plating is strengthened and tied together by means of a system of frames. The system consists of transverse and longitudinal framing. Frames are known as *continuous* when they are unbroken and *intercostal* when they are interrupted. The systems are identified by the type of framing. There are three general systems of framing: transverse; longitudinal; cellular or Isherwood.

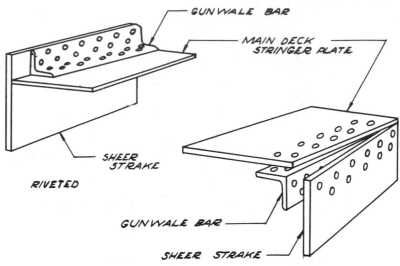

Fig. 12. Two methods of attaching gunwale bar.

The transverse system consists of closely spaced continuous transverse frames and more widely spaced fore and aft members, called longitudinals. (*See* Fig. 13 for a transverse system of framing.)

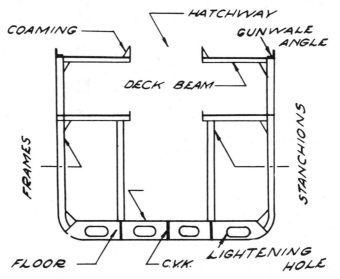

Fig. 13. Transverse system of framing.

The longitudinal system consists of closely spaced continuous longitudinal members and more widely spaced deeper transverse frames, called deep frames or web frames. (*See* Fig. 14 for a longitudinal system of framing.)

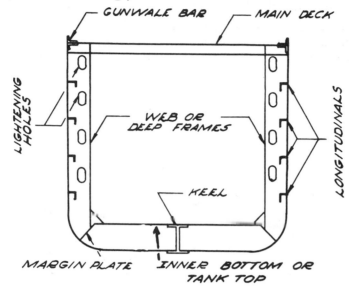

Fig. 14.   Longitudinal system of framing.

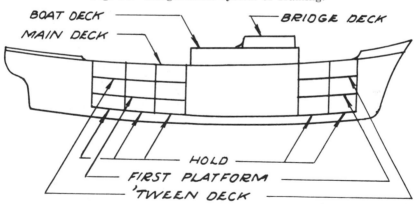

Fig. 15.   Decks.

Decks. A ship is subdivided by the installation of decks, which add longitudinal stiffness and strength to the ship. The main deck is the strength deck and is the uppermost continuous deck from the stem to the stern. The main deck is also the top flange of the hull girder.

As structural members, all other decks are secondary in importance to the main deck. Most decks are watertight, except for 'tween decks. 'Tween decks are half-decks, located in the upper holds of merchant vessels.

Figure 15 shows the deck nomenclature of a typical merchantman.

Structural Members. The vessel is tied together through combination of its structural members; i.e., keel plating, framing, decks, bulkheads, stanchions, etc. Figure 16 shows the relation of most structural members.

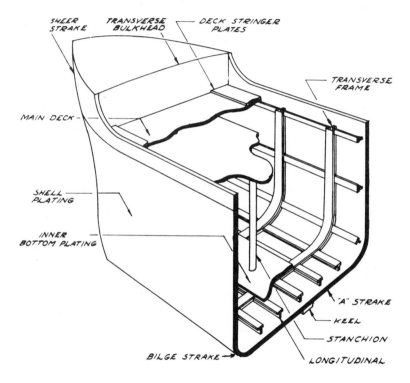

Fig. 16.   Diagrammatical section of a ship showing the relation of the structural members.

Methods of Joining Plates. Plating on welded vessels is joined by the methods illustrated in Fig. 17. Plating on riveted vessels is joined by the methods illustrated in Fig. 18.

SHIP WELDING

To build the bridge of ships needed during World War II, welded construction was advanced to a high degree of speed and efficiency. Consequently, most ships sailing today are of welded construction. It is

necessary, therefore, that the salvage engineer have a good working
knowledge of the science and technology of welding as it applies to
ship structures.

The following discussion, with illustrations and examples, will
prove valuable to those charged with the responsibility of salvage
operations.

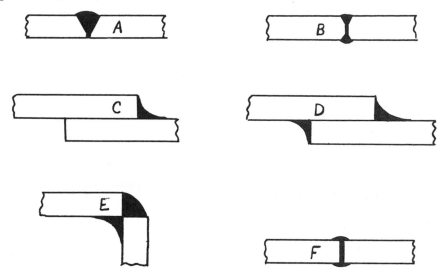

Fig. 17. Methods of welding plating. A. Vee butt joint; B. Double vee butt
joint; C. Single fillet lap joint; D. Double fillet lap joint; E. Full open corner
joint; F. Square butt joint.

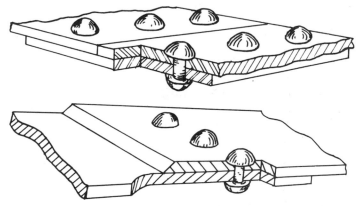

Fig. 18. Two methods of joining plating together. Top: Single riveted butt
strap joint. Bottom: Single riveted lap joint.

WELDING TERMINOLOGY

Because many terms commonly used in welding are foreign to engineering, the following definitions will be presented first:

Actual, or working stress—The load or stress placed upon a material divided by the cross-sectional area of the material.

Compression—The tendency to compress the fibers in any material or to shorten a material.

Concave weld—A weld whose center line is below the plane of the material it joins, or a fillet weld with a surface below a 45-degree plane.

Elastic limit—The limit beyond which the material will stretch when subjected to maximum load limit.

Factor of safety—The ratio between the ultimate strength of a material and the allowable or working stress.

Fatigue failure—The failure resulting from a progressive enlarging crack due to repeated cycles of stress.

Fatigue stresses—The stresses sustained by a material without failure with continual stress loading.

Impact—The load, or blow, sustained by a weld.

Shear—A scissors action that tends to cut a material in a vertical or horizontal plane.

Stress—An internal resistive reaction to an externally applied force.

Stress, thermal—Caused by differences in temperature, or coefficients of expansion.

Stress, residual—Stress remaining as a result of heat or mechanical treatment.

Stress, unit—The stress in a unit of area expressed in square inches.

Tension—The tendency to stretch the fibers of a material, or to lengthen them.

Tortional stresses—The stresses that are produced from a twisting action on a piece of material.

Ultimate strength—The greatest stress attained in a material prior to failure.

Welding sequence—The sequence, or order, in which the component parts of a structure are welded.

STRENGTH OF WELDS AND MATERIALS

Refer to Figure 19 for the ultimate strength of steel plating that is subjected to water pressure.

The throat determines the strength of the weld. The size of a concave fillet weld is the altitude of the throat. Size is the width of the contact side (*see* Fig. 20). The throat of a butt weld is equal to the size of the thinner throat (*see* Fig. 20A).

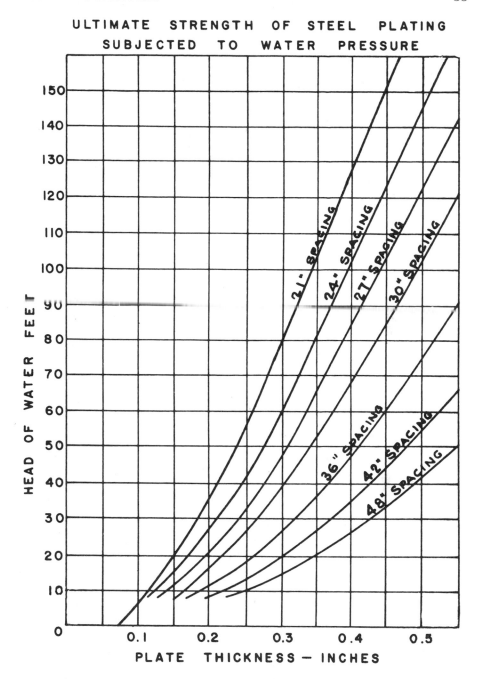

Fig. 19. Ultimate strength of steel plating subjected to water pressure.

Ship salvage work brings great forces into play. For example, beach gear is capable of developing a pull of 40 to 60 tons on the standing part, which must be secured to the structure of the vessel at a cleat, or bitt. It must be ascertained before any pulling operation is commenced whether the cleat, or bitt, and the surrounding bulkheads,

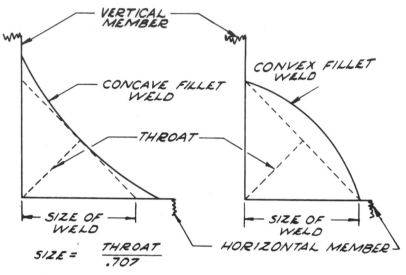

Fig. 20.   Measuring sizes of concave and convex welds.

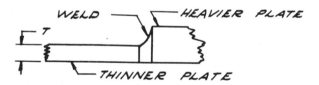

Fig. 20A.   Throat of butt weld.

decks, and structural members are strong enough to withstand the stress loading that will be applied by the standing part of the beach gear. No small part of this investigation will involve the condition of the welds. This examination should concern itself with the state of deterioration of the weld, the size of the weld, and the workmanship of the weld.

Several various types of welds will be encountered in ship structure; included are the single and double fillet, the intermittent and the chain-intermittent. The last two are modifications and variations of the double fillet weld. *See* Fig. 21, which will indicate the ultimate strength of a double fillet weld with loading in any direction. Use half the value given on the curve in order to obtain the safe working load.

The maximum unit stress for each type of weld is as follows: 13,600 pounds per square inch for fillet weld; 13,000 pounds per square inch for butt weld; and 20,000 pounds per square inch, tension and compression.

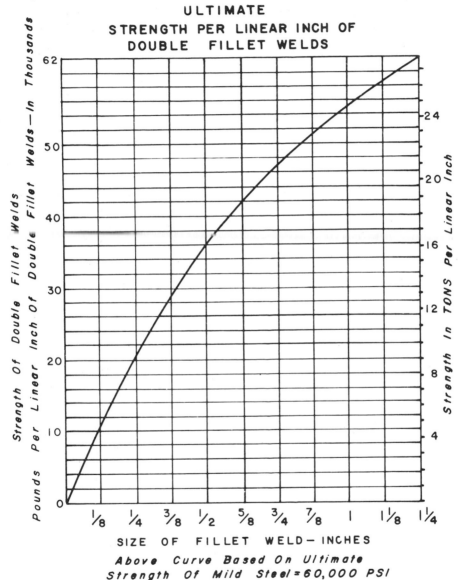

Fig. 21.   Ultimate strength of double fillet weld.

The selection of the type of joint will depend upon the following:

1. Strength of the weld (the weld resulting from the fusion of the weld metal and the base metal).

2. The type of weld.

3. Location of the weld in relation to the parts joined and adjoining.

a. The square butt joint is used for thinner plates and requires complete fusion.

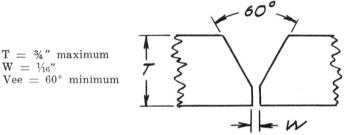

T = ⅛″ maximum
W = No separation
T — ¼″ maximum
W = ½ T minimum

b. The single vee butt joint is used for heavier conditions of loading.

T = ¾″ maximum
W = ¹⁄₁₆″
Vee = 60° minimum

c. The double vee butt joint is used for heavier loads, where the joint is accessible from both sides.

T = 1½″ maximum
W = ⅛″
Vee = 60° minimum

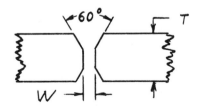

d. The square tee joint is used for longitudinal shear.

T = ½″ maximum
W = ⅛″

e. The single bevel tee joint is used for greater longitudinal shear, where work can be welded from one side only.

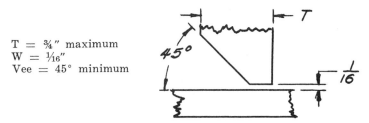

T = ¾″ maximum
W = ¹⁄₁₆″
Vee = 45° minimum

Note: Do not use when the root of weld is subject to tension bending.

f. The double bevel tee joint is used for joining heavy plate in heavy longitudinal and transverse shear loads, where the joint is accessible from both sides.

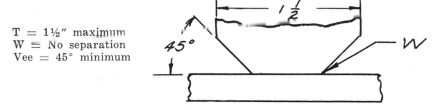

T = 1½″ maximum
W = No separation
Vee = 45° minimum

g. The single fillet lap joint is used for any thickness plate, where loading is not too severe.

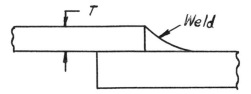

h. The double fillet lap joint is used for joining any thickness plate, where stresses and compression loading are severe.

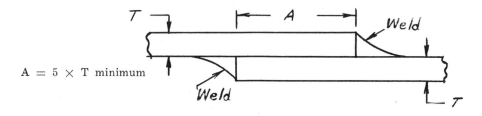

A = 5 × T minimum

i. The full open corner joint is used for joining plates, where fatigue and impact loading are severe and the joint is accessible from both sides.

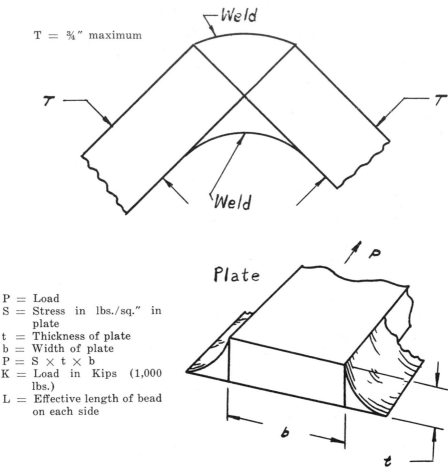

T = ¾″ maximum

P = Load
S = Stress in lbs./sq." in plate
t = Thickness of plate
b = Width of plate
P = S × t × b
K = Load in Kips (1,000 lbs.)
L = Effective length of bead on each side

1. 13,600 lbs. shear on throat area
2. Load value of 1 inch fillet weld in longitudinal shear
   $.707 \times 13{,}600 = 9{,}600$ lbs./linear inch
   (shielded arc electrodes)
3. Two beads of equal lengths and size equal to plate thickness—
   Total bead capacity $= 2 \times t \times 9{,}600$ lbs./linear inch
4. Since load $= S \times t \times b$, the effective length of weld per side would be:

$$\frac{S \times t \times b}{2 \times t \times 9{,}600} \quad \text{or} \quad \frac{S \cdot \times b}{2 \times 9{,}600}$$

5. Assume: S = 16,000 lbs./sq." unit stress
   (unit stress of structural steel = maximum 20,000 lbs.) then:

$$\frac{16{,}000 \times b}{2 \times 9{,}600} = .833b$$

6. Unit stress in plate expressed in Kips (1,000 lbs.): multiply this
   by plate width (inches) and divide by 19.2 to obtain effective
   length of bead per side:

$$L = \frac{b \times K}{19.2}$$

To determine the ultimate strength of steel plating under water
pressure, *see* Fig. 19.

Angle Iron

t = Thickness of angle
a = Length of leg
A = Area

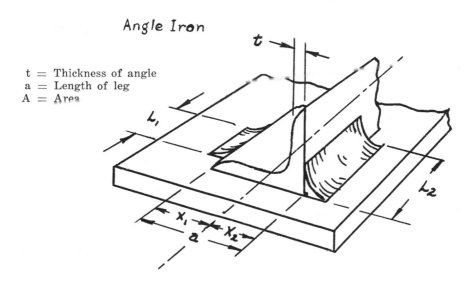

1. A = t(a+a—t)
   = t(2a—t)
   = 2ta—t²;   t² may be dropped
   Area becomes 2ta
   Load = 2ta × S
   Assume load capacity = t × 9,600

$$\frac{2ta \times S}{t \times 9{,}600} = \frac{2aS}{9{,}600} = \text{total bead length}$$

2. The shorter bead (at toe of angle) will be ⅓ of total bead length since the distance from c.g. to heel of angle is ⅓ a.
The shorter bead will be:

$$\frac{1}{3} \times \frac{2aS}{9,600} = \frac{2a}{3} \times \frac{K}{9.6} = \frac{aK}{14.4}$$

Angle is 3″ × 3″, and 18,000 lbs. unit stress

$$\frac{3 \times 18}{14.4} = 3.75 \text{ inches}$$

The longer bead will equal twice the shorter, or 7.5 inches.

$$\frac{aK}{14.4} = \text{Shorter bead}$$

Longer bead is twice this value

Strength of Angle Iron
6″ × 4″ × 5⁄16″ angle
5⁄16″ fillet weld at 3,000 lbs. per square inch
$$\frac{30,000}{3,000} = 10″ \text{ of weld needed}$$
Place 5″ of weld at each end, or 3″ at each end and 4″ at the bottom

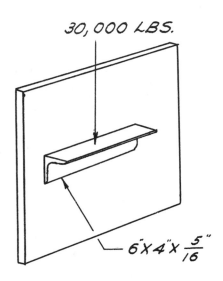

30,000 LBS.

6″×4″×5⁄16″

Padeyes. Investigate the back-up structure and ascertain if it is strong enough to support the padeye. The points to check on are:

1. The support of the deck plating to which the attachment is made. Secure the padeye as close as possible to a main structural member.

2. Determine if the designer placed similar attachments in the vicinity of the one you are planning to install. This will indicate probable strength of the surrounding structure.

3. Examine installed welds for signs of deterioration and failure. The most prevalent signs are near the waterline fittings; i.e., padeyes used to install propellers. These padeyes are located in the vicinity of the oxter plates.

Example:

For 40.8 lb. plate, use 1″ fillet weld
5″ + 1″ = 6″ of double fillet weld
55,000# × 6″ = 330,000 lbs.

$$\frac{330,000 \text{ lbs.}}{2,240 \text{ lbs.}} = 147.3 \text{ long tons}$$

$$\frac{147.3}{2} = 73.6 \text{ safe load in long tons}$$

Always convert to long tons.

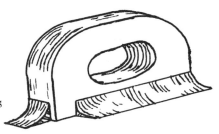

Strength of Butt Welds. Assume the strength of a butt weld is equal to the net cross-sectional area through the weld (the length of the weld times the thickness of the thinnest plate being connected, multiplied by the working shear stress).

Length (L) × thickness (t) × shear stress (S)
L × t × S equals the strength of a butt welded joint.

Merchant Marine Design Stresses.
Shear 7,950 lbs. per sq. in.
Tension 15,000 lbs. per sq. in.
Compression 15,000 lbs. per sq. in.

WELDING PRACTICE

SHELL PLATING WELDING SEQUENCE

Lock in stress at 1 with later welds 2 and 3. (Liberty ships failed, among other causes, due to a poor welding sequence.)

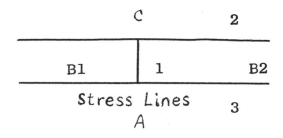

Side fillet weld is designed for sheer.

Locate center of gravity (angle iron). Greatest welded bead should be the shortest side from the center of gravity.

Whenever turning action is involved, always have welds well spaced.

A.

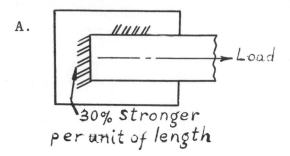

30% Stronger
per unit of length

B.

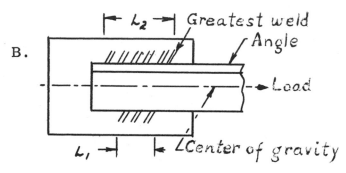

L_2 — Greatest weld
Angle
Load
L_1 — Center of gravity

C.

Underneath
Load

D.

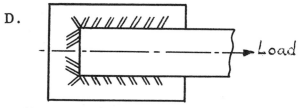

Load

Hook weld here on corners
for long welds

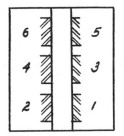

Control stress as in welding sequence

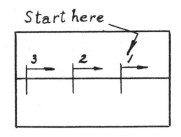

Step Back Method

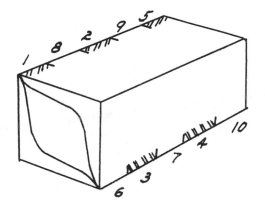

Two Angles:

Weld as in numbered sequence

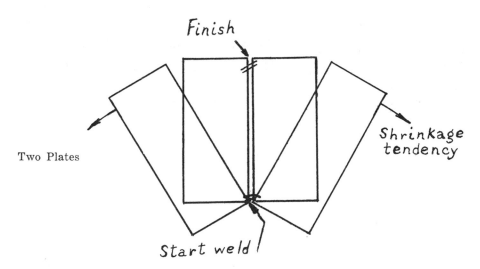

Two Plates

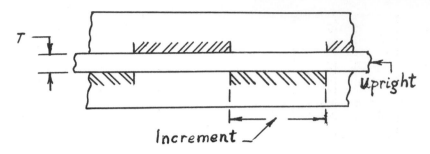

Staggered Intermittent Welded Tee Joint

Note: Length of increment—Minimum of four times the size of the weld; not less than 1 inch. Maximum of sixteen times the thickness of the thinner member; not to exceed 12 inches.

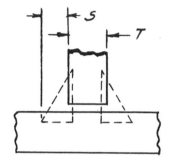

S - T Max.—The maximum center-to-center spacing between increments on the same side of the joint shall be thirty-two times the thickness of the thinner member; but in no case shall this spacing between adjacent increments on the opposite sides of members exceed 2 inches.

Chain Intermittent Welded Tee Joint (*see* note above).

The maximum center-to-center spacing between increments shall be sixteen times the thickness of the thinner member and shall not exceed 12 inches.

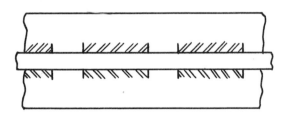

WELDING STRESSES

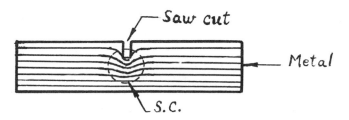

S. C. = Stress Concentration: A hacksaw cut sets up stress concentration as indicated.

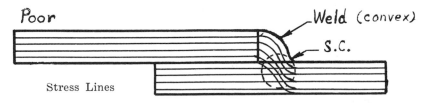

Stress lines tend to find each other in metals.

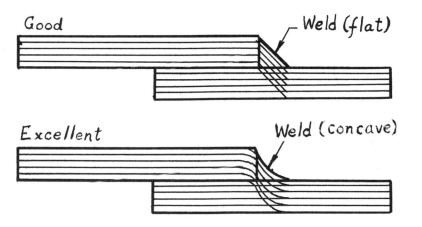

For heavy or repeated loads stress concentrations should be minimized.

WELD DESIGN

The following points should be remembered in designing a weld:
1. The throat will determine the strength of a weld.
2. The throat of a fillet weld is the altitude of the side.
3. The size of a weld is the width of the contact side.
4. The throat of a butt weld is equal to the size of the thinner plate joined.
5. Design the weld for shear, not for tension or compression.
6. In calculating welds, always add ¼ inch to the start and finish.
7. Design the weld so that a bending or prying action is minimized.
8. Symmetrical joints are stronger than longitudinal joints.

To determine the section modulus of a beam whose cross-section is known, proceed as follows:

Assume the dimensions of the beam are as shown.

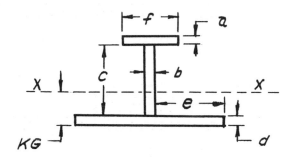

Then,

1. $I = \frac{1}{3} \left[(a+c+d)^3 f + 2d^3 e - (c+d)^3 (f-b) \right] - (fa + bc + 2de + db)(KG)^2$

$$KG = \frac{af(\frac{a}{2}+c+d) + b(c+d)\frac{(c+d)}{2} + d^2 e}{fa + bc + d(2e+b)}$$

$= $ Distance from base to center of gravity

2. $Y = $ KG, or $[(a+c+d) - KG]$, whichever is the greater

Dividing equation 1 by equation 2, we arrive at the section modulus (often defined as the letter Z).

For ease in computation, Table I is useful. This is especially helpful when the sizes of the members are known. Values of Z can easily be picked from Table I, with no further computation.

TABLE 1. WELDED TEE BEAMS AND STIFFENERS

| Standard Section | | | Z — Section Modulus (Including 30 T of Plate) | | | | |
| D x W — Tw/Tf | | | | | | | |
Ins. x Ins. — Lb./Ft.			5 lb.	7. 65 lb.	10. 2 lb.	12 lb.	15 lb.
3 x 2	—	7. 6/9	1. 65	1. 73	1. 82	1. 87	2. 0
4 x 2	—	7. 6/9	2. 20	2. 46	2. 61	2. 68	2. 77
4 x 3	—	9/15	2. 73	4. 80	5. 13	5. 3	5. 5
4 x 3	—	10. 2/20	2. 97	5. 22	6. 46	6. 7	7. 0
5 x 2	—	7. 65/9	2. 9	3. 27	3. 48	3. 58	3. 71
5 x 3	—	9/15	3. 62	6. 18	6. 63	6. 85	7. 11
5 x 3	—	10. 2/20	3. 97	6. 70	8. 3	8. 6	9. 0
6 x 3	—	9/15	4. 34	7. 59	8. 01	8. 2	8. 42
6 x 3	—	10. 2/20	4. 69	8. 1	10. 11	10. 39	10. 71
6 x 3	—	10. 2/25		8. 3	11. 97	12. 33	12. 75
6 x 4	—	12/25		8. 8	13. 5	16. 7	17. 36
6 x 5	—	12/30		9. 09	14. 0	18. 24	25. 14
7 x 3	—	10. 2/20		9. 68	12. 08	12. 39	12. 77
7 x 3	—	10. 2/25		9. 92	14. 26	14. 67	15. 15
7 x 4-1/2	—	12/25		10. 54	16. 03	19. 82	20. 57
7 x 5-1/2	—	12/30		10. 9	16. 57	21. 48	29. 67
8 x 3	—	10. 2/20		11. 14	14. 12	14. 48	14. 91
8 x 3	—	10. 2/25		11. 62	16. 70	17. 08	17. 63
8 x 4-1/2	—	12/25		12. 40	18. 63	23. 04	23. 87
8 x 5-1/2	—	12/30		12. 80	19. 24	24. 81	34. 29
9 x 3	—	10. 2/25		13. 4	19. 03	19. 57	20. 17
9 x 4-1/2	—	12/25		14. 34	21. 31	25. 33	27. 26
9 x 5-1/2	—	12/30		14. 81	22. 0	28. 24	39. 0
10 x 3	—	10. 2/25			22. 04	22. 33	22. 83
10 x 3-1/2	—	10. 2/25			24. 83	25. 17	25. 73
10 x 4	—	10. 2/25			27. 60	27. 97	28. 62
11 x 3-1/2	—	12/25			28. 92	29. 28	29. 78
11 x 4	—	12/25			31. 96	32. 37	32. 92
11 x 4-1/2	—	12/25			35. 02	35. 48	36. 09
11 x 5	—	12/25			38. 07	38. 57	39. 24
12 x 4	—	12/30			41. 13	41. 63	42. 30
12 x 5	—	12/30			49. 16	49. 77	50. 58
13 x 5	—	12/30			53. 86	54. 53	55. 41
13 x 5-1/2	—	12/30			57. 39	58. 92	59. 88

CURVES OF FORM

The "curves of form" is a common term used to identify the displacement and other curves usually found aboard merchant and naval vessels. The curves are used to determine various physical characteristics of a vessel. The characteristics are necessary in order to solve certain problems that are peculiar to the salvage operation. A typical set of curves of form is reproduced in Fig. 22 and includes the following curves:

1. Displacement in salt water.
2. Displacement in fresh water.
3. Vertical position of center of buoyancy.
4. Longitudinal position of center of buoyancy.
5. Areas of waterlines.

6. Longitudinal position of center of gravity of waterline (center of flotation).
7. Tons per inch immersion.
8. Area of midship section.
9. Outline of midship section.
10. Height of transverse meta-center above base line.
11. Longitudinal metacentric radius (BML).

12. Moment to change trim one inch.
13. Correction to displacement when vessel is trimmed one foot by the stern.
14. Area of wetted surface.
15. Curve of sectional areas up to normal load waterline.
16. Outboard profile, showing location of frames.

When the curves are not available, the various physical characteristics required in salvage work can be estimated by using the equations on Pages 51 and 52.

The primary function of the curves of form is to determine the displacement of a vessel by draft readings. The ordinates on the curves are drafts in feet, and the abscissas indicate displacement in tons and apply only to curves 1 and 2.

The abscissas of all the other curves are obtained by applying the scale factor given on each curve to the scale of tons at the top of the chart. The ordinates, which indicate drafts in feet, are the same for all curves.

To use the curves of form (Fig. 22), proceed as follows:

Curves 1 and 2, displacement in salt water and fresh water; enter the ordinates at the mean draft and proceed horizontally to intersect curve 1. The displacement is read on the abscissa in tons directly above this intersection. Use the same procedure for curve 2.

Curve 3, vertical position of center of buoyancy; enter the ordinates at mean draft and intersect the curve, diagonal for center of buoyancy and transverse metacenter above base line. Follow a vertical line through this intersection downward to curve 3. Follow a horizontal line through the intersection of curve 3 back to the draft scale ordinates and read the height of the center of buoyancy in feet above the base line.

Curve 4, longitudinal position of center of buoyancy; enter the ordinates at mean draft and intersect curve 4. The tons are read on the abscissa directly above this intersection. Apply the scale factor indicated on curve 4 and change tons to feet.

Curve 5, areas of waterlines; enter the ordinates at mean draft and intersect curve 5. The tons are read on the abscissa directly above this intersection. Apply the scale factor indicated on curve 5 and change tons to square feet.

Curve 6, longitudinal position of center of gravity of waterline (center of flotation); enter the ordinates at the mean draft and intersect curve 6. The tons are read on the abscissa directly above this intersection. Apply the scale factor indicated on curve 6 and change tons to feet.

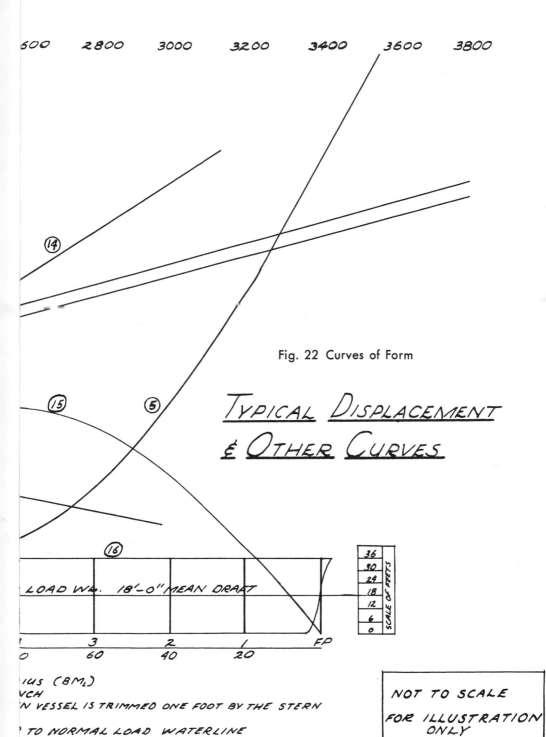

2600   2800   3000   3200   3400   3600   3800

(14)

Fig. 22 Curves of Form

(15)   (5)

TYPICAL DISPLACEMENT
& OTHER CURVES

(16)

LOAD WL.   18'-0" MEAN DRAFT

| 36 |
| 30 |
| 24 |
| 18 |
| 12 |
| 6 |
| 0 |

SCALE OF FEETS

3   2   1   FP
60   40   20

ius (BM₁)
VCH
N VESSEL IS TRIMMED ONE FOOT BY THE STERN

TO NORMAL LOAD WATERLINE

NOT TO SCALE
FOR ILLUSTRATION
ONLY

Curve 7, tons per inch immersion; enter the ordinates at the mean draft and intersect curve 7. The tons are read on the abscissa directly above this intersection. Apply the scale factor indicated on curve 7.

Curve 8, area of midship section; enter the ordinates at mean draft and intersect curve 8. The tons are read directly above on the abscissa. Apply the scale factor indicated on curve 8 and change tons to square feet.

Curve 9, outline of midship section; enter the ordinates at the desired draft and intersect curve 9. The half-breadth of the midship section is read in feet on the vertical scale after applying the scale factor indicated on curve 9.

Curve 10, height of transverse metacenter above base line; enter the ordinates at the mean draft and intersect the curve, diagonal for center of buoyancy and transverse metacenter above base line. Follow a vertical line upward through this intersection to curve 10. Follow a horizontal line through this intersection back to the draft scale ordinates and read the height of the transverse metacenter above the base line.

Curve 11, longitudinal metacentric radius; enter the ordinates at mean draft and intersect curve 11. The tons are read on the abscissa directly above this intersection. Apply the scale factor indicated on curve 11 and change tons to feet.

Curve 12, moment to change trim one inch; enter the ordinates at the mean draft and intersect curve 12. The tons are read on the abscissa directly above this intersection. Apply the scale factor indicated on curve 12 and change tons to foot-tons.

Curve 13, correction to displacement when vessel is trimmed one foot by the stern; enter the ordinates at the mean draft and intersect curve 13. The tons are read on the abscissa directly above this intersection. Apply the scale factor indicated on curve 13 and multiply the result by the number of feet in trim. The product in tons is added to, or subtracted from, the displacement, as indicated.

Curve 14, area of wetted surface; enter the ordinates at the mean draft and intersect curve 14. The tons are read on the abscissa directly above this intersection. Apply the scale factor indicated on curve 14 and change tons to square feet.

Curve 15, curve of sectional areas up to normal load waterline; at any desired point along the ship's length, follow a vertical line and intersect curve 15. Measure the distance between the base line and the intersection in inches. Apply the scale factor indicated on curve 15 and change inches to square feet.

Curve 16, outboard profile; this drawing shows the shape of the centerline plane and the location of frames.

CROSS CURVES OF STABILITY

The cross curves of stability are drawn up in order to determine the stability of a vessel through all angles of heel that the vessel will experience up to the angle of heel at which the vessel capsizes. Two sets of curves are utilized in considering the stability of a vessel: cross curves of stability and the curve of statical stability.

A set of cross curves of stability is illustrated in Fig. 23. The cross curves are plotted as contours of degrees of heel, displacement in tons, and righting arms (GZ) in feet. By knowing the displacement, the righting arm (GZ) may be determined for all angles of heel. The curves are plotted for several conditions of loading; that is, there are additional sets of curves to those shown in Fig. 23.

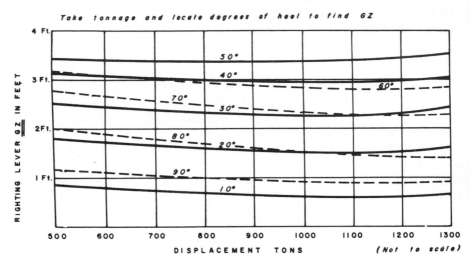

Fig. 23. Cross curves of stability.

The specific angle of heel is followed horizontally to the intersection of a vertical line drawn from the known displacement in tons. A horizontal line is drawn back to the left-hand vertical scale, and the righting arm (GZ) is read directly in feet.

CURVE OF STATICAL STABILITY

The curve of statical stability is plotted from the cross curve of stability, and it is used to analyze the vessel's stability at a specified condition of loading. The curve shows at a glance the righting arms (GZ) for all angles of heel, from upright through capsizing. Separate curves must be drawn up for various conditions of loading.

The curve of statical stability is illustrated in Fig. 24, and the following values may be determined from this curve:

1. Maximum righting arm is the highest point on the curve.

2. Angle of maximum righting arm is the angle indicated on the abscissas of the scale directly below the intersection of the highest point on the curve.

3. Range of stability is the range of degrees of heel where the curve lies above the horizontal base line.

4. Dynamic stability is the measure of the area between the curve and the base line, and it is a means of computing the work, or moments, necessary to heel the vessel.

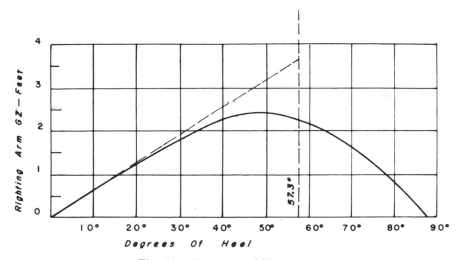

Fig. 24.   Statical stability curve.

5. Initial metacentric height may be determined by drawing a tangent to the curve at its origin and extending the tangent to intersect a vertical drawn at 57.3 degrees to the base. The height of this intersection is read as the initial metacentric height. One (1) radian equals 57.3 degrees.

ESTIMATING PHYSICAL CHARACTERISTICS

When no curves of form are available, the various physical characteristics of a vessel must be determined by formulae in order to successfully resolve many salvage problems. The following equations may be used to approximate, within reason, the unknown characteristics:

1. Displacement:

$$\Delta \text{ (Tons salt water)} = \frac{BL \times Hm \times b}{35}$$

2. Volume of displacement:
$$V = BL \times Hm \times b \text{ (cubic feet)}$$

3. Vertical position of center of buoyancy:
    1. Feet above base line
$$KB = \frac{11}{20} Hm$$
    2. Feet below base line
$$VCB = \frac{Hm}{3} \left(\frac{1}{3} + \frac{6}{p} \right)$$

4. Vertical position of center of gravity:
$$KG = \frac{11}{20} D \text{ (feet)} \quad D = \text{Depth in feet from keel to main deck}$$

5. Area of waterplane:
$$Awp = LBp \text{ (square feet)}$$

6. Tons per inch immersion:
$$T = \frac{LBp}{420} \text{ (tons per inch)}$$

7. Area of midship section:
$$A\text{⊠} = BHm \text{ (square feet)}$$

8. Moment to trim one inch:
$$MT1 = \frac{BL^2 \times p^2}{5040} \text{ (foot-tons)}$$

COEFFICIENTS OF FORM

Coefficients of form are useful in evaluating various physical characteristics of a vessel, which is required in ship salvage work. The coefficients are comparisons between one hull and a standard hull. The coefficients most generally used in ship salvage work are the block coefficient, the midship section coefficient, and the coefficient of the waterplane area. Coefficients of form are not necessary when curves of form are available.

Block Coefficient (b) is the ratio between the volume of displacement of the ship in question and the volume of a similar rectangular block having sides equal to the length, breadth, and draft of the vessel. This value will vary with the type of the vessel being considered. Table II will give an idea of the range of this value. The coefficient is determined by the following formula: $b = V \div LBHm$.

Midship Coefficient (m) is the ratio between the area of the midship section and the area of a rectangle having dimensions equal to the draft and breadth of the vessel being considered. The coefficient is determined by the followed formula: $m = A\phi \div BHm$. The midship coefficient indicates the shape of the outside hull amidship and reflects the amount of deadrise and tumblehome.

Waterplane Coefficient (p) is the ratio between the area of the water-plane at the designer's waterline and the area of a rectangle having dimensions equal to the breadth and length of the vessel being considered. The coefficient is determined by the following formula: p = Awp ÷ BL.

TABLE II. COEFFICIENTS OF FORM

TYPE	BLOCK COEFFICIENT b	MIDSHIP COEFFICIENT m	WATERPLANE COEFFICIENT p
Ocean Liner	.597	.956	.725
Large Cargo	.775	.992	.848
Large Tanker	.757	.978	.845
Great Lakes Freighter	.874	.990	.918
Yacht	.565	.938	.724
Harbor Tug	.585	.892	.800
Lifeboat	.600		

The above figures are used for estimating displacement when the ship is on the bottom or the displacement is unknown.

TRANSVERSE STABILITY

Anyone undertaking small salvage jobs will not require a detailed knowledge of buoyancy and stability principles; however, a salvage man engaged in major salvage operations must thoroughly understand and have a complete working knowledge of all the principles involved in stability problems. Not to know and apply these principles may result in the failure and abandonment of an otherwise successful salvage effort.

Initial Stability. When a body is at rest, it tends to remain at rest and is said to be in *equilibrium.*

If, when inclined or heeled over, the body tends to right itself to its former position at rest, it is said to be in *stable equilibrium.*

If a body tends to remain at rest, regardless of the position to which it is heeled, it is known to be in *neutral equilibrium.*

If a body, when inclined, tends to develop an increasingly upsetting moment, it is known to be in *unstable equilibrium.*

The tendency of a body to right itself when heeled is called *statical stability.*

Center of Buoyancy. In a floating body, the sum of the buoyant forces acting upward through one point of the underwater body is called the *center of buoyancy*; it is usually located at the geometric center of volume of the submerged underwater body. When a vessel is at rest and zero heel, the forces of the center of buoyancy are generally exerted vertically upward through the centerline.

The **center of gravity** is the point through which the weight of the ship acts downward. This is usually a fixed point and does not change position when the ship is listed or heeled, unless there is a weight shift aboard the vessel. Generally speaking, the center of gravity will always be assumed to be on the centerline at the midship section.

Metacenter. Whenever a vessel is inclined or listed, due to any reason (wave, weight shift, etc.), an angle of heel will develop—the degree of the angle depending upon the force exerted to incline the vessel. This angle of heel is called *theta*.

The shape of the displaced volume of water is changed because of the change of the shape of the underwater body of the vessel when heeled to small angles. The shape of the displaced volume is changed so as to cause a shift in the center of the underwater volume toward the direction of the list or heel and away from the centerline. This shift in the center of the underwater volume causes a reactive shift in the upward forces of the center of buoyancy, because the center of buoyancy is always considered as acting vertically upward through the center of the underwater volume.

A vertical line drawn upward through this new center of buoyancy will intersect a vertical line that was extended upward through the center of gravity (G) and center of buoyancy when the vessel was at zero angle of heel. The point of this intersection is known as the *transverse metacenter* (M). The location of this point remains on the centerline for small angles of heel not exceeding 10 degrees.

For larger angles of heel, a decided shift will be noted in the location of the center of buoyancy (B). The distance of the shift will vary in direct relation to the degree of heel.

The **center of gravity remains fairly constant**, acting downward through the centerline; however, as was quoted, the center of buoyancy shifts, causing two equal and opposite forces to come into play, which are separated by a distance referred to as the righting arm (GẒ), as shown in Fig. 25.

When an angle of heel causes the transverse metacenter to lie above the center of gravity, a *couple* (a pair of equal and parallel forces, usually in opposite directions) is produced that exerts a righting moment on the vessel.

When a small angle of heel causes the transverse metacenter (M) to lie at the center of gravity (G), a glance at Fig. 26 will readily indicate that no righting arm is developed; consequently, no couple is produced, and the vessel remains at the angle of heel and does not return to its original position of zero heel. The vessel is said to be in neutral equilibrium.

When an angle of heel causes the transverse metacenter (M) to lie below the center of gravity (G), a study of Fig. 27 will indicate that an upsetting couple is produced, which exerts ever increasing upsetting moments and resultant greater degrees of heel. The vessel is unstable and will capsize.

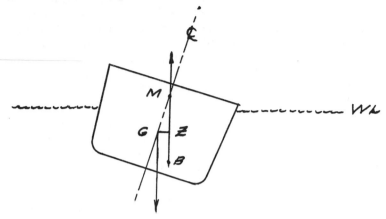

Fig. 25   Positive metacentric height (stable equilibrium).

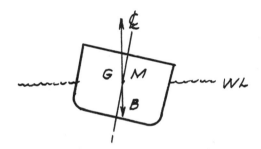

Fig. 26.   Neutral equilibrium.

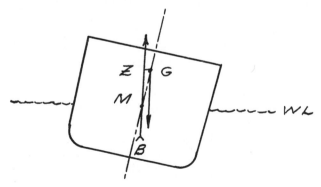

Fig. 27.   Unstable equilibrium.

The **metacentric height** is the distance between the center of gravity (G) and the metacenter (M). The metacentric height has direct bearing upon the stability of a vessel. Large metacentric height will develop large righting arms and will return the vessel rapidly to its original position of rest. A vessel with large metacentric height is said to be "stiff." Small metacentric height will develop small righting arms and will return the vessel slowly to its original position of rest. A vessel with small metacentric height is said to be "tender."

Passenger vessels usually have small metacentric height because riding comfort is a prime requisite to the trade.

The **Righting Moment** is the product of the righting arm and the displacement of a vessel. It is expressed in foot-tons and determined by the formula:

Righting moment (R) $= \Delta G\overline{Z}$ (foot-tons)

Where $\Delta =$ The displacement

The **metacentric radius (BM)** is the distance between the center of buoyancy (B) and the metacenter (M) at small angles of heel. The metacentric radius can be calculated for any given draft from the formula: $BM = I \div V$.

Where I is the *moment of inertia* of the vessel's waterplane about a longitudinal axis, V is the volume of the underwater body (or displacement multiplied by 35) $(V = 35\Delta)$.

$$I = \frac{b^3 \; l \; p^2}{12}$$

Where: $b =$ Breadth

$l =$ Length

$p =$ Waterplane coefficient

Effect of Shifting Weights. If one or a part of a system of weights is moved, the center of gravity of the total system moves in the direction of the weight shift; *ergo*, the distance can be determined from the formula:

$$GG_1 = \frac{ws}{\Delta}$$

Where $GG_1 =$ Distance center of gravity of total system shifts.

$w =$ Weight moved

$s =$ Distance weight is moved

$\Delta =$ Weight of total system, in this case the weight displacement of the vessel

As an illustration, assume that a weight (w) already on board a vessel is shifted a certain distance (s) vertically upward. First, the shift in the center of gravity of the ship must be computed from the preceding formula.

Note: The center of gravity will shift in the direction of the weight shift. In this case, the weight shift of the center of gravity will be vertically upward.

Referring to Fig. 28, it will be seen that the righting arm (G$\not{Z}$) is less, as a result of this shift of G to G_1. Since the angle "theta" Θ is the same for any given angle of heel for both triangles formed,

$$\text{sine } \Theta = \frac{\text{loss of righting arm}}{\text{shift of CG (or } GG_1)}$$

Or,

Loss of righting arm $= GG_1 \text{ sine } \Theta$

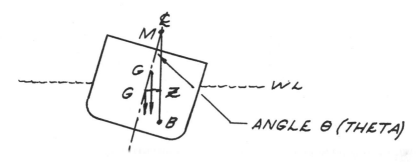

Fig. 28.   Effect on righting arm of weight shift.

Now it becomes necessary to transpose the amount of this loss of righting arm onto a statical stability curve, drawn up for the displacement (G). The application of the loss of righting arm is necessary in order to correct the stability curve for a vertical rise of the center of gravity.

To correct a statical stability curve for vertical shift of the center of gravity, refer to Fig. 29, and proceed as follows:

1. Lay off a vertical distance GG_1 on the statical stability curve at 90 degrees of heel.

2. At each 10 degrees of heel, lay off a new value of GG_1, sine Θ, where Θ is equal to the degree of heel along the abscissas.

3. Intersect these points with a curve. This curve is known as the "sine correction curve."

4. Measure the distance between the sine correction curve and uncorrected statical stability curve at each angle of heel (10, 20, 30 degrees, etc.) and lay off this distance from the base vertically upward. Intersect these new points with a new curve, which is called the "corrected statical stability curve."

For a horizontal weight shift, we assume the center of gravity shifts to GG_2, then

$$\text{Cosine } \Theta = \frac{\text{loss of righting arm}}{GG_2}$$

Or,

Loss of righting arm $= GG_2 \text{ cosine } \Theta$

Bearing in mind that the cosine of 0 degrees equals 1 and the cosine of 90 degrees equals 0, the statical stability curve can now be corrected for horizontal shift of center of gravity. Referring to Figure 30, proceed as follows:

1. Lay off a distance of GG_2 on the statical stability curve at 0 degrees.

2. At each 10 degrees of heel, lay off a new value of GG_2 cosine Θ, where Θ is equal to the degree of heel along the abscissas.

3. Intersect these points with a curve. This curve is known as the "cosine correction curve."

4. Measure the distance between the cosine correction curve and the uncorrected statical stability curve at each angle of heel (10, 20, 30 degrees, etc.) and lay off this distance from the base. Intersect these new points with a new curve, which is called the "corrected statical stability curve."

Note: It should be remembered that in both horizontal and vertical weight shifts there is a loss of maximum righting arm, angle of maximum righting arm, range, dynamic stability, and righting arm at all angles of heel.

The value of GM for a horizontal weight shift does not change in the upright position.

GM prevailing at any angle of list is less than when the vessel is upright for both horizontal and vertical weight shifts. A diagonal weight shift is treated as two problems: vertical and horizontal.

Effect of Changing Weights. If a weight is removed from or added to a vessel, calculations must be made for a shift of the center of gravity. To calculate the effect on the center of gravity of adding weight, proceed as follows:

1. Determine the amount of weight taken aboard and add it to the displacement ($\Delta + w$).

2. Draw the new curve of statical stability from the cross curves of stability, using the new displacement.

3. Shift the weight to its final location and calculate the new position of G, as described under Effect of Shifting Weights.

4. The curve of statical stability must then be corrected from the cross curves; or

$$GG_1 = \frac{\Delta + w}{w \times s}$$

Where GG_1 = Shift in center of gravity
      w = Weight added
      s = Distance weight is moved from CG
      Δ = Displacement of the vessel

To calculate the effect on the center of gravity of removing weight, proceed as follows:

1. Shift the weight to the center of gravity of the ship and calculate the new center of gravity, using the following formula:

$$GG_1 = \frac{ws}{\Delta - w}$$

2. Draw the new curve of statical stability from the cross curves of stability, using the new displacement ($\Delta - w$).

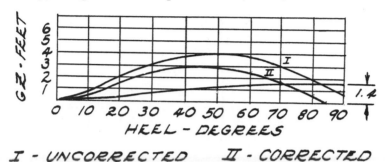

Fig. 29.   Correcting a statical stability curve for vertical weight shift.

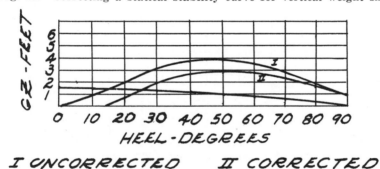

Fig. 30.   Correcting a statical stability curve for horizontal weight shift.

NEGATIVE METACENTRIC HEIGHT

When a vessel is inclined and tends to develop an increasingly upsetting moment, it is known to be in unstable equilibrium and has *negative metacentric height.*

Negative metacentric height obtains when, for some reason, the metacentric (M) falls below the center of gravity (G) when the vessel is inclined. As indicated in Fig. 31, an upsetting couple is produced that tends to capsize the vessel.

In many cases, negative metacentric height may obtain through small initial of heel, with the vessels developing positive righting arms beyond an angle of "loll." *See* Fig. 32 for statical stability curve of a vessel in this condition.

The vessel may heel over to either port or starboard and remain at the angle of "loll" unless rolled to the opposite side by outside forces; i.e., sea, weather, etc.

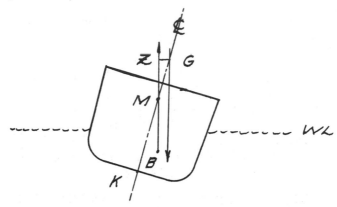

Fig. 31.   Negative metacentric height.

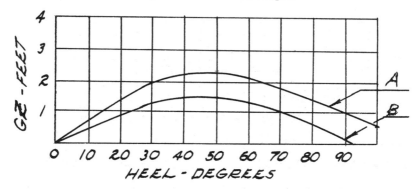

Fig. 32.   Statical stability curve for vessel with angle of "loll." A. Before flooding; B. After flooding.

A vessel in this condition is in danger of capsizing if weights are changed or shifted topside. Therefore, if a vessel develops a list, it should be determined before corrective measures are taken whether the cause is from an off-center weight or from negative metacentric height.

To remove a list caused by negative metacentric height, proceed as follows:

1. Insure that there is no free surface in any tank. The tanks should be pressed full or pumped dry.

2. Equal topside weight should be removed from both port and starboard sides; that is, the amount removed from the port side should be removed simultaneously from the starboard side.

3. Lower weights to a position on the same side of the vessel; that is, do not lower weights diagonally.

4. Add solid weight low in the vessel on both port and starboard sides.

To remove a list caused by off-center weight, proceed as follows:

1. Remove weight from low side or add weight to the high side.

2. Shift weight from the low side to the high side. Caution: Do not try to correct for negative metacenter height by taking the steps for off-center weight, because the vessel will probably capsize.

INCLINING EXPERIMENT

The *inclining experiment* is conducted as a means of determining the actual location of the center of gravity of a vessel. In all our previous discussions, the location of the center of gravity was assumed.

The experiment requires listing or heeling the vessel by shifting a known weight a measured distance athwartship and then recording the angle of heel or list developed by the vessel. By applying the foregoing factors, known and determined, to a formula, GM can be computed. KM (the distance from the keel to the metacenter) can be taken from the curves of form. By subtracting GM from KM, the center of gravity, KG, can be found.

The following equipment is required:

1. Weights of a known size that are heavy enough to list the ship several degrees when the weights are moved from the centerline athwartship. (Obtain a list of approximately 3 degrees.)

2. A crane, track, or dolly to move the weights transversely.

3. A clinometer, or makeshift pendulum with a bob immersed in a bucket of oil to dampen any oscillations. A ruler or scale, to be located in front of the plumb line of the pendulum.

An accurate knowledge of the displacement of the ship is very important when conducting the inclining experiment.

Following is an outline of a test experiment:

1. The vessel lies in calm water with zero list and trim.

2. All fuel, water, oil, and ballast tanks should be either full or empty.

3. The vessel should be moored with little or no wind blowing and slack on all the mooring lines.

4. Use two or more pendulums if possible.

5. Shift the weight athwartship and record the size of the weight, the distance the weight is moved, the length of the pendulum, and the deflection of the pendulum.

6. Apply the information obtained to the formula:

$$GM = \frac{ws}{\Delta \frac{c}{L}}$$

Where: w = Size of the weight in tons
        s = Distance the weight is moved (feet)
        c = Deflection of pendulum (feet)
        L = Length of pendulum (feet)
        Δ = Accurate displacement of the vessel (tons)

Stability estimate from period of roll. Occasionally a salvage engineer must make a rough estimate of stability based on the natural period of roll of the vessel. The roll should be easy and not forced by wind or sea. In calm waters, the vessel can be sallied to effect a roll. The results obtained are sufficiently accurate for a rough stability check.

To estimate the metacentric height from the period of roll, use the following formula:

$$GM = \frac{0.16\ B^2}{T^2}$$

Where: GM = Metacentric height
       B = Breadth of vessel (feet)
       T = Time required for one complete roll from port to starboard and back to port (seconds)

Proceed as follows to obtain the time of a complete roll:

1. Sally the vessel in calm water until the vessel is rolling approximately 5 degrees.

2. Time the interval for ten consecutive cycles of rolling and divide this time by ten to get an average period of roll.

3. Repeat the experiment several times to check results.

4. All units in the formula are in feet and seconds.

Example: If the beam of a vessel is 40 feet and the period of roll is 10 seconds, the GM would be 2.56 feet.

FLOODING

Flooding exists when water is admitted into the hull of a vessel. Flooding can be either controlled or uncontrolled. An example of controlled flooding is the ballasting with sea water of tanks or holds aboard a vessel. Controlled flooding rarely presents a problem except on tankers.

Uncontrolled flooding may result from any number of causes: a vessel may start flooding in compartments that have sustained damage due to a collision with another vessel, structure, etc.; a hold, engine room, or double bottom tank may start flooding as a result of grounding. Heavy weather, striking submerged objects, and pipe or sea valve body failures are some other causes of flooding.

Regardless of the cause of uncontrolled flooding, the effect almost always is detrimental to transverse stability.

In studying the effect on transverse stability, flooding is usually classed under three types: (1) solid; (2) partial, without free communication; and (3) partial, with free communication.

Solid flooding is the complete filling of a tank or compartment. The effect is the same as that of adding any solid weight.

The center of gravity of the vessel will be lowered if the flooding occurs low in the ship; and, if the ship does not sink as a result, the stability is probably increased.

Partial Flooding Without Free Communication. When a compartment, hold, or tank remains intact and fills partially, the liquid is said to have *free surface*; that is, the level of the surface of the water is free to rise and fall as the liquid shifts due to rolling or pitching of the vessel.

If free surface is permitted to exist, its effect is a virtual rise in the center of gravity, even though the weight shift is in a horizontal direction, as indicated by the shift of the wedge of water AGB to A'GB' in Fig. 33.

$$\text{\Lambda} GGv = \frac{i}{V}$$

Where: $\text{\Lambda} GGv$ is the virtual rise in the center of gravity

V = displacement volume of vessel (cubic feet)

i = moment of inertia of free surface area about a longitudinal axis and is calculated from the following formula:

$$i = \frac{b^3 \, l \, p^2}{12}$$

Where: b = Breadth of vessel

l = Length

p = Waterplane coefficient (*see* Table III)

Or,

$$\text{\Lambda} GGv = \frac{b^3 \, l \, p^2}{12V}$$

The loss of righting arm for any angle of heel is then computed by the formula:

LRA = GGv sine Θ

Where: Θ = angle of heel

The breadth of the vessel has the greatest influence on the loss of righting arm.

Partial Flooding with Free Communication. Figures 34 and 35 illustrate a vessel subjected to effects of partial flooding with free communication to the sea. As the vessel rolls, the hole in the shell is alternately submerged and exposed with the flooding and partial draining of the compartment.

TABLE III

TYPE	WATERPLANE COEFFICIENT p
Ocean Liner	.725
Large Cargo	.848
Large Tanker	.845
Great Lakes Freighter	.918
Yacht	.724
Harbor Tug	.800
Barge	.95

The above figures are used for estimating displacement when the ship is on the bottom or the displacement is unknown.

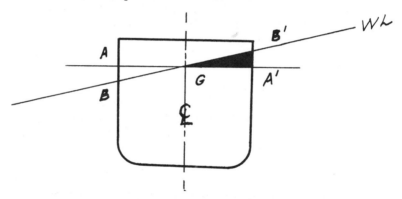

Fig. 33.   Shift of free surface liquid.

The effect of the additional weight is similar to partial flooding and causes a virtual rise in the center of gravity.

$$GGv = \frac{AY^2}{V}$$

Where: $\blacktriangle GGv$ = Virtual rise in center of gravity

A = Cross-sectional area of surface of water in compartment

Y = Perpendicular distance (feet) between center of gravity of water in compartment and centerline of ship

V = Displacement volume of ship (cubic feet)

The effect of free communication can be calculated by the formula:

$$\Lambda GGv = \frac{i + AY^2}{V}$$

The loss of righting arm for any angle of heel is then computed by the formula:

$$LRA = \frac{i + AY^2}{V}\text{sine } O$$

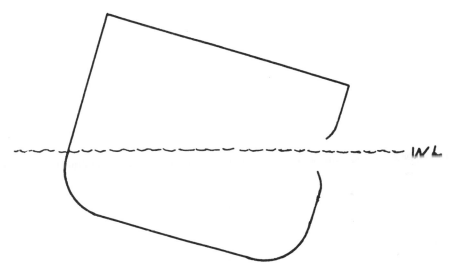

Fig. 34. Level of water when heeled toward damage.

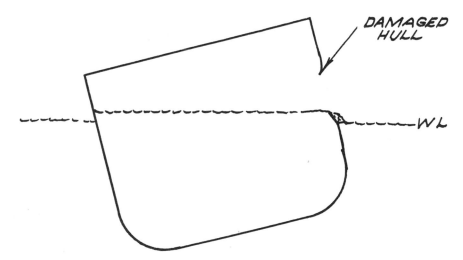

Fig. 35. Level of water when heeled away from damage.

LONGITUDINAL STABILITY

The measure of the ability of a vessel to return to a position of equilibrium after being inclined in a fore and aft direction is *longitudinal stability*.

Vessels, as a general rule, do not have longitudinal stability problems; however, certain principles will be covered here, as they are necessary to resolve trim problems, which are usually encountered in strandings.

Longitudinal Metacentric Height. The procedure for finding the longitudinal metacentric height is the same as that used to find the transverse metacenter. Because the longitudinal height is so great, it is rarely calculated in salvage work and usually is estimated from the rule:

GML $=$ 100 GM

Or,

GML $=$ One or two times the ship's length

Trim and Trimming Moment. The fore and aft inclination of a vessel is called trim, and it is the difference between the forward and after draft readings. When a weight is shifted fore or aft, it produces a *trimming moment*. The trimming moment is equal to the weight multiplied by the distance moved.

The following equation is used to determine the moment to change trim one inch:

$$MT_1 = \Delta \times GML \times \frac{1}{12L}$$

Where: $MT_1 =$ Moment to change trim one inch
$\Delta =$ Displacement of vessel
$GML =$ Longitudinal metacentric height
$L =$ Length between perpendiculars

To determine the change of trim from a weight shift, use the following equation:

$$\mathfrak{t} = \frac{ws}{MT_1}$$

Where: $\mathfrak{t} =$ Change of trim
$w =$ Weight shifted
$s =$ Distance moved
$MT_1 =$ Moment to change trim one inch

To determine the change of trim from a change (addition or removal) of a weight, proceed as follows:

1. Assume the weight is added or removed at the center of flotation and calculate the change in mean draft:

$$Hm = \frac{w}{T}$$

Where: Hm = Change in mean draft
    w = Weight added or removed
    T = Tons per inch immersion

2. Next, determine the distance the weight is then shifted longitudinally and calculate for change of trim:

$$\iota t = \frac{ws}{MT_1}$$

CHAPTER IV

EQUIPMENT AND STRUCTURES
USED IN SALVAGE

Salvage work requires men of dedication of purpose. All too often the work is long, hard, and exhausting, and the results, when analyzed, are believed to be hardly worth the effort. The work requires resourceful men of infinite patience and tenacity of purpose.

A salvage diver must have a thorough knowledge of the uses of underwater pneumatic tools, underwater welding and cutting, and the preparation and placing of explosive charges. In addition, he must be able to perform, topside, any job that may be required under water; for, if a diver cannot perform a particular evolution out of the water, he certainly cannot do it while submerged.

A salvage vessel may range in size from a small boat to a large ocean-going vessel: any vessel, in fact, that is used to perform salvage work. Generally speaking, though, a salvage vessel is considered to be a large vessel used for offshore salvage work. A salvage vessel should be outfitted with the following minimum equipment, or suitable substitutions, in order to provide an effective plant for salvage operations:

1. Two 10″ portable centrifugal gasoline-engine-driven pumps.

2. Two 6″ portable centrifugal gasoline-engine-driven pumps.

3. Flexible and pipe suction and discharge hoses, couplings, foot valves, strainers, gaskets, tools, etc., in sufficient quantities for the job intended.

4. Electrical submersible pumps (aluminum casings), if power is available.

5. Portable steam- or gasoline-engine-driven pumps: 2½″ to 4″ pumps may be substituted for half of the recommended 6″ and 10″ pumps.

6. Air compressors: two 100–200 cubic-foot capacity at 100 pounds per square inch.

7. Minimum of two heavy, portable winches, preferably with torque clutches, gasoline-engine-driven.

8. Hydraulic force pump with jetting nozzle and hose.

9. Wire and Manila ropes, chain and tackle in sufficient quantities to supply anticipated needs.

10. Timbers, shores, steel plates and shapes, wood plugs, and sheet plywood to be used for patching and cofferdam construction; the quantity will depend on the salvage plan.

11. Cement, bricks, gravel, and sand for patch work and for plugging leaks.

12. Oxgen-acetylene cutting apparatus for above-water use.

13. Oxygen-hydrogen or oxy-arc cutting apparatus for underwater use.

14. Welding machine and electrodes.

15. Pneumatic drills for rock and steel, and augers for timber boring.

16. Pneumatic saws for cutting timber under water.

The workshop should contain a smithy's forge, lathe, drill press, pipe threaders, dies, taps, band saw, vices, small bending slab, blow torches, and all hand tools. The amount of equipment required will depend upon the size and scope of the work to be undertaken.

TUGS

To be considered for any major salvage operation, a salvage tug should have a main engine capable of developing approximately 3,000 HP. The tug should carry aboard the minimum gear listed above for a salvage vessel. The number of tugs and the total horsepower required will vary with the size and scope of the salvage operation.

A salvage tug should be capable of maintaining sustained offshore operations, and it should be outfitted to provide reasonable comfort for the salvage crew.

The salvage tug should be outfitted in port, before leaving on any job, with all the equipment that can be anticipated for the job. The necessity of returning to port for additional required equipment may spell the failure of the venture; consequently, it is better to delay a departure, in order to properly outfit a salvage tug, than to depart hastily without an adequate salvage plant. In this connection, it is well to remember that the necessity to return for additional equipment may involve a voyage of hundreds or even thousands of miles and a lapse of days or even weeks. It is needless to say what can happen to the costs of the job and the all-important weather in the interim. The salvage plant aboard the tug should be sighted to insure that all the equipment that may be used is actually on board.

A tug, or salvage vessel, will develop approximately a 1-ton pull for every 100 HP of the main engine.

A well-laid set of beach gear will develop approximately a 40–60-ton pull. A minimum of two sets should be aboard.

Fig. 36. Typical salvage tug and crane in salvage operation.

The tug should be equipped with a tow engine and tow wire suitable for the job intended.

Figure 36 is a photograph of a typical salvage tug.

BEACH GEAR

Beach gear is a combination of anchors, purchase blocks, carpenter stoppers, shackles, and wire used to free a grounded vessel. The anchor is planted to seaward and is connected to the stranded vessel with large-diameter wires, called anchor pendants. The purchase wires are led from a winch, rove through the fourfold purchase blocks and connected to the anchor pendants with carpenter stoppers.

A well-laid set of beach gear will develop up to a 60-ton pull, and it is the most effective and efficient force that can be applied to free a grounded vessel.

A standard set of beach gear generally consists of the following:

1. One 8,000-pound patent anchor, usually the Eells type.
2. Two 100 fathoms of $1\frac{5}{8}''$, 6 × 37, high-grade plow-steel wire rope with a thimble fitted to each end for connecting shackles.
3. One 50 fathoms of $1\frac{5}{8}''$, 6 × 37, high-grade plow-steel wire rope with a thimble fitted to each end for connecting shackles.
4. One 15 fathoms (one shot) of $2\frac{1}{4}''$ chain.
5. Three small plate-type connecting shackles.
6. One large plate-type connecting shackle.
7. Two $1\frac{5}{8}''$ carpenter stoppers (wire cable grips).
8. Heavy purchase gear consisting of the following:
    a. One standing block, four sheaves.
    b. One running block, four sheaves.
    c. One 1,200' of $\frac{5}{8}''$ wire rope.
    d. One fairlead block for $\frac{5}{8}''$ wire rope.
    e. One fairlead block for $1\frac{5}{8}''$ wire rope pendant.
    f. One anchor buoy (spar buoy or can buoy).
    g. One crown line: 15 to 20 fathoms of 8" Manila or $\frac{7}{8}''$ wire rope.

Figure 37 is a photograph of beach gear purchase tackle. Figure 38 is a photograph of a salvage, or Eells, anchor.

To lay out the beach gear, proceed as follows: The fourfold purchase blocks, $\frac{5}{8}''$ purchase wire rope, carpenter stoppers, and fairlead blocks are placed aboard the stranded vessel.

Reeve the $\frac{5}{8}''$ purchase wire rope through the purchase blocks. One recommended method of reeving a fourfold purchase is illustrated in Fig. 39. This method tends to limit the turning of the running block and the resultant friction caused by the twisting of the purchase wires. There are other methods of reeving, and the particular method employed will reflect the experience and choice of the salvor.

Fig. 37.   Beach gear purchase tackle ranged on deck of wreck.

Fig. 38.   Salvage, or Eells, anchor.

One carpenter stopper is connected to the running block of the pur-chase gear, as illustrated in Fig. 40. The other carpenter stopper is secured to a cleat or bitt at the offshore end of the vessel. This second stopper is a back-up stopper, and it is connected to hold the 1⅝″ wire pendant while the running block is being overhauled.

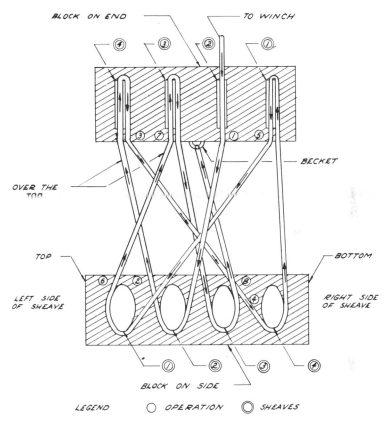

Fig. 39. Method of reeving a four-fold purchase.

The standing fourfold purchase block is secured to bitts well for-ward on the vessel, to insure maximum reach. The bitter end of the purchase wire is led to a deck winch or to a portable salvage winch. The ⅝″ fairlead block may be used to obtain a more direct lead for the purchase wire to the winch. The remainder of the beach gear is rigged aboard the tug, or salvage vessel.

Hang the Eells anchor out over the side of the tug, well forward, and stop off with four turns of 5″ Manila rope or a pelican hook. Con-nect the 15 to 20 fathoms of ⅞″ crown wire or 8″ Manila rope to the crown of the anchor and hang the crown line over the side in several loops. The bitter end of the crown line should be led forward and secured to the anchor buoy at the bow. The buoy should have sufficient positive buoyancy to support the crown line, and it should just watch at the surface of the water after the anchor is laid.

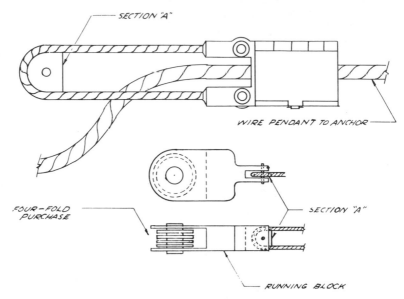

Fig. 40.   Carpenter stopper.

The 50-fathom length of $1\frac{5}{8}''$ wire pendant is connected to the anchor, using the large plate shackle. Connect the shot of $2\frac{1}{4}''$ chain and two 100-fathom lengths of $1\frac{5}{8}''$ wire pendants successively, using the three small plate shackles. The chain and wire are hung out over the side and stopped off with $2''$ Manila rope. The bitter end of the pendant, with a small buoy and line attached, is led aft and laid out on the after deck or fantail of the tug. A vessel rigged for laying beach gear is illustrated in Fig. 41.

The tug, or salvage vessel, is positioned for letting go the beach gear anchor. In determining the location of the anchor, consideration should be given to the depth of the water and the desired scope and catenary of the anchor pendants. The anchor is dropped by severing the Manila rope or by tripping the pelican hook. The vessel steams toward the wreck, allowing the $2''$ Manila stoppers to part as a strain is developed on each of the loops of anchor pendant. The bitter end of the pendant is passed to the stranded vessel and secured to the carpenter stopper on the running block of the fourfold purchase. The general layout of beach gear, rigged aboard a stranded vessel, is shown in Fig. 42.

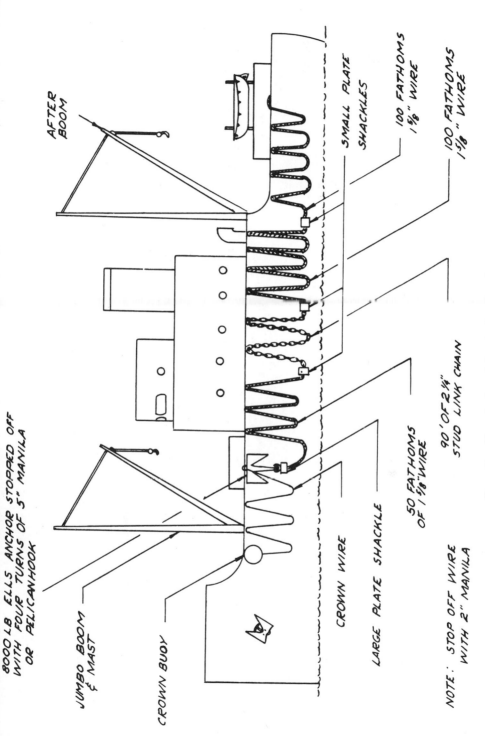

8000 LB ELLS ANCHOR STOPPED OFF
WITH FOUR TURNS OF 5" MANILA
OR PELICANHOOK

AFTER BOOM

SMALL PLATE SHACKLES

100 FATHOMS 1⅝" WIRE

100 FATHOMS 1⅝" WIRE

JUMBO BOOM & MAST

CROWN BUOY

CROWN WIRE

LARGE PLATE SHACKLE

50 FATHOMS OF 1⅝"WIRE

90' OF 2¼" STUD LINK CHAIN

NOTE: STOP OFF WIRE
WITH 2" MANILA

Fig. 41. Vessel rigged for laying beach gear.

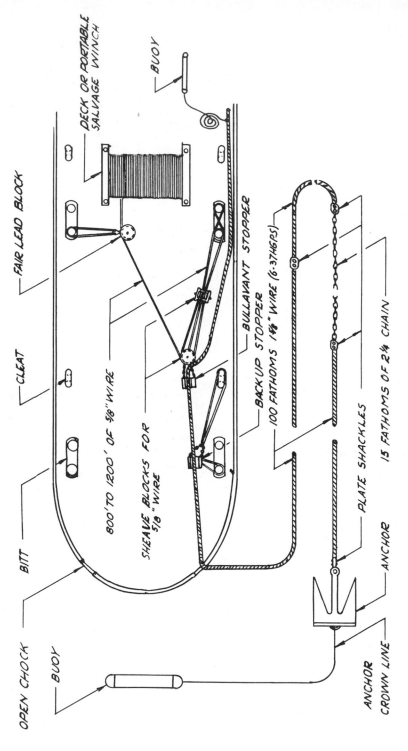

DECK OR PORTABLE SALVAGE WINCH

BUOY

FAIR LEAD BLOCK

BULLAVANT STOPPER

CLEAT

BACK UP STOPPER

100 FATHOMS 1⅝" WIRE (6-37/16FPS)

800' TO 1200' OF ⅝" WIRE

SHEAVE BLOCKS FOR ⅝" WIRE

15 FATHOMS OF 2¼ CHAIN

PLATE SHACKLES

BITT

OPEN CHOCK

BUOY

ANCHOR

ANCHOR CROWN LINE

Fig. 42.   Beach gear layout on deck of stranded vessel.

In some cases, the salvage vessel will reverse the procedure for laying the beach gear, by passing the bitter end of the anchor pendant to the stranded vessel first, where it is connected to the carpenter stopper. The salvage vessel then steams on a planned course, using markers on the stranded vessel to maintain position, and the anchor is dropped after the entire pendant is laid out. This method is described in Chapter V, under Salvage Plan.

WINCHES, PUMPS, AND COMPRESSORS

Winches. The winches generally used for salvage are the gasoline-engine-driven type with attached variable torque clutch (a salvage winch is pictured in Fig. 43). The winches are portable, though they are cumbersome and heavy. The size and weight of the salvage winch sometimes make it difficult to transfer the winch to a wreck, particularly during inclement weather with a sea running. When the winch cannot be transferred to the wreck, it may be rigged on a barge with the beach gear purchase tackle and the barge towed to the vicinity of the wreck.

Fig. 43. Salvage winch. (Photo courtesy Pacific Towboat and Salvage Co., Long Beach, Calif.)

It should be remembered that the deck winches powered by steam-driven reciprocating engines can be adapted to compressed air, in the event that weather conditions do not permit the transfer of portable salvage winches. In cases of this nature, a compressed air hose is floated to the stranded vessel and connected to a manifold fitted with hose leads to the steam winches. The winches can then be used to power the purchase tackle of the beach gear.

Where shore power is available, the electric-motor-driven winches on a wreck can be similarly activated.

A small salvage diving boat should be fitted with at least one small portable air winch. This air winch can be used for numerous functions on the boat itself, and it is easily transferred to a wreck for unloading cargo, wreckage clearance, patch construction, etc.

Fig. 44.   Ten-inch salvage pump.

Pumps. Pumps are considered the most important items of equipment used in any salvage operation. A salvage pump is pictured in Fig. 44. The pump most generally used is the centrifugal, self-priming type, driven by a gasoline engine. This type of pump is capable of passing objects in excess of 25 per cent of normal diameter of suction and discharge.

Salvage pumps are manufactured in the following sizes: 10″, 6″, 3″, 2½″. The size of the pump is determined by the diameters of the suction and discharge, which are of the same dimensions. Refer to Table IV for 3″, 6″, and 10″ salvage pump capacities.

For efficient operation, a salvage pump must be located so that the suction lift will not exceed 10 to 15 feet. In many cases, this necessitates removing the pumps below decks during salvage operations. The 10″ salvage pump weighs approximately 1¼ tons, so it can be seen that moving this heavy pump will require some planning. The accessibility of doors, passageways, and compartments must be considered, as well as locations of structural members to which chain falls and tackle may be attached.

TABLE IV. SALVAGE PUMP CAPACITIES
Gallons per Minute

TOTAL HEAD	10 Feet	15 Feet	20 Feet	25 Feet
	10" PUMP			
15 Feet	3200			
20 "	3140	2870		
25 "	3070	2850	2600	
30 "	2980	2810	2580	1780
40 "	2800	2680	2460	1700
50 "	2520	2480	2290	1580
60 "	2100	2100	2020	1400
70 "	1380	1380	1380	1200
	6" PUMP			
25 Feet	1500			
30 "	1480	1280	1050	790
40 "	1450	1230	1020	780
50 "	1350	1160	950	725
60 "	1220	1050	900	680
70 "	1050	900	750	600
	3" PUMP			
25 Feet	325	280	225	
30 "	310	270	220	160
40 "	290	250	210	160
50 "	260	220	190	155
60 "	225	180	160	140
70 "	160	150	130	120

The self-priming, centrifugal type of pump is preferable in salvage operations because no harm will be done to the pump impeller if the water drops below the end of the suction hose, and pumping will commence immediately when the water again rises above the end of the suction hose.

Care should be taken to insure that applicable manufacturer's instructions and operating procedures are followed. The pumps are installed on the job and securely mounted to wood bases. Suction and discharge pipes or hoses are connected, the pump primed, and the engine started. After starting, operate the engine at approximately half-throttle until it is warmed up. Should the pump fail to prime immediately, the following should be checked:

1. Air leaks in the suction line.
2. Clogged strainers.
3. Suction lift too high.
4. Shaft seal leaking.
5. Worn thrust collar.
6. Impeller clearance too great.
7. Suction check valve (foot valve) jammed.
8. Pump prime recirculation line clogged.

Do not allow the pump to operate for prolonged periods with insufficient water in the impeller housing, as heating of the shaft may result. Should the pump fail to prime, speed up the engine for a short duration before shutting down the engine. The speeding up sometimes causes the pump to pick up a suction.

The pumps should be equipped with the following minimum accessories:

PUMP ACCESSORIES

10" PUMP

8-foot lengths of rubber hose	12 each
8-foot lengths of metal pipe	12 each
3-foot lengths of metal pipe	8 each
5-foot lengths of metal pipe	15 each
2-foot lengths of metal pipe	8 each
90-degree elbows	8 each
22-1/2-degree elbows	8 each
Foot valves	2 each
Strainer	1 each

6" PUMP

8-foot lengths of rubber hose	12 each
8-foot lengths of metal pipe.	12 each
5-foot lengths of metal pipe	15 each
3-foot lengths of metal pipe	8 each
2-foot lengths of metal pipe	8 each
90-degree elbows	8 each
45-degree elbows	8 each
22-1/2-degree elbows	8 each
Foot valves	2 each
Strainer	1 each

3" PUMP

10-foot lengths of rubber hose	8 each
25-foot lengths of fire hose	8 each
Spanner wrenches	2 each

The 6" electric submersible salvage pump is a combination all-positive induction motor and centrifugal pump, built as a compact self-contained unit to operate in shallow water. The pump will operate in any position. The three-phase, 220–440-volt induction motor is built integrally with the pump sealed in a watertight casing filled with a special non-hydroscopic oil of high dielectric strength, to provide electric protection, as well as lubrication and cooling for the motor.

The pump is enclosed in a heavy bronze casing; however, recent developments by the A. O. Smith Corporation have produced a pump with an aluminum casing that reduces the weight of the pump considerably.

Compressors. Air compressors used in salvage diving operations range in rated capacity from approximately 50 to 100 cubic feet of air per minute.

When a compressor is used for diving purposes, air filters should be installed on the manifold in the compressor discharge line: one filter for each diver's air hose. Care should be taken to insure a fresh supply of air to the compressor intake. Sometimes it is necessary to attach an extension hose to the intake, in order to prevent the gaso line engine exhaust fumes from entering the intake of the compressor.

Compressors used for de-watering purposes in raising sunken vessels using compressed air should have a rated capacity of approximately 200 cubic feet per minute at 100-pounds-per-square-inch pressure. Compressors of this size are very heavy, and, although they are fairly compact, they are difficult to handle because of their weight.

AIR LIFTS

An air lift is used to lift mixtures of water, grain, sand, mud, and similar materials from the holds of ships during salvage operations. In some cases of stranding, the air lift may be used to clear away sand and mud from the side of the vessel.

The air lift, basically, works on a pressure differential principle. Air is introduced into the lower end of a partially submerged pipe. The combining of air bubbles with the liquid in the pipe forms a mixture that is of less density than the liquid outside the pipe. The lighter density results in less head pressure inside the pipe than outside, which causes the mixture to rise in the pipe. The amount of liquid lifted will depend upon the size of the air lift, submergence of the pipe, air pressure and volume used, and the discharge head.

The air lift is constructed of two basic parts, as illustrated in Fig. 45: the discharge pipe and the foot piece, or air chamber. The size of the discharge pipe will range from approximately 3″ to 14″ in diameter, depending upon the amount of work to be done and the service intended. The air chamber should be located approximately 20″ to 30″ from the end of the pipe.

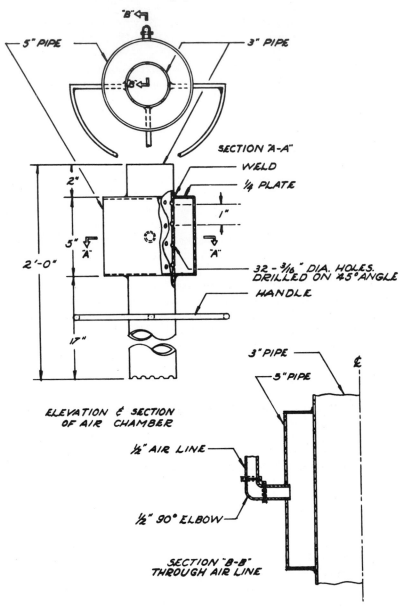

Fig. 45.   Air lift.

The following table may be used as a guide in selecting the size of discharge pipe and air line, taking into consideration the air available and the job to be done.

DIAMETER OF PIPE	DIAMETER OF COMPRESSED AIR LINE	GALLONS PER MINUTE	CUBIC FEET OF AIR
3"	1/2"	50-75	15-40
4"	3/4"	90-150	20-65
6"	1 1/4"	210-450	50-200
10"	2"	600-900	150-400

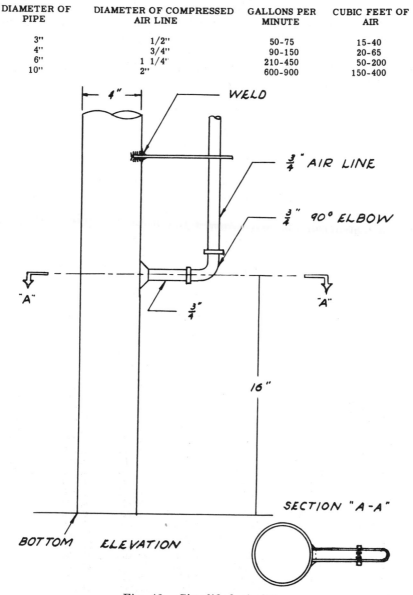

Fig. 46. Simplified air lift.

The operation is as follows: The discharge pipe is submerged in the mixture to be lifted, to a depth of approximately 50 to 70 per cent of the total length of the pipe. The air is turned on, and the lifting operation should commence almost immediately.

Sometimes considerable experimentation is necessary to determine the amount of air required to operate the lift efficiently.

Figure 46 shows a more simplified, though less efficient, air lift than that illustrated in Fig. 45; however, it can be quickly manufactured for immediate use.

MARLINSPIKE SEAMANSHIP

The gear and operations, which are usually classed under the heading of marlinspike seamanship, will be discussed, generally, in this section.

Fiber Rope. Manila rope is made from the combed fibers of the abacá plant, which are first spun into yarns, then twisted into strands—three or four of which compose the finished rope. The yarns are generally twisted right-handed, the strands left-handed, and the ropes right-handed. These alternating twists help to counteract the tendency of the rope to unlay.

For comparative strengths of fiber ropes, refer to Table V.

TABLE V. MINIMUM SPECIFIED STRENGTH IN POUNDS OF FIBER ROPE

Circumference	Diameter	Manila 100%	Composite 90%	Mixed Sisal 75%	Sisal Hemp 70%	Jute 60%
5/8	3/16	450		340	310	270
3/4	1/4	600		450	420	360
1	5/16	1,000		750	700	600
1 1/8	3/8	1,350		1,010	950	810
1 1/4	7/16	1,750		1,310	1,230	1,050
1 1/2	1/2	2,650		1,990	1,850	1,590
1 3/4	9/16	3,450		2,590	2,410	2,070
2	5/8	4,400		3,300	3,080	2,640
2 1/4	3/4	5,400		4,050	3,780	3,240
2 1/2	13/16	6,500		4,880	4,550	3,900
2 3/4	15/16	7,700		5,780	5,390	4,620
3	1	9,000		6,750	6,300	5,400
3 1/4	1 1/16	10,500		7,870	7,350	
3 1/2	1 1/8	12,000		9,000	8,400	
3 3/4	1 1/4	13,500		10,120	9,450	
4	1 5/16	15,000		11,250	10,500	
4 1/2	1 1/2	18,500	16,600	13,900	12,950	
5	1 5/8	22,500	20,300	16,900	15,800	
5 1/2	1 3/4	26,500	23,800	19,900	18,500	
6	2	31,000	27,900	23,200	21,700	
7	2 1/4	41,000	36,900	30,800	28,700	
8	2 5/8	52,000	46,800	39,000	36,400	
9	3	64,000	57,500	48,000	44,800	
10	3 1/4	77,000	69,300	57,800	53,900	
11	3 5/8	91,000	81,900	68,200	63,700	
12	4	105,000	94,500	78,800	73,500	

In the event that definite information is not at·hand concerning the strength of a rope, the following formula may be used:

B = Breaking stress, in pounds or long tons (2,240 pounds)

P = Safe working load: viz., safe tension for a single part of the rope

C = Circumference in inches

B = C × 900 pounds

A factor of safety must now be applied to the breaking stress, in order to obtain the value of P. Generally speaking, the factor of safety used will depend upon the condition of the rope and the service for which it is intended. Accordingly, the factor of safety will vary from approximately one-eighth to one-fourth of the breaking stress.

In determining the circumference of Manila rope necessary to lift a given load, P equals the load in tons and C equals the circumference of the rope.

Exposing Manila to high temperatures or stowing it away in a wet condition will cause it to deteriorate rapidly. A sharp nip may weaken Manila from approximately 25 to 50 per cent. A well-made splice weakens Manila rope approximately 5 to 10 per cent. The breaking stress of Manila is equal to approximately the working load for wire rope.

The comparative strength of two similarly constructed ropes of different sizes is equal to the squares of their circumferences; for example, a 3″ rope is to a 4″ rope as 9 is to 16.

When a load is applied with a sudden jerk, it effects a double strain on the rope.

Table VI shows, by size, the comparative strengths of wire and Manila ropes. Wire rope is approximately six times as strong as Manila rope.

Hemp will not be discussed in detail here, as it is used mostly in "small stuff." In this category are small cordage, designated by the

TABLE VI. SIZE OF WIRE ROPES TO REPLACE MANILA LINES

Manila Rope		Spring Lay Wire Rope		6 x 12 Wire Rope Type "G"		6 x 24 Wire Rope Type "J"		6 x 37 Wire Rope Type "E"	
C	S	D	S	D	S	D	S	D	S
Inches	Pounds	Inches	Pounds	Inches	Pounds	Inches	Pounds	Inches	Pounds
4	15,000	3/4	17,500	5/8	17,700			1/2	18,600
5	22,500	1	29,300	3/4	25,400			9/16	23,200
6	31,000	1 1/8	37,100	7/8	34,500	3/4	36,900	3/4	40,000
7	41,000	1 3/8	54,600	1	44,800	7/8	49,300	7/8	53,400
8	52,000	1 1/2	70,200	1 1/8	56,700	1	64,000	1	69,400
9	64,000	1 5/8	81,900	1 1/4	69,400	1 1/16	72,200	1	
10	77,000	1 3/4	95,500	1 3/8	83,300	1 3/16	89,900	1 1/8	87,600
11	91,000	1 7/8	109,200	1 1/2	99,300	1 1/4	99,400	1/4	108,000
12	105,000	2	117,000	1 5/8	115,000	1 3/8	120,000	3/8	130,000

Note:. C - Circumference: D - Diameter: S - Strength

number of threads it contains, such as 15-thread, 21-thread, etc., and tarred hemp, referred to as seizing, marline, etc.

Weights of various sizes of fiber ropes are listed in Table VII.

Nylon is not used as a general practice in salvage work. However, it is gaining wider acceptance for use in the make-up of coastal and, sometimes, offshore tows.

TABLE VII. COIL WEIGHT AND COIL LENGTH OF FIBER ROPE

Circumference	Minimum Length	Approximate Weight
5/8 inches	3,000 feet	45 pounds
3/4	2,750	55
1	2,250	65
1 1/8	1,620	66
1 1/4	1,200	63
1 1/2	1,200	90
1 3/4	1,200	125
2	1,200	160
2 1/4	1,200	200
2 1/2	1,200	234
2 3/4	1,200	270
3	1,200	324
3 1/4	1,200	375
3 1/2	1,200	432
3 3/4	1,200	502
4	900	432
4 1/2	900	540
5	900	670
5 1/2	900	805
6	600	645
7	600	875
8	600	1,145
9	600	1,450
10	600	1,795
11	600	2,200
12	600	2,610

Wire Rope. Wire ropes are the most reliable of any used in ship salvage work. The steel used in wire ropes is a composition resulting from a blending of different iron ores. Some steels used are iron, cast steel, extra-strong cast steel, plow steel, improved plow steel, and high-grade plow steel. It is then processed through rolls into small rods of approximately 1/4″ to 1/2″ in diameter. These rods are then drawn cold through dies to form wire of the desired diameter. The cold-drawn wire is annealed, lubricated, and quenched in order to offset the hardening effect of the drawing, which tends to make the wire brittle.

Six wires laid around a center wire form what is known as a strand, used for haulage rope. An additional layer of twelve wires forms a nineteen-strand wire rope, used for hoisting, etc. The finished strands are wound around a hemp or Manila core. The hemp or Manila core tends to add flexibility to the wire rope. When subjected to a pull, the stretching effect on the wire rope will tend to cause the center strands to lay against the Manila or hemp core, thus providing a cushioning effect in the setup.

The Manila core will absorb some of the lubricants that are sluiced on the wire rope from time to time as a preservative. This absorption of oil will tend to provide lubrication for the interior wires and reduce the interior friction under heavy pulls.

Wire rope is galvanized during the manufacturing process. The galvanizing will provide adequate protection from the corrosive action of moisture and salt water. However, it will not last indefinitely; and when it wears away, the corrosive action on the wire is greatly increased. When the outer wires are worn down to half their original diameter, the wire rope should be discarded.

The center hemp or Manila core can be examined by laying open the strands with a marlinspike. The core should appear lubricated and soft.

As previously noted, wire rope is approximately six times stronger than Manila rope of the same size; and Table VI should be referred to for the comparative strengths.

A sharp nip may weaken a wire from approximately 25 to 50 per cent.

If a load is applied with a jerk or sudden shock, the effect of the load is doubled and should be allowed for in calculating the size of the rope required.

To determine the strength of wire rope when definite information is not available, use the following formula:

B = Breaking stress in pounds or tons (2,240 pounds)
D = Diameter of wire rope
$B = D^2 \times 25$

A factor of safety should be applied. This factor of safety will vary from one-eighth to one-fourth of the breaking stress, depending on the condition of the rope and the service for which it is intended.

To determine the safe working load for wire, use the following formula:

P = Safe working load
D = Diameter

$$P = \frac{D^2 \times 25}{6}$$

Depending upon conditions, add or subtract 30 per cent to the foregoing value of P.

Note: The working load for wire rope is approximately the same as the breaking stress for Manila rope.

To determine the diameter of wire rope necessary to lift a given load, use the following formula:

D (inches) $= \frac{1}{2} \sqrt{P}$
P $=$ Desired weight to be lifted

Splices. Splicing is a method of joining the bitter ends of two lines or of forming a permanent loop in one line by bending back the bitter end of the line. Splicing rarely weakens the line if done properly. A splice is much stronger than a knot and the splice permits running through a sheave more readily.

These two splices are the most often used:

1. The *eye splice* is installed to form a loop and is made by bending the bitter end of the line back upon itself. An eye splice may or may not have a thimble inserted into it. For any eye splice, three tucks are usually sufficient, one over and one under each, against the lay.

2. The *short splice* is for joining together the bitter ends of two lengths of line. Three tucks on both sides of the short splice are sufficient to hold for the maximum breaking strength of the rope.

In Manila, approximately 12″ to 24″ should be allowed for tucking for both the eye splice and the short splice. When the bitter end of a rope tends over and under a strand, it is called a *tuck*.

Another splice not as frequently used as either of the foregoing is the *long splice*. The long splice provides a much neater and less noticeable joint between two ropes, and it allows for an easier passage through the swallow of a block than the short splice. Most reference books on seamanship will contain instructions on making a long splice.

EYE SPLICE IN WIRE ROPE

Diameter of Rope, in Inches	Length to Allow for Tucking, in Feet
1/4″ to 3/8″	1′
1/2″	1 1/2′
5/8″ to 3/4″	2′
7/8″ to 1″	2 1/2′
1 1/8″	3′
1 1/4″	3 1/2′
1 1/2″	4′

The foregoing lengths should be adequate for splicing five tucks into 6 x 37 wire rope. Refer to Fig. 47 for dressing an eye splice.

Wire straps are always measured in a straight line from pull to pull as shown:

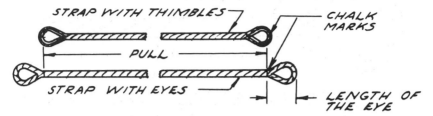

The rules for measuring the length of wire rope for a strap to be fitted with a thimble are:

1. Insure that the bitter end is ready for splicing.

2. Lay off on the wire rope the amount needed for tucking and one-half the distance around the thimble.

3. Chalk this point.

4. Lay off the length necessary for the strap, plus three times the diameter of the wire for each thimble.

5. Chalk this point.

6. Measure half the distance around the thimble, plus the amount needed for tucking.

7. Indicate the point to be cut by a clove hitch.

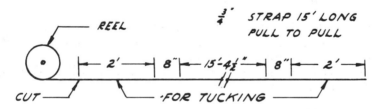

Note: Seize the wire on both sides of the cut before the cut is made.

Proper servings are shown in the following table:

SERVINGS

Size of Wire Rope	Serve With
3/8"	marline
1/2"	marline
5/8"	marline
3/4"	houseline
*1"	thread seizing stuff
*1 1/2"	

*One-inch wires and larger should be wormed before parceling and serving.

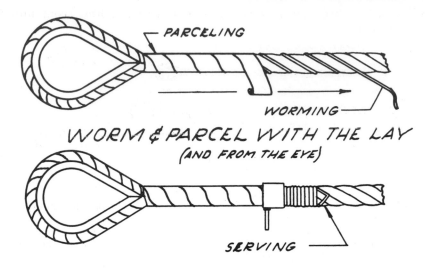

Fig. 47.   Dressing an eye splice.

Seizings. Unless the bitter end of a rope is fitted with an eye splice or socket or is attached to a permanent fitting, it must be seized in order to prevent it from unwinding.

Seize the wire so that the unlaying of the wire will tend to tighten the seizing, as shown in Fig. 48.

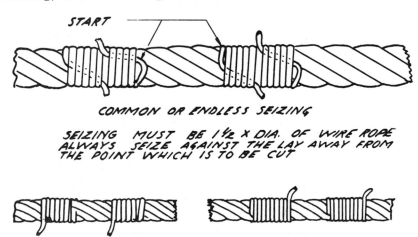

Fig. 48.   Methods of seizing rope.

TABLE VIII. SEIZINGS RECOMMENDED

Rope Diameter in Inches	Number of Seizings	Length of Seizings in Inches	Distance Between Seizings in Inches	Approximate Size of Seizing Wire in Inches
1/2 and smaller	2	1/2	1	.020-.030
9/16 to 7/8	3	1	2	.040-.060
1 to 1 1/4	3	1 1/2	2	.060-.090
1 3/8 to 1 5/8	4	2	2	.080-.125
1 3/4 to 2	4	3	2	.105-.125
2 1/2 and larger	4	4	3	.105-.125

The following represent the percentages of the total rope strength obtainable by the various methods of rope fastenings:

METHOD OF ROPE FASTENING	PERCENTAGE OF TOTAL ROPE STRENGTH
Wire rope socket (attached with zinc)	100
Thimble or eye splice in rope with four or five tucks	90
Thimble placed in the end of rope and fastened with wire rope clips	85
Three wire rope clamps	75

Clips. Clips are used to secure the bitter end of a wire over a thimble or to secure the bitter ends of two wires together.

To properly install the clip, the "U" bolt should bear on the short or bitter end of the rope. When installed this way, the flat base of the clip will rest on the side of the rope under tension, thus preventing injury to the rope by crimping. The "U" bolt section will grip the bitter end by its crimping action. The clips should be spaced approximately six times the diameter of the rope on centers. The bitter end should extend a minimum of six inches from the last clip and should be properly seized. Figure 49 shows the correct and incorrect methods of attaching clips.

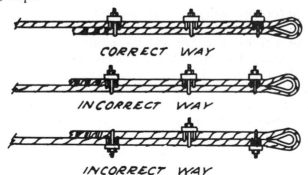

Fig. 49. Correct and incorrect methods of attaching clips.

To determine the proper number of clips to use, consult the following chart:

ROPE DIAMETER IN INCHES	NUMBER OF CLIPS FOR EACH END OF ROPE
3/16 to 7/16	2
1/2 to 3/4	3
7/8 to 1	4
1 1/8 to 1 1/4	5
1 3/8 to 2 1/2	6

Following is the formula for a Liverpool eye splice (Fig. 50):

Measure off 2 to 4 feet from the end of the rope and seize wire with marline to prevent unraveling while splicing. Unlay the strands back to the seizing, cut out the heart close to the seized end and whip the end of each of the six strands.

6	under	DE	With butt of spike (the rest go in with the
5	"	D	point).
1	"	ABC	
2	"	BC	
3	"	C	
Heart	"	ABC	
4	around	D	This is first tuck.
5	"	E	
6	"	F	
5	"	E	
4	"	D	Run up four and five tucks.
Heart inside splice			Even-numbered strands get five tucks.
3	"	C	Odd-numbered strands get four tucks.
2	"	B	
1	"	A	

Using a nonferrous mallet, pound the splice away from the thimble and well up into the standing part. This will make for a tighter splice. To get a tight splice, spread the points of the thimble. Apply all seizings against the lay. When the splice is completed, tar the parceling and serving.

A popular variation of the Liverpool eye splice is made by reversing the position of strands 3 and 4. In the merchant marine, this splice is sometimes referred to as a "lock splice" because, by reversing strands 3 and 4, a lock is formed.

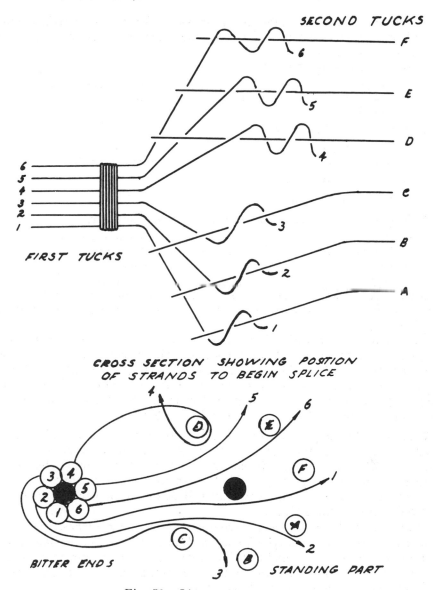

Fig. 50. Liverpool eye splice.

Knots. Knots are used temporarily to secure a line to a bitt or cleat or to secure one line to another line or to secure the line to itself. A knot tends to weaken a line and should never be used permanently where a splice can be made.

Knots are discussed in detail in most books on seamanship, and it will be necessary here to list only the knots most commonly used in salvage operations:

1. Bending two lines together.

    a. Square knot.
    b. Becket or sheet bend (single or double).

    c. Carrick bend (single or double).

2. At the end of the line.

    a. Overhand knot.
    b. Figure-8 knot.

    c. Bowline.
    d. Running bowline.

3. In the bight of a line.

    a. Bowline on a bight.

4. Knots for securing a line on a ring, boom, or spar.

    a. Clove hitch.
    b. Two half hitches.
    c. Round turn and two half hitches.

    d. Fisherman's bend.
    e. Rolling hitch.
    f. Stopper hitch.

Blocks. A block is a pulley or sheave in a strapped frame, through which ropes are rove to gain fairlead or advantage for hoisting or hauling.

The primary parts of a block are the frame (wood or steel), one or more sheaves (pulleys), and a strap. The secondary parts of the block are the hook, swallow, becket, and the cringle. Blocks take their names from their type of construction or the number of sheaves; or they may be named by the purpose for which they are used aboard ship. Some typical blocks are illustrated in Fig. 51.

Tackles. A tackle is a purchase made up of ropes or falls and blocks, used to gain an advantage in power. A stationary block gives no gain but only serves as a fairlead for the rope; however, if the block is installed on the load and the hook is secured to a stationary point, the advantage is twofold. Any multiplication of power in blocks is derived from movable blocks.

Many methods have been developed in reeving blocks, most of which have their own particular advantages. It is to be remembered in reeving blocks that consideration must be given to minimizing the loss due to mechanical friction and to minimizing the chafing action of lines upon other lines and lines upon sheaves.

The center-to-center method, as used and developed at the United States Naval School of Salvage, Bayonne, New Jersey, is probably one of the best methods for rigging heavy purchase gear. This system is illustrated in Fig. 39.

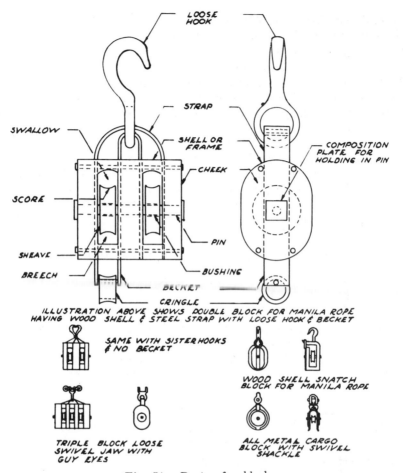

Fig. 51.   Parts of a block.

In order to determine the power developed by the blocks, count the number of lines leading to and from the moving block and multiply by the power on the hauling part.

The following nomenclature is used in describing tackles:

Falls—The rope used in the tackle.

Handy-billy—A small light tackle, with small wood or steel blocks, used for miscellaneous small work.

Hauling part—The part of the falls to which power is applied.

Overhaul—To separate and lay off the blocks in preparation for hauling.

Reeve—To rig a purchase by reeving the falls through the swallows of the blocks and over the sheaves.

Standing part—The bitter end of the falls that is made fast to one of the blocks.

Two-blocked—When the two blocks are close together after hauling, sometimes called "chock-a-block."

To find the size of wire rope to be used when rove in a tackle and to lift a given weight, proceed as follows:

D (inches) $= \frac{1}{2}\sqrt{P}$

Where P = Desired weight

To P, add $\frac{1}{10}$ of its value for every sheave to be used in hoisting. This gives the total resistances, including friction; then divide this by the number of parts at the movable block for the maximum tension on the fall.

Example: To lift ten tons with a threefold purchase where the hauling part is led from the upper block, determine the size of the Manila rope needed. Total resistance, including the friction, equals the weight of the load plus the number of sheaves multiplied by the weight of the load divided by the percentage of loss per sheave, or:

$$10 + \left(\frac{6 \times 10}{10}\right) = 16 \text{ tons}$$

The maximum tension on a single part of the fall is:

$\frac{16}{6}$ or 2.6. The size of a single part is:

C (inches) $= \sqrt{15 \times P}$ (tons)

Fairleads. A fairlead is a fitting used to change the direction of a rope or line from that which the line tends to lead. It is generally used to prevent chafing and to clear obstructions. In addition to the fairleads illustrated in Fig. 52, certain types of snatch blocks are also used.

CLOSED CHOCK   ROLLER CHOCK   OPEN CHOCK

Fig. 52.   Fairleads.

Securing ana Mooring Fittings. The fittings illustrated in Fig. 53 are used for securing and mooring purposes.

Hooks and Shackles. Because the hook is invariably the weakest part of any block, the strength of the hook is the measure of the strength of the block. Sometimes the hook can be reinforced by mousing (*see* Fig. 54), but for most heavy work the hook should be substituted with a shackle.

To determine the strength of a hook, use the following formula:

P $= \frac{2}{3} D^2$ tons

D = Diameter at back of hook

To determine the strength of a shackle, use the following formula:

P = 3 D² tons
B = Diameter at sides

A shackle is approximately five times as strong as a hook.

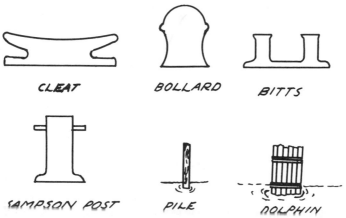

Fig. 53. Securing and mooring fittings.

Fig. 54. One method of mousing a hook.

Spars. In many cases in ship salvage work, it is necessary to use various lengths and thicknesses of booms and spars. It is well to know in advance the safe load that can be applied to the boom or spar before it is used.

To determine the strength of a spar to resist compression, use the following formula:

T = Safe thrust in tons
C = Constant
R = Radius of spar in inches
L = Length of spar in feet

Example: to find the safe thrust of a spar eight inches in diameter (fir), fifteen feet long,

$$T = \frac{C \times R^3}{L^2}$$

$$T = \frac{4 \times 4^3}{15^2} = 4.5 \text{ tons}$$

Note: the constant 4 is safe for most ordinary woods; however, when oak mahogany, or very strong woods are used, the multiplier, 4, can be increased as much as 50 per cent.

PATCHES

A patch is used to temporarily close a hole or opening in the shell of a vessel and is a temporary repair, installed after suffering hull damage, to restrict flooding, so that the vessel will maintain positive buoyancy and remain afloat. Any temporary patch requires considerable planning, design, and time for installation.

In most cases where a patch is needed, the emergency that exists does not allow for the time required to install a temporary patch; consequently, a *collision mat* is employed to cover the hole quickly. One type of collision mat is illustrated in Fig. 55.

The mat design will vary, depending upon the location and size of the hole. For smaller holes, a mattress or a piece of canvas, fitted with lowering and hogging lines, may be substituted. A grommet is fitted into each corner of a square piece of canvas. Lowering lines are secured to the two top corner grommets. The bottom corner grommets are fitted with lengths of chain to prevent chafing on the vessel's bottom and to provide negative buoyancy to the mat so that it will sink into position over the hole. For greater effectiveness, the canvas may be doubled. Both lowering and hogging lines should be long enough to lead to a winch on deck.

Installation is accomplished by lowering the mat into position over the hole, using the lowering lines. The hogging lines are led under the bottom of the vessel and up on deck on the opposite side. After the mat is positioned, a strain is taken on the lowering and hogging lines to haul the mat taut.

A *salvage mat* is used, instead of a patch, wherever possible, to cover moderate-sized holes in the shell of a vessel. Whereas a large wood patch requires considerable time and labor, the salvage mat is more easily and quickly constructed; however, it lacks the strength of the wood patch.

A typical salvage mat is illustrated in Fig. 56. The mat is positioned over a hole on the outside of the hull, so that the planks are horizontal and the wire ropes are vertical. The lower ends of the wire ropes are led down and under the vessel and up on deck on the opposite side. A strain is taken on all wires and the mat is hogged to the ship's side, making for a fairly watertight covering.

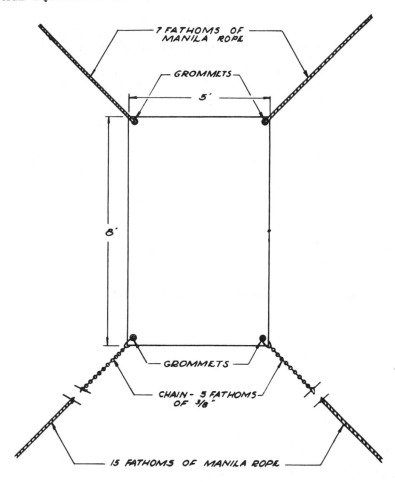

Fig. 55.   Collision mat.

Pumping is commenced, and, as the water level inside the ship drops in way of the hole, the outside water pressure forces the planks tighter against the oakum-filled canvas mat, increasing the watertightness of the joint.

The dimensions of the planks, size of the wire ropes, and thickness of the mat used will vary considerably, depending upon the size of the hole and the depth of the water.

For construction of a mat larger than that illustrated in Fig. 56, four or more wire rope straps should be stapled to larger planks.

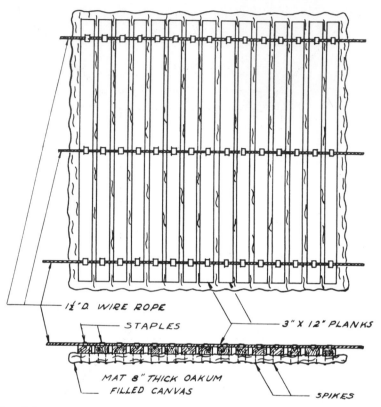

Fig. 56.   Salvage mat. Wire rope is secured to planks with staples. Planks are
spaced 3 inches apart and mat is spiked to planks.

Small Patches. Holes of small diameter usually present no great
problem, and they can be covered or plugged by the installation of
small patches.

Figure 57 illustrates a small patch using tongue and groove planking nailed on 4" x 4" timber frame. The construction is fairly simple,
and the patch can be made in a short time. After the patch is constructed, two or more holes are drilled into the tongue and groove
planking to receive the ell bolts. The ell bolts are fitted with butterfly
nuts. The patch is fitted with a small pudding gasket.

The patch is fitted over the hole so that the gasket rests around
the periphery and against the hull. The ell bolts are turned so that
they bear against the plating at the edge of the hole, and the butterfly
nuts are then taken up so that the patch seats firmly. In any patch
construction, tongue and groove planking provides greater watertightness than any other type of planking.

Figure 58 illustrates a small patch made by nailing together two layers of planks at right angles. This patch is not as watertight as the patch illustrated in Fig. 57; however, it is easier to make and can be constructed quickly when time is of the essence. Ell bolts and butterfly nuts are used to secure the patch and make for a watertight joint at the gasket. The size of the planks will depend upon the depth of the water and the size of the hole to be covered.

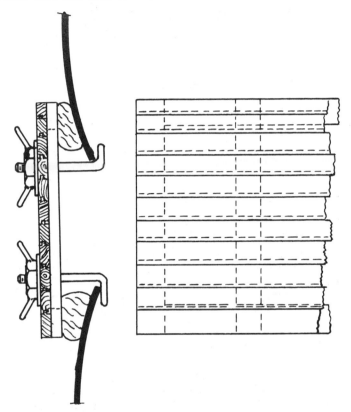

Fig. 57.   Small patch, made of 2-inch tongue-and-groove planking on 4″ × 4″ timber frame.

Figure 59 is a photograph of a small steel patch installed over a crack. This type of patch is called a *doubler*. Figure 60 is a photograph of a large steel patch.

Tooker Patch. The tooker patch is a patch used to close port light openings in a sunken vessel. The patch, when properly constructed, is as strong, if not stronger, than the port light cover. Figure 61 shows the construction of a typical tooker patch. The patch is con-

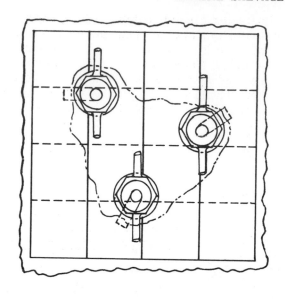

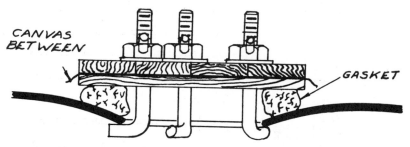

Fig. 58. Small patch, made by nailing together two layers of planks at right angles.

structed in two halves of tongue and groove planking. The halves are joined together with hinges so that the patch may be folded.

The hinged patch is folded and inserted inside a porthole. The patch is then unfolded and the eyebolts are inserted through the holes in the strongback, or brace. The strongback is braced against the porthole coaming, and nuts are screwed on the exposed threads of the eyebolts. A wrench is used to take up on the nuts, causing the patch to seat and the gasket to bear against the inside port light rim, forming a watertight joint.

Large Patches. Holes of large diameter require covering by patches of heavy construction, necessitating considerable design, extensive construction work, and detailed planning for installation.

The design of a large wood patch will depend upon the depth of the water, the size of the hole, and the location of the hole.

Fig. 59. Small doubler patch. (Official U.S. Navy photo.)

Fig. 60. Large steel patch. (Official U.S. Navy photo.)

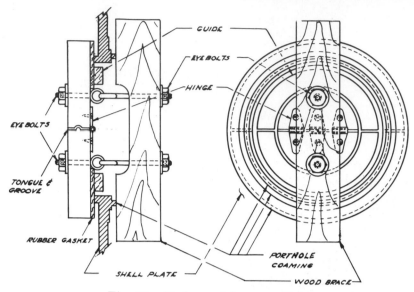

Fig. 61. Tooker patch on porthole.

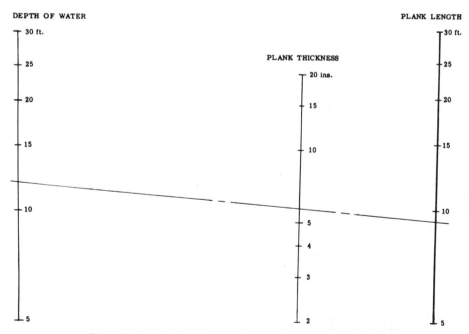

Fig. 62. Plank thickness for underwater patches.

Figure 62 should be consulted to determine the size of planks necessary for the depth of the water where the hole is located. In determining the depth of water, the measurement should be taken from the waterline to the bottom of the hole.

The extent of the damage is next determined by the use of a plumb line. A weight is attached to the end of a line, and the weight and line are lowered over the side of the vessel in the vicinity of the hull damage. A diver descends and places the weight at the extreme forward end of the hole. This position is marked on deck. He then places the line at the extreme after end of the hole, and this position is also marked on deck, topside. These marks determine the length of the hole. Next, the line is placed at several positions along the length of the hole, and the diver places the weight alternately at the upper and lower extremities of the hole at each station in turn. These locations are marked on deck, topside, so that after all stations have been marked longitudinally along the deck an accurate plan of the size of the hole is obtained. Figure 63 shows a method of using a plumb line.

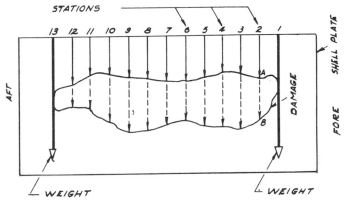

Fig. 63.   Method of using a plumb line.

The three types of large patches that are commonly used to cover large holes in a ship's underwater body are the American Patch, the British Standard Patch, and the Plank-by-plank Patch.

The *American Patch* is the easiest to make and install and requires a minimum amount of work to be done by the diver. Any size hole can be covered by this patch, or by a combination of several patches.

After the general dimensions of the patch have been determined by using a plumb line, a wood template is constructed in order to determine the general shape the patch is to take. Figure 64 illustrates a typical wood template.

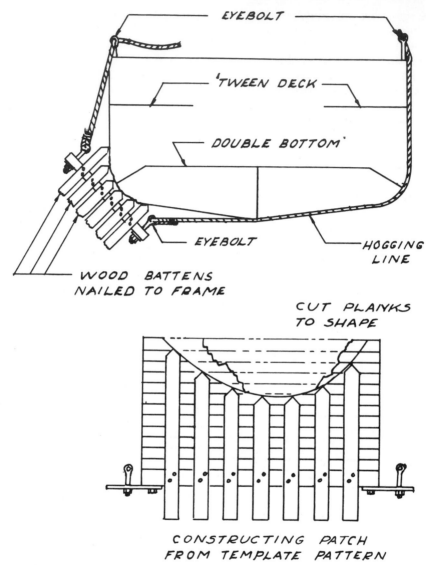

Fig. 64.   Wood template.

In lieu of a wood template, a batten frame may be constructed, as illustrated in Fig. 65. The batten frame is constructed of light wood. Holes are drilled around the periphery of the frame to receive movable picket batten rods of wood or steel.

The frame is lowered into position over the hull damage, and a diver descends and adjusts the rods so that each touches the hull.

The diver burns or drills holes in the shell of the vessel in line with the picket battens. The frame is then taken aboard, and the general shape of the hull, in way of the damage, is determined from the outline formed by the positions of the battens. The pattern formed by the positions of the battens is used to construct the frame for the American Patch.

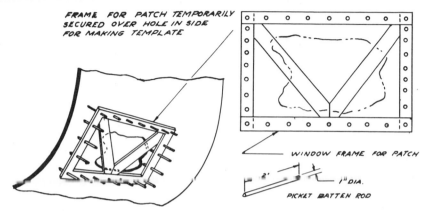

FRAME FOR PATCH TEMPORARILY SECURED OVER HOLE IN SIDE FOR MAKING TEMPLATE

WINDOW FRAME FOR PATCH

1" DIA.

PICKET BATTEN ROD

Fig. 65.   Frame for American type patch.

A heavy timber frame is constructed to the shape of the template, or batten frame. To the frame timbers are nailed, or spiked, heavy tongue and groove planking. The shaped side of the frame timbers is fitted with suitable gasket material to make a watertight joint in way of the hull. Holes are drilled in the frame timbers in line with the picket battens.

The completed American Patch is usually very heavy and cumbersome. To aid in installing the patch, "A" frames of steel construction are mounted on deck over the damage to facilitate lowering and positioning the patch. A general arrangement of a mounting technique is illustrated in Fig. 66.

The "A" frames are fabricated from pipe sections and welded to the deck. The frames are footed in steel pipe shoes of larger diameter than the pipe frame. These shoes afford greater strength and should be mounted on suitable deck doublers or pieces of steel plate welded to the deck to distribute the load and provide additional strength.

Because the lowering and hogging lines are used only to position and hold the patch over the hole while it is being throughbolted to the hull, Manila or hemp rope may be used. However, if it is anticipated that the Manila or hemp rope hogging lines may chafe considerably in way of the vessel's bottom, then chain or wire rope should be substituted.

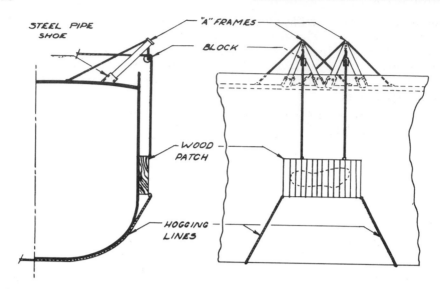

Fig. 66. Mounting a patch, using "A" frames. Patch is positioned with lines from "A" frames. Patch is secured by hauling taut hogging lines.

If the vessel is lying on rocky or coral bottom so that the hogging lines cannot be passed under the hull, the lines must be fairleaded and taken aboard on the same side of the ship on which the patch is located. The fairlead must be installed so that the patch is, in effect, hogged against the side of the vessel when a strain is taken on the hogging lines. Figure 67 illustrates a typical method of attaching the blocks for a fairlead. Holes are cut in the hull well below the patch. "T" bolts or hook bolts are inserted in the holes, and the hooks of the fairlead blocks are inserted in the eyes of the bolts. Lines secured to the lower corners of the frame of the patch are rove through the fairlead blocks and led topside on deck. The lines should extend diagonally from the corners, tending slightly forward and aft. The bitter ends of the lines on deck should be led to the niggerheads of winches.

Before any holes are burned in the hull to receive the "T" or hook bolts, an investigation should be made to determine whether a fuel tank is located in the vicinity.

The completed patch is lowered into position and drawn to the ship's side, using tackle rigged from inside the ship through the back of the patch and secured in two bolt holes, as illustrated in Fig. 69. The patch is then throughbolted from the frame to the shell of the ship.

After the patch is throughbolted and firmly secured in place, the lowering and hogging lines may be removed.

As the water lowers inside the hull during pumping operations, the patch will be seated more firmly by the greater pressure of the water outside the hull.

When the hole is too large for one patch, it may be covered by the installation of two smaller patches (*see* schematic diagram in Fig. 68).

Large patches must be shored internally to prevent their collapse during pumping operations, as illustrated in Fig. 68.

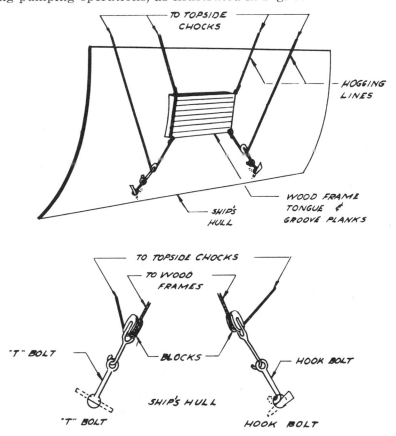

Fig. 67. Hogging a patch to ship's hull. Drive wedges in hook holes; use tongue-and-groove planking; "T" bolts installed beneath turn of bilge; inert fuel tanks before burning holes.

Figure 69 illustrates a completed American-type patch.

During the construction and fitting of large patches, it is necessary for divers to have easy access to the inside of the hull and patch, in order to facilitate the rigging of wires, the installation of shoring, and the fastening of throughbolts.

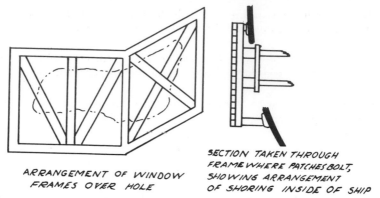

ARRANGEMENT OF WINDOW
FRAMES OVER HOLE

SECTION TAKEN THROUGH
FRAME WHERE PATCHES BOLT,
SHOWING ARRANGEMENT
OF SHORING INSIDE OF SHIP

Fig. 68.   Large hole in ship's side covered by two American type patches.

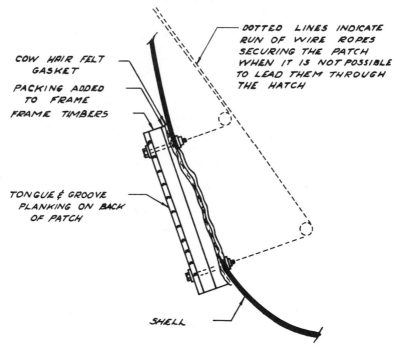

COW HAIR FELT
GASKET

PACKING ADDED
TO FRAME

FRAME TIMBERS

DOTTED   LINES INDICATE
RUN OF WIRE ROPES
SECURING THE PATCH
WHEN IT IS NOT POSSIBLE
TO LEAD THEM THROUGH
THE HATCH

TONGUE & GROOVE
PLANKING ON BACK
OF PATCH

SHELL

Fig. 69.   End view of a completed American type patch.

The necessary access may be provided in the form of a door installed directly in the planking of the patch. The construction of a typical door in a patch is illustrated in Fig. 70.

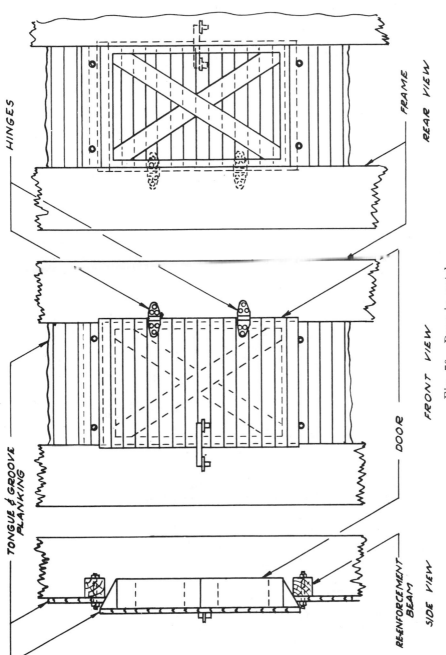

Fig. 70. Door in patch.

The access door eliminates the necessity for additional time-consuming dives inside the vessel, which would otherwise be required.
The horizontal tongue and groove planking of the door is mounted on,
and secured to, an internal beveled frame and cross braces. The bevel
of the frame is fitted with suitable gasket material of canvas or split
fabric rubber hose in order to form a watertight joint when the door
is closed.

When the water level inside the vessel is pumped down below the
height of the door, the outside water pressure will force the door
inward to increase the tightness of the joint. Because of this force
inward and the weakened patch structure in way of the door opening,
reinforcement beams are installed transversely behind the patch
planking between frames in way of the top and bottom planks against
which the door bears.

The door must be large enough for a diver to pass through easily
without getting hung up.

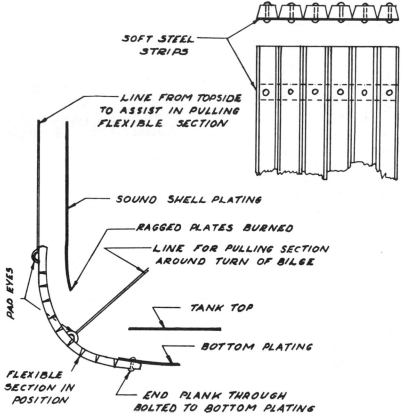

Fig. 71.   British standard patch. Planks are chamfered to form curve, and are
bolted to thin flat bars of soft steel.

The *British Standard Patch* requires considerably more work to be done by the diver than the American Patch; however, it is constructed ashore and can be manufactured in standard sizes, which eliminates considerable on-the-scene patch construction.

To construct this patch, horizontal chamfered planks are bolted to vertical soft metal strips or thin flat bars. The edge of the hole to be patched must be trimmed by burning or cutting, to remove jagged steel.

The patch is installed by lowering it into position over the hole and throughbolting the bottom plank to the hull plating.

Lines are secured to internal padeyes mounted on the patch, about mid-height. These lines are used to haul the patch inboard to the shape of the bilge or ship's side. Lines are also secured to padeyes mounted on the top end plank for hauling the flexible section after the bottom end plank is secured.

The patch is then hauled into position, as shown in Fig. 71, and completely throughbolted. A wood form is constructed internally, in way of the hole, and concrete is poured to cover and overlap the entire hole. The shell, in way of the patch, is shored and stiffened, as illustrated in Fig. 72.

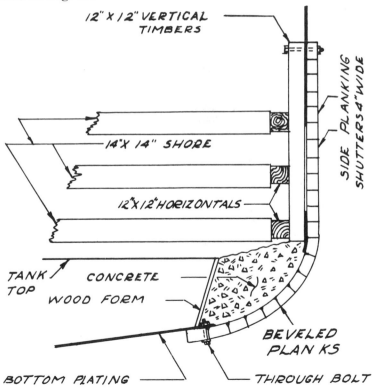

Fig. 72. British standard patch.

The *Plank-by-plank Patch* is used for patching holes too large for the small patch and not as large as those covered by the American or British patches.

The Plank-by-plank Patch is not suitable for patching holes of very large diameter. This type of patch is a custom-built job and consequently requires more work to be done by the diver.

The patch is constructed on the job, so construction is combined with installation. Each plank is lowered to the damage area and bolted separately, starting at the top of the hole and finishing at the

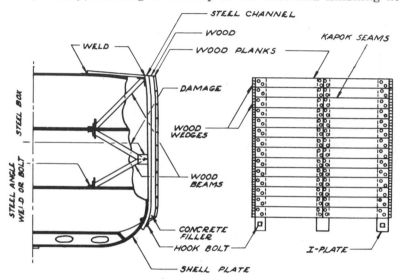

Fig. 73.   Plank-by-plank patch.

bottom. After the first plank is installed, the second plank is lowered and fitted against the bottom of the top plank. A tight fit is insured because the buoyancy of the second plank tends to cause the plank to rise, forming a tight seal. In this way, the pressure of the water is utilized to aid in the construction of a watertight patch. Before the patch is installed, the hull plating in the way must be cleared of jagged edges so that the planks will seat firmly.

Figure 73 illustrates a typical Plank-by-plank Patch; and Figs. 74 and 75 show a variation of the Plank-by-plank Patch.

Figure 76 illustrates a method of obtaining a watertight joint between a patch and the shell plating.

The most common bolts used to secure patches are the *hook bolt, ell bolt, tee bolt, tumbler bolt,* and *double hook bolt,* illustrated in **Fig. 77.** The nuts used in conjunction with these bolts are installed by divers; consequently, it has been found that the butterfly nut is perhaps the

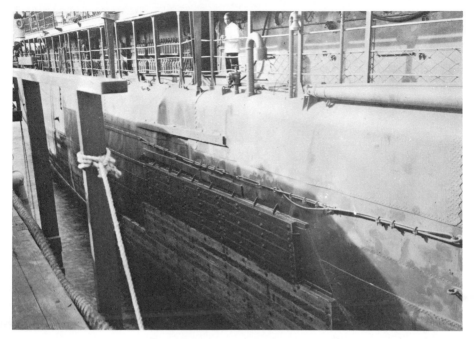

Fig. 74. Plank-by-plank patch. (Official U. S. Navy photo.)

Fig. 75. Plank-by-plank patch. (Official U. S. Navy photo.)

handiest to use under water. The butterfly nut may be manufactured simply by welding two steel rods, three to eight inches in length, to the opposite sides of a nut.

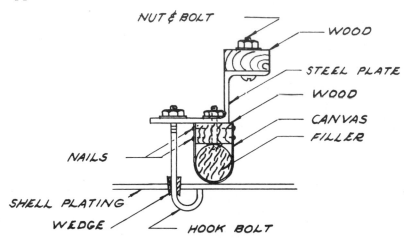

Fig. 76.   Watertight joint for hull patch.

Regardless of the type of patch used, a certain amount of preparation of the hull structure, in way of the hole, must first be accomplished. Jagged and ragged plating must be cut away; fractured, distorted, or otherwise weakened structural members must be stiffened, shored, or strengthened; and debris must be cleared away to facilitate working.

A patch is only as good as the workmanship that went into it. The best materials available will not, in themselves, insure a satisfactory patch. The patch must be well made and carefully installed. Figure 78 shows one method of securing a patch.

COFFERDAMS

A cofferdam is a large, watertight fence or wall constructed around a hatch or completely around the periphery of the weather deck of a submerged vessel in order to obtain freeboard. The cofferdam extends from the deck to the surface of the water, and it is supported by frames and stanchions and held in place by shoring. When construction is completed, the top edge of the cofferdam should reach just above the mean high water level.

The suction hoses of the pumps are placed inside the cofferdam, and the vessel is pumped out and refloated. In order to use the cofferdam successfully, the hull must be comparatively watertight, so that any leaks will not overcome the capacity of the pumps.

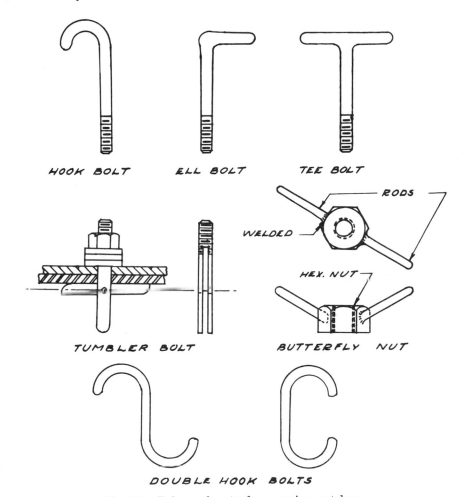

Fig. 77.   Bolts and nuts for securing patches.

There are two general types of cofferdams: partial cofferdam, which is fitted around hatches or small deck openings; and complete cofferdam, which extends completely around the edge of the main deck in way of the gunwale bar.

Partial Cofferdam. The partial cofferdam is most generally used on cargo-type vessels where deck openings are at a minimum or on other vessels where there is little or no main deck damage. Figure 79 shows a partial cofferdam. The partial cofferdam is most often used in commercial ship salvage because of the greater cost of installing a complete cofferdam.

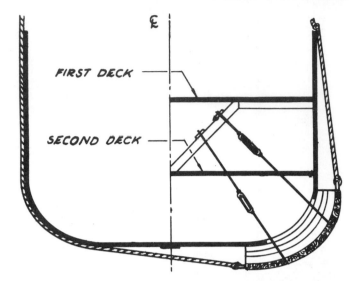

Fig. 78.   Method of securing patch. Where possible use tongue-and-groove lumber, otherwise chamfered. For additional holding power, use turnbuckles and strong-back, as shown. In addition to hogging line, tie rods can be fastened to stanchions or other ship's structure.

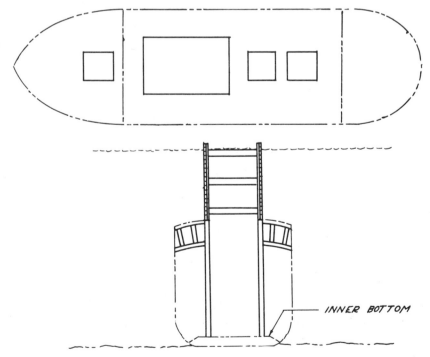

Fig. 79.   Partial cofferdam. Solid lines indicate shoring and partial cofferdams.

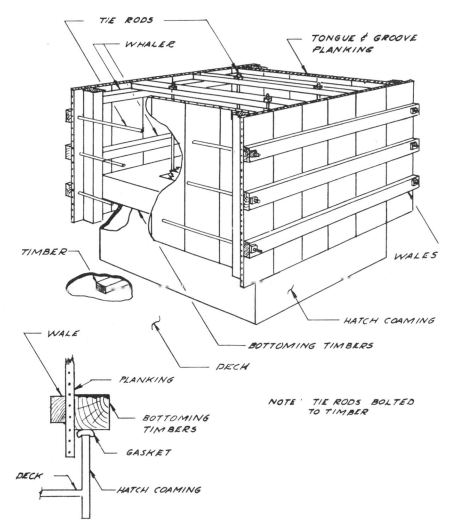

Fig. 80. Wooden cofferdam for small hatch. Tie rods are bolted to timber.

A partial cofferdam is similar in construction to the complete cofferdam, except that it is smaller and is usually fitted around hatches and engine-room skylights. The greater area of the deck left outside the cofferdam is subjected to the weight of the water above it; consequently, more work is required to be performed by divers, shoring internally, to enable the main deck to support the abnormal weight. This shoring is usually carried down to the tank tops. The shores are approximately 12″ × 12″ timbers, or 2½″ pipe; however, the sizes of the shores will vary, depending on the depth of water and strength required.

Wood shores should be weighted to overcome their inherent positive buoyancy, so that the divers can easily submerge and install them. All shoring should be accomplished prior to the start of pumping operations.

As opposed to a complete cofferdam, the submerged vessel is more unstable during refloating operations when using a partial cofferdam; therefore, this method is best used in conjunction with pontoons or large floating cranes.

The deck area outside the cofferdam must be included in the total area of free-surface when stability calculations are made. Figures 80 and 81 illustrate two methods of partial cofferdam construction.

Among the factors to be considered in constructing a cofferdam are (1) materials available, (2) maximum differential in pressure, (3) tides and weather conditions, and (4) facilities for construction.

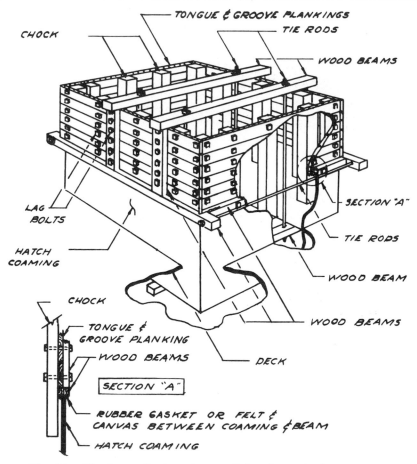

Fig. 81.   Wooden cofferdam for small hatch in shallow water.

Complete Cofferdam. The complete cofferdam is more easily adaptable to passenger vessels and vessels having numerous main deck openings. Because of the comparatively flimsy construction and necessarily large exposed area, the complete cofferdam is susceptible to the effects of adverse winds and seas and should not be constructed unless the vessel lies sunk in shallow water near the shore or in a protected harbor. Figure 82 illustrates a complete cofferdam.

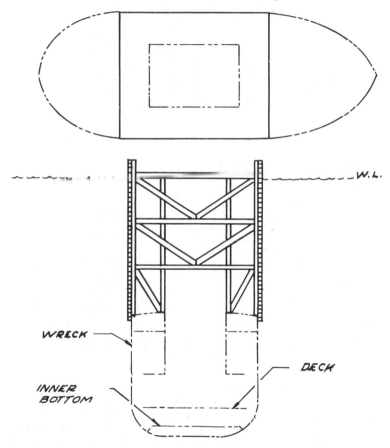

Fig. 82.   The complete cofferdam is indicated by solid lines.

The construction methods of the complete and partial cofferdams are similar, so that one general discussion on cofferdam construction can be applied to either.

The cofferdam illustrated in Fig. 83 is usually made in vertical sections approximately eight to twelve feet in width, the height being sufficient to extend above the surface of the water at high tide.

The sections are constructed using tongue-and-groove planking bolted
to horizontal timber wales. The wales are 12″ × 12″, spaced approximately on four-foot centers for large vessels. The size of the timber
and the thickness of the planking will be determined by the depth of
the water. Refer to Fig. 62, which depicts the size and thickness of
cofferdam planking.

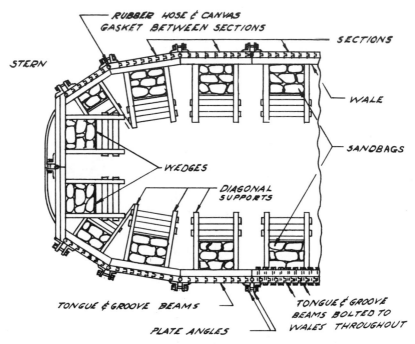

Fig. 83.   Complete cofferdam attached to ship's rail. Sections are bolted together
at plate angles.

The vertical sections should be weighted sufficiently to overcome
the positive buoyancy of the wood. The bottom planking is fitted with
a gasket of rubber hose and throughbolted to the ship's rail. The
cofferdam vertical sections are braced internally to the main deck
with diagonal shoring. The foundations of the shorings are wedged,
to force a pressure against the gasket at the rail, which will create a
watertight joint. Rubber hose and canvas gaskets are fitted between
the vertical sections and drawn together with bolts through fitted
plate angles to make for a watertight vertical joint.

In some instances, cofferdams are not complete, in the sense that
they do not extend completely around the vessel. They may cut across
the bow and stern sections, eliminating approximately twenty, thirty,

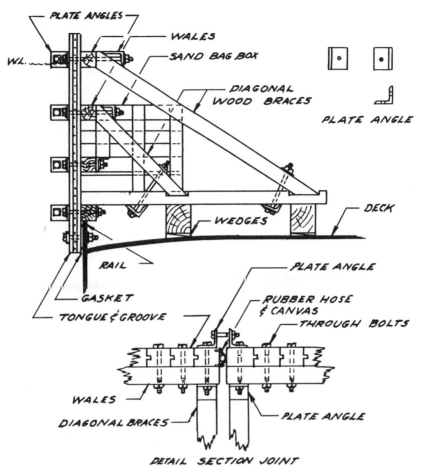

Fig. 84. Complete cofferdam attached to ship's rail.

or forty feet at each end. The bow and stern sections thus eliminated are usually over the forepeak or the afterpeak tanks. The main deck over these tanks must be watertight, and the cofferdam sections at the bow and stern may only be stopped at frames that are particularly strong. The exposed sections of the main deck outside the cofferdam will be subjected to the weight of the water above; therefore, the load must be distributed through several decks by shoring.

Any deck plating outside a cofferdam will be subjected to the considerable weight of water over it after pumping commences; consequently, the decks must be shored and stiffened from underneath to prevent collapse. In order to be effective, the shoring should be carried down to the tank tops or to the keel.

Cofferdams are used to give freeboard to the sunken vessel; consequently, the shell plating must be watertight, or made so.

The two general methods of bottoming complete cofferdams to the hull are the American and the British. Bottoming is a term used to define the method of securing the bottom of the cofferdam to the deck of the sunken vessel, illustrated in Fig. 84. The American practice is to secure the cofferdam on the deck edge, in way of the gunwale bar. The British practice is to bolt a strake of heavy timber, longitudinally on the sheer strake, approximately one foot below the main deck edge, completely around the periphery of the vessel. The bottom of the

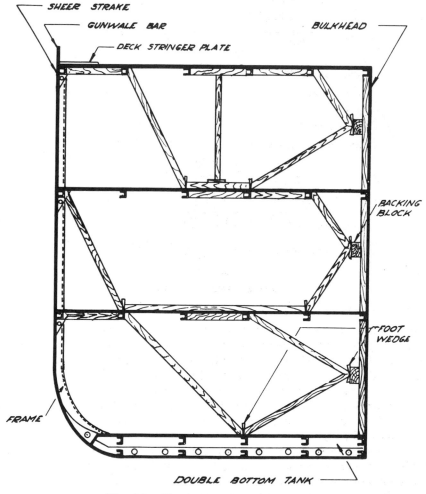

Fig. 85.   Shoring decks and bulkheads.

vertical section of the cofferdam is then secured to this heavy timber. This practice involves considerable time and labor in drilling the steel hull plates and fastening the timbers with throughbolts.

The use of a complete cofferdam requires the removal of much of the upper structure and appendages, such as masts, stacks, etc. In many cases, most of the superstructure must also be removed.

SHORES

Shores are lengths of timber or pipe used to strengthen bulkheads, decks, or overheads.

In ship salvage work, shoring is usually installed in a vessel where the pressure of water or air may cause a collapse. Shores are also used to overcome weakness where structural members have been damaged.

Wood shores used in ship salvage work are usually pine, oak, or fir.

The shoring should be installed so that the load is distributed over a large area. The directional force should be downward on any shore that may float away: shore decks to bulkheads, overheads to decks, etc.

The maximum length of a shore should not exceed thirty times the shortest dimension. The pressure point of a shore on a bulkhead should not be less than approximately one-third the height of the bulkhead. Fittings and structural members already installed aboard should be used to secure shoring. Figure 85 illustrates some general methods of shoring.

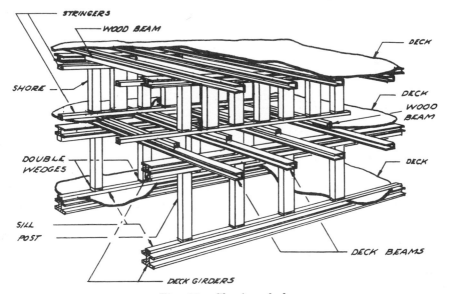

Fig. 86. Shoring decks.

Wedges. Shoring is secured and stiffened by the use of wedges. Two wedges are used simultaneously beneath the foot of the shore, and they are driven with a sledge hammer or maul from opposite directions. A proper wedge is as wide as the shore, with one-inch taper for every six inches of wedge. Sand, iron filings, etc., may be used to increase the grip or friction of a wedge. Figure 86 illustrates a method of shoring decks.

Vertical wood shores are installed between the steel deck beams and the deck plating. The vertical shoring bears against longitudinal wood stringers at the top, in line with and beneath longitudinal deck girders and longitudinal wood sills at the deck, in line with and above longitudinal deck girders. The vertical wood shores are wedged in place by driving on double wedges installed between the shores and the longitudinal wood sills.

CONCRETE

The qualities of ship salvage concrete must include strength, watertightness, and steel adhesiveness. Although concrete sets in approximately 45 minutes, it does not reach maximum strength before approximately four weeks. Rarely is concrete allowed to set to maximum strength in ship salvage work.

The holding power of concrete is determined by its weight and is equal to approximately 150 pounds per cubic foot.

Mixtures. The intended use for concrete will determine its mixture with other materials. In marine use, concrete is mixed for ballast and patches. Concrete for ballast need not have the strength of patch concrete; consequently, the mixture is leaner.

Ballast:	Portland cement	1 part
	Sand	2½ parts
	Gravel	5 parts
Patch:	Portland cement	1 part
	Sand	1½ parts
	Gravel	2 parts

Mix in approximately six gallons of water to every bag of cement. Concrete to be used under water should be a comparatively dry mixture; that is, it should contain very little water. The sand and cement are mixed first; then the water and gravel are folded in until a thoroughly homogenized mixture that may be placed by one of the following methods is obtained: pouring; tremie funnel; cement gun.

Pouring. Pouring concrete for a small patch presents no great problem. A form is constructed around the hole and adequately shored, or otherwise stiffened. A pipe drain is installed prior to pouring the concrete so that excess water may be removed to enable the concrete to set. Figure 87 illustrates this type of concrete patch. Note

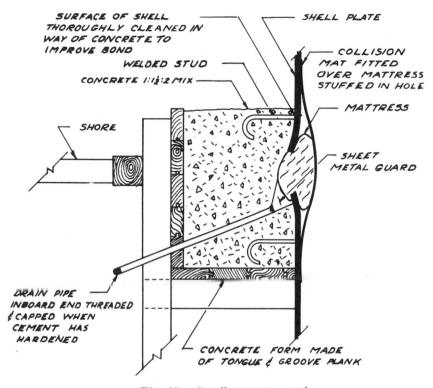

SURFACE OF SHELL
THOROUGHLY CLEANED IN
WAY OF CONCRETE TO
IMPROVE BOND

WELDED STUD

CONCRETE 1:1½:2 MIX

SHELL PLATE

COLLISION
MAT FITTED
OVER MATTRESS
STUFFED IN HOLE

MATTRESS

SHORE

SHEET
METAL GUARD

DRAIN PIPE
INBOARD END THREADED
& CAPPED WHEN
CEMENT HAS
HARDENED

CONCRETE FORM MADE
OF TONGUE & GROOVE PLANK

Fig. 87.   Small concrete patch.

that the drain pipe is threaded so that it may be capped with a standard pipe cap after the concrete has hardened.

Wherever possible, metal surfaces should be thoroughly cleaned before concrete is poured, in order to improve the bond between the concrete and the metal surface.

The large concrete patch illustrated in Fig. 87A requires considerably more preparatory work for the installation than does a temporary wood patch of studding and tie rods.

Tremie Funnel. A tremie funnel is used to pour concrete under water. The tremie funnel is basically a funnel welded to the top of a large-diameter pipe. The pipe is long enough to extend from the bottom of the patch to above the surface of the water.

Figure 88 illustrates a simple tremie and its use in bulkhead construction. The bulkhead is made watertight at the shell of the ship by pouring concrete, using a tremie. After the form is constructed, in way of the junction of the temporary bulkhead and the shell of the ship, the tremie is lowered to the bottom of the form and concrete is poured into the funnel. As the level of the concrete rises in the form, the tremie is also raised; however, the end of the pipe should always be kept below the surface of the concrete in the form. The same procedure is followed where concrete is poured in any type of patch construction.

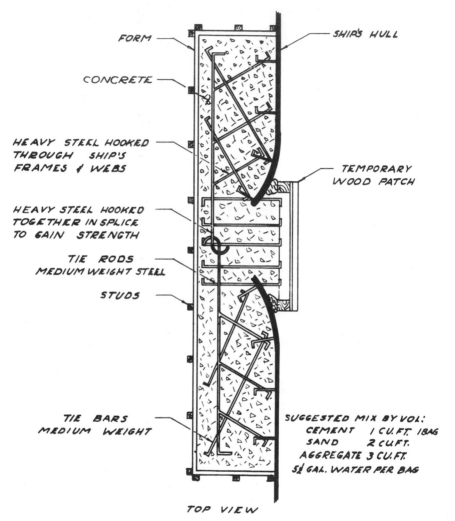

FORM

CONCRETE

HEAVY STEEL HOOKED
THROUGH SHIP'S
FRAMES & WEBS

HEAVY STEEL HOOKED
TOGETHER IN SPLICE
TO GAIN STRENGTH

TIE RODS
MEDIUM WEIGHT STEEL

STUDS

TIE BARS
MEDIUM WEIGHT

SHIP'S HULL

TEMPORARY
WOOD PATCH

SUGGESTED MIX BY VOL:
CEMENT   1 CU.FT. 1 BAG
SAND   2 CU.FT.
AGGREGATE 3 CU.FT.
5½ GAL. WATER PER BAG

TOP VIEW

Fig. 87A.   Large concrete patch. Studding is employed to prevent form bulging while pouring concrete. Leave a 3-inch clearance between form and tie rods.

Cement Gun.   The cement gun is used to pour cement where water pressure prevents the cement from flowing readily.   Figure 89 illustrates one type of cement gun.

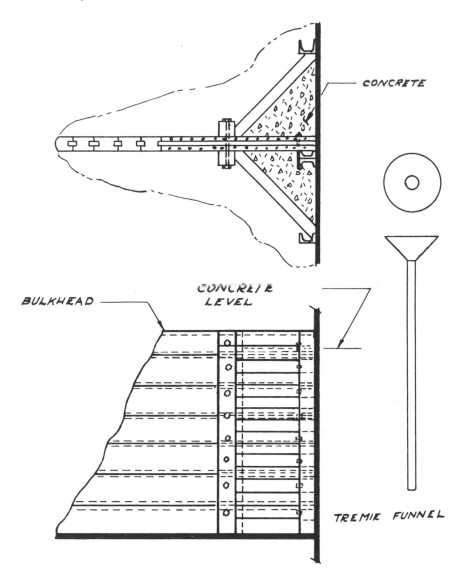

CONCRETE

BULKHEAD

CONCRETE LEVEL

TREMIE FUNNEL

Fig. 88.   Bulkhead construction; Tremie funnel is used in pouring cement.

The concrete gun is especially useful for pouring cement into partially opened or jammed valves that must be made watertight. The
cement gun is cumbersome, awkward to handle, and should be fitted
with a lifting ring for use with a block and tackle, handy-billy, etc.

After the chamber is filled with a cement mixture, the cover is fitted and the air hose is connected to a fitting on the cover. The large-diameter hose at the lower end of the chamber is lowered to the position where cement is to be poured. Air pressure is applied to the chamber, which forces the cement through the hose.

When the chamber is emptied, the air is secured and the cover valve is opened to bleed off any air pressure remaining in the chamber. The cover is removed, and the chamber is filled with another charge of cement mixture.

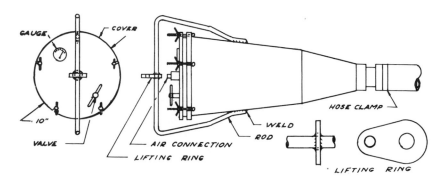

Fig. 89.   Gun for pouring underwater cement. Gun cover is made from blank flange.

CHAPTER V

SALVAGE PRACTICE

Having studied the basic fundamentals of naval architecture and acquired a working knowledge of salvage equipment and the structures employed in salvage operations, we may now pass on to the practical problems of marine salvage operations.

Although each individual salvage job is unique in its combination of problems, there are certain proven methods that are used for each category of salvage: stranding, sinking, or towing (rescue). The necessary steps to be followed in each of these will be outlined, although all steps indicated may not be necessary in every salvage case. The steps that are actually used in a salvage venture will depend upon the information accumulated in the survey.

STRANDINGS

There are many factors that will influence the salvage plan in the case of strandings. A partial list follows:

1. Character of bottom: slope; composition (sand, rock, coral, old wrecks).
2. Depth of water: range of tide.
3. Area of the vessel's bottom in contact with the ground.
4. Character and size of ship.
5. Drafts and loading.
6. Stability.
7. Structural strength.
8. Damage in stranding.
9. Relative position of ship to shore.
10. Surf.
11. Presence or absence of swell.
12. Currents.
13. Visibility under water.
14. Prevailing weather conditions.

Upon notification of a stranding, the first steps to be taken are sometimes found, in the final analysis, to be the most important. For, upon these first steps, the success or failure of the venture may often rest.

Charts, tide tables, and weather conditions relating to the specific area involved should be consulted. If it is found that a successful venture is possible, then the next step is to proceed to the scene immediately with an adequate salvage plant.

131

Upon arrival, an investigation should reveal whether proper pre-cautionary measures have been taken to prevent the vessel from going further aground. Broaching and riding farther up on the beach can be overcome by setting one or more anchors to seaward. The object is to keep the vessel in as stationary a position as possible until such time as a salvage plan can be evolved and put into action.

Following an initial investigation, a salvage plan should be drawn up based on information accumulated from an external and, if pos-sible, internal survey. This plan should take into consideration the power and equipment available at the site. Forms and records that may be useful in determining a workable salvage plan are shown in the Appendix.

In the event that an anchor to seaward is urgently·needed, the salvage vessel or tug should proceed toward the stranded vessel and pass as close aboard as possible. The bitter end of the chain of one bower anchor should be passed to the stranded vessel, with a 7″ or 8″ messenger. If no power is available aboard the wreck, a bight of the messenger should be passed aboard and inserted in a snatch block. The tug's winch can then be used to haul on the bitter end of the messenger and haul aboard the anchor cable. The bitter end of the anchor chain is secured aboard the wreck, and the salvage vessel then steams seaward until all the anchor chain is paid out; then the anchor is dropped. Because the purpose of the anchor is to keep the vessel from riding harder aground or from broaching, a steady strain should be maintained on the ground tackle. It is well to provide maximum scope to the anchor cable, so that sudden surges caused by waves and swells will not result in dragging the anchor. The use of explosives in way of the anchor flukes will help to obtain a satisfactory bight on rocky or coral bottoms.

Upon finding his vessel stranded, the first action of the master is usually to throw the engines full speed astern. In most cases this is not the correct course of action to pursue without a prior investigation of the condition of the underwater body of the stranded vessel. If the vessel has struck a rock and is holed, it is likely that backing off the rock without isolating the damage may result in sinking. If the hole is very large and the underwater damage extensive, the chances are that lives may be lost as a result of the immediate, inevitable sinking. If the vessel lies on a soft, sandy, or muddy bottom, the chances are that the main engines, if maneuvered, will become inoperative due to the admittance of sand, mud, etc., into the condensers, thereby disabling the main unit. In addition to the foregoing hazards, the maneuvering of the engine on a single-screw vessel, stranded forward, may cause the vessel to broach. Therefore, all factors that may tend to increase or jeopardize the vessel's safety should be considered when making a decision as to whether the engines should be maneuvered immediately.

Should it be decided that the vessel cannot be backed off immediately, attempts should be made to place an anchor to seaward, as described above. By keeping a steady strain on the cable of this anchor, sometimes the vessel may come free unexpectedly. This may be caused by a combination of the slight rise and fall of the swells and currents acting on the vessel with a constant strain maintained by the offshore cables. As is the case in most strandings, an anchor is needed to seaward almost immediately, but the time and work involved in rigging a bow anchor astern may delay the securing of the stern to seaward and result in possible broaching. Because of this possibility, it is sometimes a better course of action to lay a small kedge anchor to seaward immediately. This smaller anchor should be easier to handle and lay and should be followed by the heavier bower anchors later. Needless to say, the anchors should be laid toward the set; that is, in the direction of any current, seas, winds, etc. which tend to affect the lie of the vessel. A buoy should be secured to the anchor with a crown line so that, in the event of parting the anchor cable, it will be easy to locate and recover. During the interim, soundings can be taken completely around and in the vicinity of the stranded vessel, and the rise and fall of the tide can be noted and recorded by a leadsman. By consulting tide tables, sailing directions, navigation charts, and such, the time of maximum high tide may be determined and the direction of tidal and coastal currents noted. If at all possible, a tug should be secured prior to any refloating effort; however, in many cases the wait for the arrival of the tug will delay the operation for days or even weeks, so the vessel must make every effort to refloat itself.

After all measures have been taken to prevent the vessel from riding farther up on the beach, the work of lightening her may be started. No attempt should be made to lighten until such time as the vessel is, in fact, stationary; that is, it will not ride farther up on the beach. Lightening the vessel should be commenced so that a minimum draft will be obtained at a maximum high tide. The lightening of the vessel may be accomplished by pumping out oil and/or ballast tanks; shifting or discharging cargo. In this connection, it is well to remember that if a vessel is aground forward a change in trim from bow to stern may sometimes be effected by pumping ballast from forward tanks to after tanks. Occasionally this change of trim is enough to effect a rise in draft forward sufficient to refloat the vessel.

In the case of a large cargo vessel, the amount of cargo that can be shifted or removed easily is a negligible amount; however, in smaller boats—sailing craft, fishing vessels, and the like—the removal of cargo and provisions can be accomplished quickly and easily by using the lifeboats and rafts. The cargo and provisions can be landed on a beach by successive trips of the boats.

On vessels of medium and large sizes, slipping the anchor cables should also be given consideration as a means of lightening the bow. Before doing this, one end of a crown line of suitable size and length should be secured to the anchor and the other end to a crown buoy to facilitate the recovery of the anchor and cables. The buoy should be large enough to support the weight of the crown line and float at the surface of the water.

In conjunction with keeping the vessel from riding harder aground by laying of anchors to seaward as a preventive measure, the vessel's double bottom tanks can be flooded with salt water. The additional weight of the salt water will increase the ground reaction as well as protect the bottom of the vessel from serious crushing and pounding damage. When the maximum effort to refloat is started, the double bottoms are pumped out so as to be empty at a maximum high tide.

Finally, it must be remembered that a vessel will come off easiest the way she went aground, although there are exceptions to this due to prevailing currents, weather conditions, locations of sand bars, and the topography of the bottom in the vicinity of the stranding—all conditions that can usually be ascertained during the course of the preliminary investigation and survey. The direction of pull for refloating the vessel must be included in any salvage plan.

SURVEYING

Surveying is the accumulation of information and data pertaining to the physical location of the vessel, its condition, and the surrounding area. Surveying is generally divided into two parts: the topside survey and the underwater survey.

Topside Survey. A topside survey includes information about the ship, its cargo, the location of the ship, depth of water, and type of bottom. It also includes information gathered concerning tides, currents, conditions of surf, visibility, and prevailing weather conditions.

Survey data should include the ship's measurements, capacities, etc. The ship's plans and curves of form are extremely valuable in developing a salvage plan.

It is useful to know the circumstances surrounding the stranding. The depth of water in the vicinity of the stranding should be ascertained by soundings. The use of a hand lead line is recommended; however, if an electric portable fathometer is available, it may be used. Soundings spaced at distances of approximately ten to twenty feet from bow to stern should be taken completely around the vessel. The soundings should extend to approximately one ship width to port and starboard and astern or offshore to deep water.

There have been occurrences where a vessel was refloated, yet, before it could be salved, the vessel required additional lightening because of a sand bar astern and outshore, which was not previously located by soundings.

The topside survey should include information gathered from the tide tables, current tables, coast pilot publications, sailing directions, and navigation charts. In addition to the foregoing publications, valuable information can be garnered from local fishermen, inhabitants, and seafarers.

A part of the topside survey should determine what machinery aboard the stranded vessel can be used in the salvage operation. It should also be determined if there is any equipment in the vessel's cargo that may be used during the salvage operation. The use of this cargo equipment will probably save considerable time and labor that otherwise would be required to transport the necessary equipment from the salvage vessel or from a distant port.

The specific gravities of any large bulk cargoes that may be carried aboard the stranded vessel should also be determined. These cargoes may be carried either in tanks or in the holds. This information will be useful later when it must be decided which cargoes are to be jettisoned and which left aboard for the refloating effort.

Weather. It cannot be stressed too strongly that weather conditions are the single most important prevailing factor in the success or failure of any offshore salvage venture. Unexpected heavy weather, adverse tides, and strong currents can spell failure; consequently, a determined effort must be made to ascertain what these conditions will be before, during, and after a salvage venture.

Wind velocities, barometric pressures, and temperatures should be recorded periodically in order that the local trends of weather may be determined.

In most cases, the success or failure of any salvage venture will be established within the first twenty-four hours of stranding. If the vessel does not suffer extensive damage upon grounding or within the first twenty-four hours of stranding, there is a good chance of successful salvage, providing the prevailing weather conditions are favorable. Again, the importance of weather conditions in any salvage operation cannot be overemphasized.

Tides. The range of tides is determined from tide tables, which are indispensable in salvage work.

The tables should be consulted to determine the height of the tide at the time of stranding, and they are most useful in determining when the maximum heaving effort should commence during the refloating operation of a stranded vessel. The tide tables must be consulted for a maximum high tide. The salvage plan should be based around a maximum high tide, with pumping operations starting early enough to obtain a minimum ground reaction at a maximum high tide.

Tides may cause a stranded vessel to change trim, which can affect her stability or result in structural failures.

Tide tables should be augmented by actual soundings at the scene of the stranding, which should be taken twice daily at high and low tides.

Currents. The local coastal currents in the vicinity of the stranding should be ascertained.

Currents have a tendency to set a vessel in the direction of the current; consequently, the general layout of beach gear and/or the direction of pull of the tug will be influenced by the force of the set.

Currents may also cause a stranded vessel to broach, i.e., ground parallel to the shoreline. Broaching makes salvage more difficult because the greater bottom area of the vessel aground increases the magnitude of the ground reaction. The increase in ground reaction will require a proportionate increase in the force required to free the stranded vessel.

Soundings. Complete and thorough soundings should be taken in the vicinity of the stranding and entered on a sounding record chart. The soundings should be taken at high and low tides, at spaced intervals, to port and starboard, and astern to deep water. During prolonged salvage operations, soundings should be taken periodically and compared with the tide tables. A lead line used for taking soundings is illustrated in Fig. 90.

The sounding chart should also be used to indicate the direction and force of prevailing winds and currents, compass bearings, position of stranded vessel, location of marker buoys, type of bottom, and any other pertinent information that may prove useful in the salvage operation.

Machinery, Pipes, Equipment. Diagrams of the vessel's piping arrangements and systems will be most helpful in determining the usefulness of any installed piping, as every effort should be made to utilize the stranded vessel's available equipment and deck machinery for power. Steam-driven winches and pumps are adaptable to air pressure.

Emergency diesel generators, which are usually located in a compartment at a high point in the superstructure, can also be utilized for auxiliary power, to operate submersible electric pumps and to provide lights and power for portable tools.

In many instances, the vessel's pipe lines and valves may be used to advantage for bilge suction, oil and water transfer, ballasting, air lifts, etc.

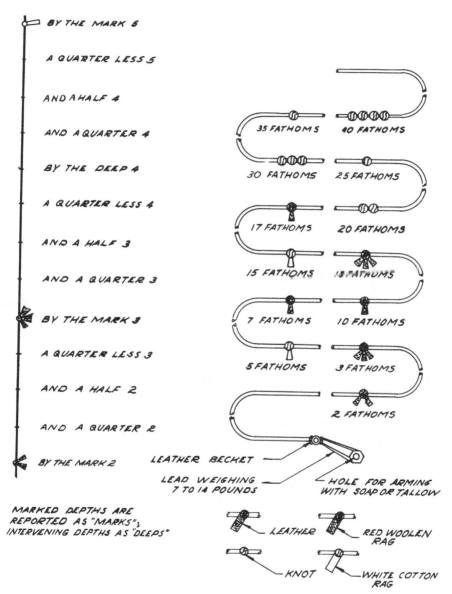

BY THE MARK 5

A QUARTER LESS 5

AND A HALF 4

AND A QUARTER 4

BY THE DEEP 4

A QUARTER LESS 4

AND A HALF 3

AND A QUARTER 3

BY THE MARK 3

A QUARTER LESS 3

AND A HALF 2

AND A QUARTER 2

BY THE MARK 2

35 FATHOMS   40 FATHOMS

30 FATHOMS   25 FATHOMS

17 FATHOMS   20 FATHOMS

15 FATHOMS   13 FATHOMS

7 FATHOMS   10 FATHOMS

5 FATHOMS   3 FATHOMS

2 FATHOMS

LEATHER BECKET

LEAD WEIGHING 7 TO 14 POUNDS

HOLE FOR ARMING WITH SOAP OR TALLOW

MARKED DEPTHS ARE REPORTED AS "MARKS"; INTERVENING DEPTHS AS "DEEPS"

LEATHER

RED WOOLEN RAG

KNOT

WHITE COTTON RAG

Fig. 90.   Marking of lead line.

Underwater Survey. The underwater survey is an inspection conducted by deep sea or shallow water divers. The purpose of the survey is to determine the condition of the vessel, topography of the ocean floor in the vicinity of the vessel, and other information that may affect the salvage plan or operation. The survey starts under water at the bow or the stern and extends progressively around the ship.

The divers must report any existing conditions that may adversely affect salvage operations. The size and location of holes and open portlights should be determined. Use of a plumb line in determining dimensions of large holes is most helpful. In many cases, particularly those of simple strandings, the condition of the bottom of the stranded vessel cannot be ascertained by a diver's inspection, due, in part, to the broad bottoms and minimum rise of floor of present-day merchant cargo vessels. On a sandy bottom, this condition is not worried about too much; however, on rocky bottoms, large holes may exist in the vessel, which cannot be observed externally by a diver. A preliminary pump-down of suspect compartments will indicate the general external condition of the hull. Observing the surface water level inside the ship at the rise and fall of the tide can also provide a good indication of the location and extent of any hull damage. An internal survey by a diver may divulge bottom hull damage.

Because of the many hazards that exist, an internal survey by divers should not be conducted unless there is specific information required or a specific job to be done. The danger of a diver in a deep sea rig falling during an internal survey is very great; therefore, he should be limited in his internal search and survey. Because of their greater freedom and neutral buoyancy, shallow water divers are more adaptable to internal search and survey, but the hazards are still great because of their comparative greater isolation and lack of positive communication. Common sense and good judgment should determine to what extent they should be employed on internal surveys.

Internal lines and piping, which may prove useful in pumping or de-watering by air, can be traced by divers. The usefulness of divers in making an underwater survey is unlimited.

All information gathered on the survey should be entered on a record sheet for future reference in determining and laying out a salvage plan.

In conclusion, it is noted that the amount of time spent on a detailed survey is well repaid in the final analysis, and it has a direct bearing upon the success or failure of any salvage venture. Therefore, it is most desirable to ascertain any and all prevailing conditions and to spend as much time on the survey as is practicable, weather permitting.

There is little to be said, indeed, for a half-completed salvage operation that discloses some basic information that should have been determined during the survey and that requires a change in salvage plans after a portion of the work has been accomplished.

CALCULATE GROUND REACTION

In most stranding cases, lightening the ship is the only major problem encountered in the actual salvage work. In making the determination as to where the vessel is to be lightened, it must first be established at which point it is aground—amidship, forward, or aft.

If the vessel is aground amidship, there is little to the problem except to remove weights throughout the vessel. The problem becomes slightly more complicated when it is aground forward or aft. Consideration must be given to the effects on trim of the vessel by the removal of weights already on board, the shifting of weights, or the addition of weights.

The point at which the vessel is aground will dictate from where the weights will be removed or shifted. The amount of weight removal or shift will depend upon the magnitude of the ground reaction, or the total tons that a vessel is aground. When a vessel is aground and not completely stranded, she generally has some buoyancy left. The buoyancy is computed by comparison of the draft readings before and after grounding. The draft readings before grounding can be learned from the ship's officers. After grounding, the draft is determined from reading the forward and aft draft marks, although in the majority of cases they can only be estimated, because conditions of sea and surf interfere with an accurate reading.

There are two generally used methods of calculating the ground reaction (R).

Parallel Rise Method. Referring to the following sketch, we assume that a vessel is aground at R. The parallel rise method assumes that we remove a weight equal to, and at the point of, the ground reaction.

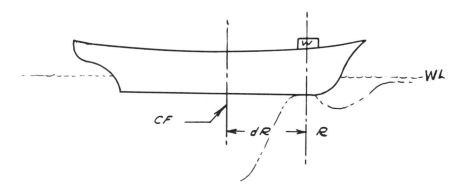

First, the mean draft before and after grounding must be determined. The forward and aft drafts before grounding are added together and are then divided by two to obtain a mean draft. The mean draft after grounding is computed in the same manner and subtracted from the mean draft before grounding. The result is converted into inches. The tons-per-inch immersion of the vessel is calculated and multiplied by the mean change in draft, in inches (*see* Page 52). The result is the amount of tons that the vessel is aground (magnitude of ground reaction).

Example: H_F = Draft forward
           H_A = Draft aft
           H_M = Mean draft
           T = Tons-per-inch immersion
           δH_M = Change in mean draft
           R = Magnitude of ground reaction
           Before grounding: H_F =   6'–0''; H_A = 8'–0''
           After grounding: H_F =   4'–0''; H_A = 9'–0''
           H_M before grounding: 7'–0''
           H_M after grounding: 6'–6''
           T   10 tons per inch
           δH_M 6''
           R = $\delta H_M \times T$
           R = 6 × 10 = 60 tons

Change of Trim Method. This is a method that is seldom used because of the difficulty in locating the center of the ground reaction. However, it may prove practical when a vessel is aground at one point, which can be located, along its length.

Example: t = Trim
           δt = Change in trim
           dR = Distance from midship to center of ground reaction
           MT_1 = Moment to trim ship one inch (*see* Page 66)
           Before grounding: H_F 6'–0''; H_A = 8'–0''
           After grounding: H_F 4'–0''; H_A = 9'–0''
           t before grounding: 24''
           t after grounding: 60''
           δt due to grounding: 36''
           MT_1 100 foot-tons
           dR   75'

$$\delta t = \frac{R \times dR}{MT_1}$$

$$36'' = \frac{R \times 75}{100}$$

$$R = \frac{100 \times 36}{75}$$

$$R = 48 \text{ tons}$$

In addition to the ground reaction, the coefficient of friction should also be determined. The coefficient of friction is the friction loss due to the contact of the vessel's bottom with various types of ground: sand, 0.4; coral, 0.5–1.0; rock, 0.9–2.0.

The magnitude of the ground reaction is multiplied by the coefficient of friction, and the result is added to the ground reaction. The result is the total ground reaction from which the salvage plan must be evolved. Weight is removed and beach gear rigged so that the total of the weight unloaded and the tons' pull developed by the beach gear and tugs will equal the total ground reaction. Figure a set of beach gear for 40 tons' pull and a tug for a one-ton pull for every 100 HP of the main engine.

The rise and fall of the tide will have a positive or negative effect on the magnitude of the ground reaction; therefore, the maximum refloating effort should be calculated to obtain at a maximum high tide.

SALVAGE PLAN

After the initial surveying is completed, the ground reaction is calculated, and weather conditions are determined, the salvage plan must be drawn up. The amount and location of weight removals or shifts, the layout plan and number of sets of beach gear, and the number and position of all tugs must be indicated. The plan should include all the phases of the heaving operations, including wrenching, pivoting, and/or scouring prior to the final heave.

In addition, a pumping plan must be devised for any flooded spaces aboard the stranded vessel or for any pumping overboard of bunkers or ballast.

Frequently, upon arrival at the scene of the stranding, it is wise to lay a set of beach gear to seaward immediately, not only to prevent the stranded vessel from riding farther up on the beach, but also to be used later in refloating efforts.

All hands involved in the salvage operations should be briefed on the salvage plan before work starts.

To determine the number of sets of beach gear for the salvage plan, proceed as follows:

1. Calculate the ground reaction.
2. Estimate the coefficient of friction (*see* Page 140).
3. Calculate the effects of weights to be shifted or changed.
4. Calculate the effects of tides, winds, and currents on the ground reaction.
5. From the ground reaction in tons and coefficient of friction, determine the number of sets of beach gear necessary, assuming one set to develop approximately 40 tons' pull.
6. Draw up deck layout plans for the beach gear purchase tackle and indicate the direction to plant the anchors.

In determining the number of sets of beach gear it must be remembered that a well-laid set of beach gear will develop from 40 to

60 tons' pull, depending upon the type of bottom and the power available; whereas a tug will only develop approximately a one-ton pull for every 100 HP of the main engine. However, tugs are extremely important, for they must control the salved vessel.

After a beach gear plan has been drawn up, range markers are used by the salvage vessel to lay the beach gear according to the plan. The salvage ship maneuvers with the beach gear swung out over the side, and bearings are taken on the markers to maintain a predetermined course.

The beach gear anchor should be hung over the bow and secured with a 5-inch Manila stopper. The stopper is cut when the vessel is in position for letting go the anchor. Many combinations of wire and chain are used in the make-up of the anchor pendants; however, it is generally desirable to include at least one shot of $2\frac{1}{4}''$ chain in the make-up. This shot of chain provides weight and flexibility to the beach gear and tends to absorb the sudden shocks that are placed upon the anchor and cables by the surges of the vessel from the effects of tides, currents, and swells. Two additional 100-fathom lengths of wire are secured to the shot of chain to complete the make-up of the anchor pendant. One of these is hung over the ship's side, and the other is figure-eighted on the after deck or fantail of the salvage vessel. Each figure eight should be secured with a $3\frac{1}{2}''$ Manila line to a padeye on deck. As the cable is being laid, the movement of the vessel will create a strain, which will part the lashings for each coil as it slips over the side.

To lay out the beach gear pendant, the bitter end is passed aboard the wreck and secured by using a carpenter stopper. Sometimes the salvage vessel cannot go alongside the stranded vessel to pass aboard the wire because of heavy weather or the proximity of rocks. In these cases, the bight of a messenger is passed to the stranded vessel and inserted in a snatch block. The bitter end of the messenger is bent onto the pendant, which is then hauled aboard the stranded vessel by the messenger, by means of the salvage vessel's power winches. The purchase blocks and gear are then laid out on the deck after the bitter end of the pendant is secured aboard.

The salvage vessel steams on course, with the markers in line on a prearranged bearing; upon reaching the maximum length of the pendant, the anchor is let go after a heavy Manila stopper is severed. This stopper is located just forward of amidship and acts as a pivot to allow the salvage vessel to maneuver into position before dropping the anchor. It should not part until it is cut.

In the event that weather and sea conditions set the salvage vessel off course, delaying the beach gear laying operations, a Liverpool bridle, rigged from the stern quarter of the vessel, may be used to maintain course and proper bearing. For the method of rigging a Liverpool bridle, *see* Chapter VI.

All beach gear anchors should be inspected visually before heaving operations commence. This can be done by a diver or by using a glass from a small boat. If the anchors lie on smooth rock or coral, explosives should be used at the flukes to secure a better bite.

The salvage plan is the basic implement from which all salvage operations evolve. No salvage operation can be considered complete without a salvage plan.

REFLOATING EFFORTS

Before heaving operations commence, a conference should be held with the supervisory personnel involved in the salvage operation. Each step in the proposed plan should be explained in detail. The importance of this conference cannot be overstressed. It must be understood by all those concerned what their duties are before, during, and after salvage efforts. Attempts should be made to anticipate problems during this conference and to resolve them prior to initiation of the plan.

There are several variations of method in rigging beach gear in addition to the standard practice illustrated in Fig. 91. The standard method, as described in Chapter IV, is to lay out the purchase tackle on the deck of the stranded vessel. There are numerous occasions, however, where adverse conditions of weather and sea do not permit the transfer of the heavy purchase tackle and portable winches to the stranded vessel. When these occasions arise, there are several alternate methods of rigging beach gear without transferring the purchase tackle aboard.

One method is to rig the purchase tackle and portable winches on a barge lying in the calm waters of a nearby cove or harbor and tow the barge to the site of the stranding. The anchors are planted to seaward, and the hauling stopper of the purchase tackle traveling block is connected to a $1\frac{5}{8}''$ wire pendant secured to bitts aboard the stranded vessel. The standing block of the purchase tackle is connected to the anchor pendant with a carpenter stopper. Figure 92 illustrates this method of rigging beach gear. Caution must be exercised when using this method, for, when the stranded vessel is pulled free of the ground, the locked-in potential force of the beach gear is converted into kinetic energy, causing the stranded vessel to move quickly to deep water. There is imminent danger of the freed vessel overriding the barge in its path unless some planned action is taken to prevent collision. Two courses of action are possible: control the freed vessel, or shift the barge.

The freed vessel may be controlled with the aid of tugs or by letting go bower anchors. The barge may be shifted quickly by hauling on wire pendants attached to anchors planted toward the set and simultaneously casting off the $1\frac{5}{8}''$ wire pendants connected to the stranded vessel and slacking off the beach gear anchor pendants. As a result, the barge will be shifted toward the set, out of the path of movement of the freed vessel. The set will tend to force the freed vessel away from the direction of movement of the barge. This is a tricky operation and should not be attempted where tugs are available. Buoy all pendants so as to enable both barge and salved vessel to cast off all lines to prevent the vessel from getting "in irons."

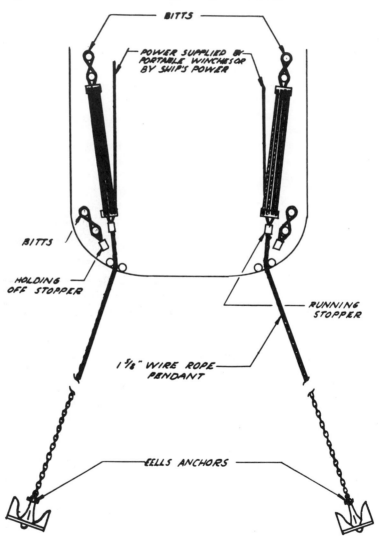

Fig. 91.   Beach gear rigged on a stranded vessel.

Figure 93 shows a second method of rigging beach gear luff on luff aboard the salvage vessel or tug.

The salvage vessel or tug plants two anchors over the bow and connects the main tow wire to the stranded vessel. The anchors are planted well to seaward for maximum reach. Each anchor pendant

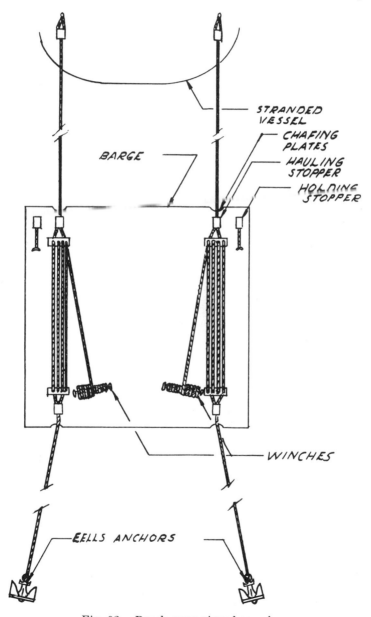

Fig. 92.   Beach gear rigged on a barge.

is connected with a carpenter stopper to the traveling block of a fourfold purchase tackle.

The hauling part of the tackle is connected to the carpenter stopper on the traveling block of a secondary set of fourfold purchase tackle. Finally the hauling part of the secondary set of tackle is taken on the drum of a winch.

Before commencing heaving operations, all purchase tackle is laid out for maximum reach and the carpenter stopper on the traveling block of the first set of tackle is connected to the anchor pendant. The tow wire, connected to the stranded vessel, is heaved in until all slack is out of the anchor pendants and a steady strain is maintained with all wires taut. The towing engine is dogged, and the tow wire is secured to the towing bitts so that it cannot pay out. Heaving operations are then commenced by using the winches. The secondary set of purchase tackle will be overhauled several times before it becomes necessary to again lay out the primary set to maximum reach.

When the stranded vessel is freed from the ground, the tug must maneuver quickly to avoid being struck astern by the moving vessel.

Heaving Operations. Heaving operations are normally commenced during high tide, when the buoyancy of the vessel is at a maximum and the ground reaction is at a minimum.

All slack should be taken out of cables before heaving operations commence, and the purchase gear should be laid out for maximum reach. At least two buoy markers should be laid, preferably in a parallel line across the stern and approximately fifty feet, or one shipwidth, to port and starboard.

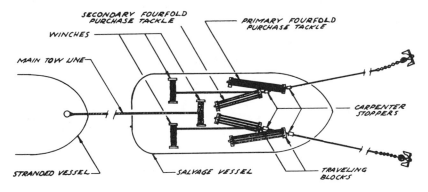

Fig. 93. Method of removing a stranded vessel with beach gear rigged luff upon luff.

It is well to set up communications between the salvage vessel and the personnel aboard the stranded vessel. If the heaving operations are to commence in darkness, simplified flashlight signals should be

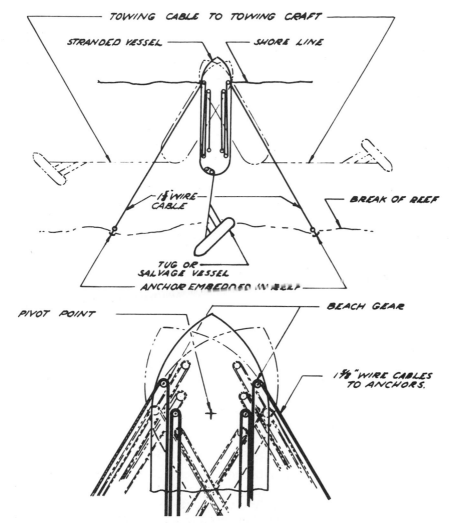

Fig. 94.   Common method of wrenching. Ghost lines indicate method in which
ship is wrenched in both directions.

prearranged between the salvage vessel or tug and the supervisor in
charge on the stranded vessel to indicate when the vessel is afloat,
when to commence maximum pull, and when to stop pulling.

All beach gear should be rigged, a tow line connected from the
salvage vessel, and heaving preparations completed.

When all is ready to pull, start the engines slow ahead and build up
speed gradually until maximum strain on the hawser is developed.
Commence hauling on the purchase tackle of the beach gear. In addition to the foregoing, the practice of "jumping the line" is sometimes
resorted to if the vessel fails to move. This sudden pull with full

power may overcome initial resistance of vessels that are hung up at one point. To "jump the line," slow the engines so that the towing hawser comes slack. Then ring full speed ahead and allow the tow wire to come taut with a sudden jerk. Anything can happen during this operation, so insure that all personnel are standing clear of the towing hawser.

Wrenching. During heaving operations, it is always helpful for the salvage vessel to sweep laterally with the tow wire hooked up, in an attempt to wrench and loosen the ship in its bed. Sometimes secondary sets of beach gear are laid at approximately right angles to the direction of the primary pull. The secondary sets, which oppose each other, are alternately hauled in and slacked off in an attempt to wrench the vessel sideways and help break the ground reaction. On smaller salvage jobs, two or more small craft can be used for wrenching. Figure 94 illustrates a common method of wrenching, using a tug and two sets of beach gear.

Scouring. Scouring with the propellers of tugs placed alongside the stranded vessel aids considerably in minimizing the ground reaction. The tugs or small craft should be trimmed by the stern and tied up alongside so that the water from their propellers is directed diagonally down and under the hull. Variable-pitch propeller craft are very useful in this type of work. The scouring vessels are moved forward and aft during the operation. Scouring, as the word implies, displaces sand and mud from under the hull through the force and movement of water agitated by the tugs' propellers.

Jetting. On salvage of small craft, jetting by divers with a high-pressure water hose can be substituted for the scouring of tugs.

PROCEDURES UPON REFLOATING

Tugs are extremely important during refloating operations, especially as the grounded ship comes off and while the beach gear is being cast off. All personnel should be thoroughly instructed in the beach gear plan, in which a sequence for casting off beach gear is indicated. Upon being refloated, the vessel is taken under control by the tugs and the beach gear is cast off as planned, when directed by the salvage officer in charge. In addition to the tug boats, one anchor aboard the stranded vessel should be made ready for letting go in the event of an emergency.

In order for a salvage operation to be truly successful, a refloated vessel must remain afloat. To accomplish this, all possible hazards due to weather, currents, tides, etc., should be anticipated in the salvage plan and a course of action predetermined.

Sometimes, in cases of stranded vessels that are pulled off the beach, damage holes are exposed on the underwater body of the vessel, which, if left exposed, might cause the refloated vessel to sink eventually. To anticipate and overcome this hazard, a collision mat should be hung over the offshore end of the vessel in readiness to apply over any holed area of the underwater body. An adequate collision mat is square in shape and made of multiple layers of canvas. The lower corners are fitted with fifteen feet, or more, of heavy chain, used to weight down the mat and cause it to sink beneath the hull. Attached to the ends of the chain are hogging lines, which are controlled from the main deck. In addition to obtaining negative bouyancy for the collision mat, the purpose of the chain is to prevent chafing against the barnacles usually found on the underwater body and along the bilge keel. With this in mind, the collision mat and the chains for the collision mat should be designed with sufficient length to overcome any chafing factor. A typical collision mat is illustrated in Fig. 55.

SINKINGS

Once the extent of the damage and the sizes of possible holes in the vessel are known, the salvage plan is evolved. It will be determined at this time whether the vessel is to be raised by using pumps or by using air. In some instances, a combination of both methods can be used, depending upon which compartments are bilged (open to the sea) and which compartments are watertight.

If a vessel has suffered extensive bottom damage, it is almost certain that it cannot be refloated by pumping methods, because the inaccessibility of most bottom holes to closure by patching prevents attaining the necessary watertight hull. If the vessel lies in fairly shallow water (less than thirty-five feet to the main deck), it may be subject to salvage by using compressed air, provided the main deck and sides are not so severely damaged as to cause serious structural weaknesses.

SURVEYING

In order to draw up an adequate salvage plan, an internal and external examination of the hull must be made. Whether the plan will involve the use of pumps or compressed air, it is necessary for divers to conduct a complete underwater survey similar to that for strandings, eliminating those phases which are not deemed applicable to a survey for a sinking.

External Survey. The survey should start from the bow and work around to the stern and back to the bow on the opposite side of the vessel. All hull openings should be noted, such as damage holes, open portholes, sea suctions, and overboard discharge. In order to determine the size and dimension of large holes, the use of a plumb line, controlled from the main deck, is most effective. The diver places it first at the top of the hole, then at the bottom of the hole. The size of the opening is then noted topside. The width of the hole can also be established by the same method. This information will be useful in determining the construction and sizes of patches needed. By conducting their examination while the compartments in the vicinity are being pumped, the divers will be aided considerably, as the pumping will cause a suction in way of the holes or cracks, which will assist in locating them.

The external survey should include soundings in the vicinity of the wreck and the location of any obstructions. In conjunction with the survey, buoy markers should also be laid at the outshore end of the vessel: one to port and one to starboard, approximately one ship breadth distant.

Internal Survey. The diver should never be used on an internal survey unless specific information is required. Although the hazard need not be defined here, it suffices to say that there is extreme danger. Only when information of this nature is required, should a diver enter within the hull: (1) condition of structural members in way of damage; (2) the type of damaged compartment; (3) the location of rocks or coral heads in bilged vessel; (4) piping that may be useful in refloating operations; and (5) the condition of doors and hatches useful to the watertight integrity of the vessel.

From the survey information, a salvage plan will be developed.

USE OF PUMPS IN SALVAGE WORK

In order to raise a vessel by pumping, there must be little or no damage to the vessel's bottom; the vessel must lie in fairly shallow water; and it must be possible to use cofferdams with a minimum removal of superstructure.

Underwater Repairs. In order to refloat a sunken vessel by using pumps, it is first necessary to make the hull watertight from the waterline to the keel. The patches used for de-watering by pumps may be less watertight than those which would be used for de-watering by compressed air. In any event, all repairs must be effected prior to any pumping operation and refloating effort. Patches should be so installed that the pressure of the water will tend to seat them more firmly. The usual underwater repairs for restoring watertight integrity may be classified as (1) minor leaks, (2) leaks of moderate size, or (3) large holes.

Minor leaks, as implied, are those that can be stopped by using wooden plugs, wedges, sawdust, and leak-stopping compounds. When using pumps, leak-stopping paste should be applied from outside the hull. If the vessel is to be salved by using compressed air, then the leak-stopping paste should be applied from within the hull.

For leaks of small size, a mixture of lambs' tallow and 10 per cent Portland cement is recommended. In cases where leaks cannot be located by the diver, and especially if they are in inaccessible locations, they may be stopped by feeding them with such materials as sawdust, straw, and bits of oakum, while pumping the adjacent compartment. The material will flow into the cracks, lodge, swell up, and eventually reduce the seepage into the hull. However, the best material to use as a salt-water plug is pine wood, as it will swell by absorption of water, thereby increasing the restriction of seepage the longer it is installed submerged.

Leaks of moderate size may often be plugged by stuffing them with pillows, blankets, mattresses, or by covering them with a collision mat. The tooker patch used over the portholes comes under the heading of moderate-sized patches, and, because of its particular design and strength, it will prove more adequate than the portlight cover itself. Figure 61 shows a tooker patch construction. Small patches are generally hauled to the ship's side with hogging lines (see Fig. 67)

Used in conjunction with collision mats, cement is sometimes poured to provide a watertight patch. Collision mat construction is illustrated in Fig. 55.

Large holes will require large patches constructed with wood, iron, steel, and cement; these patches are commonly known as the British Standard, American, and Plank-by-plank. The construction of these patches is described in detail in Chapter IV.

Concrete is used extensively in ship salvage work to make a hull watertight, usually in conjunction with other patches, and is rarely used to patch a hole or plug a leak unless poured into a form or box.

For best results, concrete should be placed above water. In order to do this, it is sometimes necessary to pump down a compartment, then place the cement in one of the previously installed temporary patches. The concrete is generally molded in a box to the desired shape and should be tamped in the box to eliminate all entrained air and should not be overwatered.

In making patches, there are many cases where concrete must be used under water, and the placing of large quantities in such circumstances is usually accomplished by the use of the tremie funnel, which is described in Chapter IV. A cement gun is also used for placing underwater cement. This operation is also described in Chapter IV.

Necessary concrete should be poured early enough in salvage work to allow sufficient time for setting, prior to pumping operations.

Cofferdam Construction. After the underwater repairs have been effected and the concrete poured, it is time to construct any cofferdams needed. In a case of a vessel sunk in shallow water that is to be raised by pumping, the construction of a cofferdam, either full or partial, is most often necessary, in order to give the vessel freeboard.

Much of the cofferdam sections can be prefabricated ashore or on the salvage vessel while underwater repairs are being accomplished. It should be determined at the beginning whether a full or partial cofferdam is required. The full cofferdam is used on passenger vessels and vessels with large superstructures and requires the removal of much of the topside masts and superstructure as an aid in maintaining stability during refloating operations. A partial cofferdam is generally used on cargo-type vessels and is constructed over hatches, coamings, and engine-room skylights, where the surrounding main deck area is generally sound. A partial cofferdam should be used when only a few internal structural failures exist, as the weight of the water on the decks, topside, is projected down through the hull; and if there are serious structural weaknesses, additional failures will occur, and perhaps the success of the refloating operation will be jeopardized. Whenever a cofferdam is used, its base must be securely mounted to the deck or hatch coaming in a watertight joint. This can be accomplished by either sandbagging, weighting down, or through-bolting. The use of cofferdams in pumping out vessels is a tricky operation, at best. The size of the cofferdam will depend upon weather conditions and strength required. The surrounding seas and weather conditions exert a considerable force upon any cofferdam, and, compared with the over-all structure of the vessel, it is usually of flimsy construction. Types of cofferdams and their construction are described and illustrated in Chapter IV.

Pumping Operations. Upon completion of the necessary underwater repairs, the construction of the patches for the leaks, casing for any required concrete, and the construction of any cofferdams desired, pumping operations should commence according to the salvage plan.

A salvage pump should be located so that the suction lift will not exceed fifteen feet. This requirement sometimes necessitates the placing of salvage pumps below decks. A procedure must also be set up to remove the pumps farther down to maintain an adequate calculated suction lift while the vessel is being pumped down. After all the pumps have been rigged, the suction lines laid out with adequate strainers, and the foot valves and discharge hoses placed overboard, the pumps should be test-run individually, and inspection should determine whether the pump will pick up suction under operating conditions and if there is a complete supply of fuel. It must be remembered that the salvage pump is used more than any other item of equipment in any salvage operation, so its condition of maximum efficiency must always be maintained. Generally, it has been determined that the best pump for moving large volumes of water in salvage operations is a self-contained, self-priming, heavy duty, centrifugal

gasoline-driven type. Besides de-watering, there should be an adequate means to counterflood the vessel in the event that stability
becomes questionable or to prevent the vessel from breaking up.

Considerable time can often be saved in pumping operations if
holes are bored or drilled in bulkheads and decks to de-water adjacent
compartments, rather than move the pump and suction hoses. Care
should be taken to insure that all compartments are adequately
venting; otherwise, failure of a bulkhead or deck in the compartments will result from developing a vacuum.

The rise and fall of the tide should be compared with the level of
the water inside of the hull. After the installation of patches, if the
water level outside drops below the water level inside, it may cause
pressure upon the outside patches, resulting in leaks or entire failure.
Therefore, it is sometimes necessary, especially during low tide, to
pump water out of the vessel in order to minimize any stresses that
may be placed on hull patches. By the same token, pumps must be
started up and water pumped into the hull upon the next flooding
tide, primarily to prevent the vessel from becoming buoyant prior to
final pumping operations. Compartments that have been patched
should be test-pumped in order to determine whether they will pump
down.

It is well to have a diver examine all patches from within the hull
prior to commencing pumping operations. In conjunction with this
inspection, it should be ascertained if there are conditions that may
give rise to free-surface effect, as a result of collections of water on
generator flats, decks, etc. Any noted accumulation of water on
decks and flats should be drilled in way of the decks to allow the water
to drain to the bilge. During pump-down operations, it is most desirable to pump one compartment dry at a time.

The effect of free surface on stability should be predetermined so
as to ascertain the maximum number of compartments that may be
pumped at one time without loss of stability in the vessel, in the event
that the pumping sequence cannot be maintained.

Pumps should be rigged on a pivot platform if the vessel lies at a
large angle of heel. Figure 95 illustrates a pivot platform.

The exhausts of salvage pumps should be led away to clear air.
There have been many cases where, when salvage pumps were located
on 'tween decks and enclosed areas, the exhaust fumes from the gasoline engines caused considerable discomfort to the pumping and salvage crews aboard the stranded vessel. In some instances, there have
been serious toxic results.

The pumping operations should commence at an ebb tide or on the
flood tide so that a minimum ground reaction will obtain on a
maximum high tide.

The salvage plan should include the approximate volume of water to be removed, the total capacity of the pumps involved, and the consequent time required to pump out the vessel, considering leaks in way of patches, etc.

Needless to say, upon refloating the vessel, it is necessary to have tugs standing by and to have an anchor ready for letting go, to prevent the vessel from riding inshore on the beach after refloating. Prior arrangements should be made to have a dry dock available to receive the salvaged vessel.

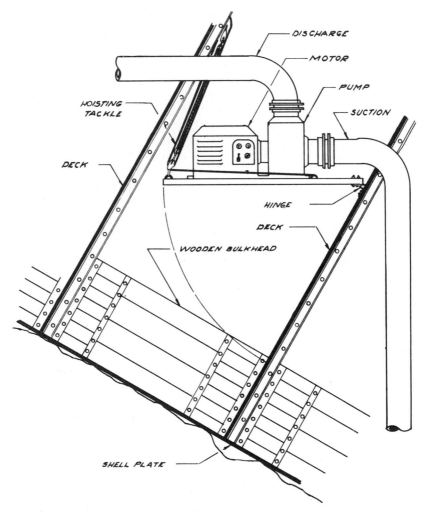

Fig. 95.   Pivot platform pump rig.

USE OF AIR IN SALVAGE OPERATIONS

The salvaging of vessels by the use of compressed air is not a common resort in salvage work of any scope. The reasons for this are manifold. Hull repairs and patches must be far more complete than for de-watering by pumps, necessitating extensive and costly hull preparatory work, including long and arduous internal shoring by divers.

Prior to determining the feasibility of de-watering by use of compressed air, there are several factors that must be given full and equal consideration: (1) the size and number of holes, (2) the number of patches required, (3) the cost of the operation, (4) the de-watering capacity of compressors, and (5) the stability calculations during the refloating operations.

Of course, any vessel that has suffered extensive bottom damage will be generally considered for de-watering by compressed air before any other method, as there is a far greater chance of success than if pumps are used, provided there is a chance of salvage at all.

The depth of water warrants careful consideration, because the operation of refloating is, at best, a tricky one. Unless there is bottom damage to some extent, arrangements must be made for adequate venting of the compartments being blown; otherwise, serious hull fractures may result due to the considerable and increasing difference between air pressure inside and water pressure as the vessel is rising.

It would be fruitless to attempt salvage of a vessel by compressed air if there were not sufficient compressors and equipment to overcome the capacity of any leaks in the hull, which should previously have been determined by divers in an extensive external hull-damage survey.

All internal patches and cofferdams must be installed by divers, which, of necessity, is a time-consuming and laborious task. All openings in the hull proper, except for the bottom, must be made sufficiently tight for compressed air. All compartments must be vented, one to the other. Because of the foregoing problems in de-watering by compressed air, the operation is usually reserved for vessels that are grounded and bilged or for sunken vessels with extensive bottom damage. In some cases of strandings, it is not unusual to find bottom damage. In order to lighten the vessel, de-watering the flooded compartment by using compressed air is probably the most practical method available, because of the inaccessibility of the bottom damage for the installation of patches. In any case, extensive bottom damage provides a natural vent for the escape of water, for, when compressed air is admitted to the upper reaches of a compartment, it forces the water out through bottom vents, which must be installed unless they already exist in the form of holes in the bottom.

In many cases, compressed air is used to expel water from compartments that cannot be reached by pumps.

The use of existing bilge line and water lines, both sanitary and fresh water, within a vessel, must be considered in planning an operation using compressed air. In many cases, the existing lines and valves may be used as vents. In this respect, tankers lend themselves very well to de-watering by compressed air because of their extensive internal piping and large diameter cargo lines, which can be used for vents.

In preparatory work for using compressed air, the decks must be shored from overhead to prevent their collapse because, in most instances, the decks are not strong enough to withstand the pressure that will be exerted on them from underneath. It must be remembered that the pressure on any deck will be from below during a de-watering by compressed air operation.

It may be found that the combination of pumping and use of compressed air will result in a satisfactory operation. There is usually water remaining in the bilges in the bottom of a vessel that has been de-watered by compressed air. In the case of large vessels, this remaining water may provoke a serious stability problem, presented by the presence of free surface of the entrained water; whereas, in pumping, most water can be removed from a compartment. In preliminary calculations to determine the method of de-watering, consideration must be given to the effect of free-surface water, which may be brought about by any remaining water in a compartment, which may or may not be a serious hazard, depending on the over-all stability of the vessel when refloated and on the existing weather conditions.

On vessels that have "turned turtle," that is, vessels that have capsized, the use of compressed air is the ideal means for refloating operation. In such cases, all, or part, of the vessel may be buoyant because of trapped air. In any case, gauges installed on a compartment to which compressed air is applied will indicate the amount of pressure within.

Although there are a few salvage operations where its use is indicated, de-watering vessels by compressed air is one of the most difficult problems in marine salvage.

There are advantages, in that there is no limit to the size of the ship that can be raised, and it is easier to rig for compressed air use.

However, the disadvantages of using compressed air are multiple, as leakage of air is four to five times greater than water; it is difficult to control the ship while lifting; an air lock is needed in order to enter the ship; a large air supply is required; and there are limitations on the work that can be done inside the ship due to inaccessibility.

Preparatory Hull Work. Extensive preparatory hull work must be accomplished to de-water a vessel by compressed air. All openings and apertures through which air can escape above or below the water-line, except those on the bottom, must be closed and made sufficiently tight to hold air. Because air will escape four to five times faster than water, the degree of tightness of the closures must be greater than when de-watering by using pumps.

All hatches, ventilators, openings, and fittings must be closed or patched. Because of the poor visibility and difficulty encountered by

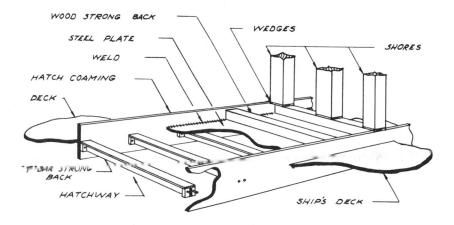

Fig. 96.   Making hatches airtight.

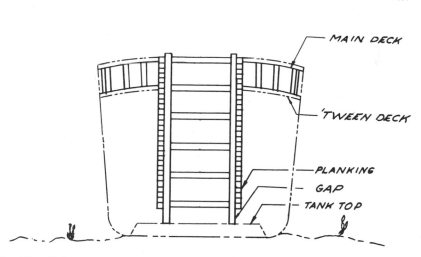

Fig. 97.   Submerged vessel's hatch shored as vent for compressed air. Solid lines indicate shoring and planking. Gap between planking and tank top is approximately 2 feet.

divers in working within a hull, patches are sometimes manufactured topside and installed by the divers. This procedure will eliminate much of the divers' underwater work (*see* Fig. 96).

With the vessel lying on the bottom in an upright position, it is raised by compressed air only if there is extensive bottom damage, which will serve as a vent. If there are no large holes in the bottom, they must be cut in the hull of a size sufficient for the purpose.

In the event a compartment is not bilged on the bottom, it is vented by installing an internal cofferdam, as indicated in Fig. 97. The cofferdam should extend from the deck down to the lowest point in the compartment, but it should terminate at approximately tank-top height to permit the free passage of any excess air. In addition, the decks and bulkheads must be made tight and the decks strengthened and shored as in any other compressed air operation (*see* Fig. 98). Because of the difficulty in pre-calculating the conditions of list and trim of a vessel during a refloating operation by compressed air, a floating crane, A-frame, or similar equipment is used to supplement the lift obtained by the air and to control the vessel's stability during the floating operation.

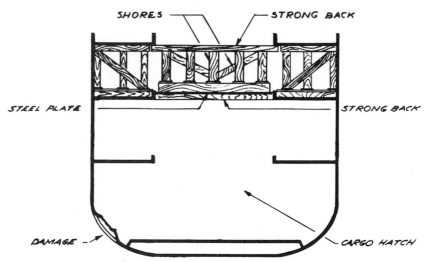

Fig. 98.   Type of shoring used between decks when shoring ship for air.

In the case of a sunken vessel lying bottom side up in shallow water, as illustrated in Fig. 99, the below-deck compartments are usually divided into groups, in order to maintain better control of list and trim as the vessel is refloated. Each group of compartments is fitted with air locks, installed by divers, similar to the illustration in Fig. 100. All hull openings must be closed, sea suctions secured, and bulkheads made watertight between groups of compartments. The vessel's hatches, which are now on the underside of the vessel, are opened, and their size usually is sufficient for venting purposes.

To de-water a vessel in deep water, using compressed air, the vessel should be raised right side up, the decks and sides must be airtight in order to retain an internal air bubble, and the decks must carry the weight of the ship. (Decks are usually designed to take 13 pounds per square inch.)

The formula to determine deck strength is as follows:

$$\text{Load in lbs. per sq. inch} = \frac{\text{Weight of ship in lbs.}}{\text{Area of deck in sq. in.}}$$

Change in pressure due to rise of ship:

a. The ship will rise when the weight of water displaced is equal to the weight of the ship.

b. The pressure on the deck of a ship when submerged equals the air pressure required to move a column of water minus the pressure of a column of water on deck.

The following formula may be used to compute the time required to refloat a vessel using compressed air:

$$\text{Time (min.) to blow ship} = \frac{\text{Volume (H}_2\text{O)} \times \left(\dfrac{\text{Depth}}{33} + 1\right)}{\text{Compressor output (cu. ft./min.)}}$$

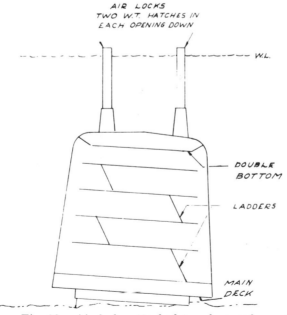

Fig. 99. Air locks attached to submerged vessel.

Air Locks and Hull Vents. To prepare a vessel for de-watering by compressed air, air locks are first fitted to each group of compartments. Figure 100 shows a typical air lock.

After the installation of the air locks, patches, and temporary shoring, a small amount of air pressure applied to the compartment will, in most cases, lower the water level in the compartment. The compartment can then be entered, and the overhead can be shored and stiffened so that it may withstand greater pressure. When the pressure is increased, the water in the compartment will lower sufficiently to allow work to commence on sides and bulkheads. If badly buckled or damaged, bulkheads may be left unrepaired and the adjacent compartment grouped with the compartment fitted with the air lock. This will reduce the amount of work necessary for internal shoring and patching. The work of shoring should continue on down through

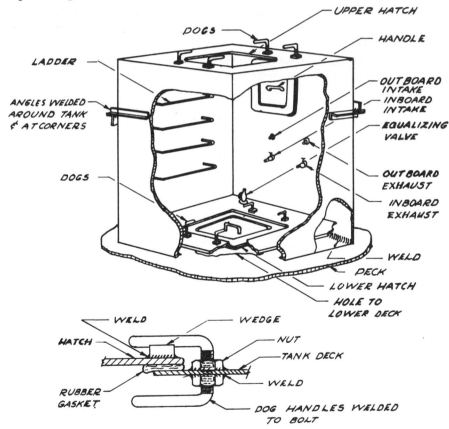

Fig. 100.   Air lock construction. Hatches swing down. Upper hatch is same as
lower hatch. Lock is welded to ship's deck.

the hull with the increased air pressure as it exposes bulkheads and decks. The work of shoring and patching continues downward until the bottom of the vent is exposed, allowing air to escape so that the water level will lower no farther. Upon completion of all internal repairs in this compartment or group of compartments, the air should be secured and the water permitted to flow back in through the vent, filling the compartments. The next group of compartments should then be repaired in the same manner. However, no more than. one group of compartments should be repaired at one time, as this may effect a condition of positive buoyancy in the sunken hull, resulting in the vessel's refloating, capsizing, or fracturing.

The methods of installing underwater patches and making underwater repairs are described in Chapter IV.

In most salvage operations, stability control is a primary consideration. Free surface, when using compressed air, may present a serious problem when refloating a vessel. The results of stability calculations on a bilged ship will also determine the sequence in which the various compartments are to be de-watered. This sequence of work is a most important factor when using compressed air. In many cases, the use of compressed air and pumps is combined. There is no limitation to the combinations that may be deemed useful and desirable.

After the initial preparatory work is done, a low-pressure relief valve should be connected to the compartment, set so that it will open when pressure reaches 13 pounds per square inch, or less, and close at 5 to 10 pounds per square inch. A quick release valve may also be used, employing a scale of predetermined pressures and depths.

When it is possible to use an air bubble farther down in the hull without upsetting the righting arm G$\not{Z}$, shoring should be used between decks above the compartment being blown.

Air can be used to advantage in the following cases:

1. To isolate compartments.
2. To right a vessel when on its side.
3. To raise a ship just enough to tow to more shallow water.

The air compressors used for de-watering vessels are numerous and varied. The standard compressor used in most salvage operations has a rating of 220 cubic feet per minute at approximately 100 pounds per square inch. Other compressors, used mainly for diving purposes, have rated capacities of between 56 and 105 cubic feet per minute. However, these are not used in large salvage operations because of their limited capacities but may be used to good advantage on small salvage jobs.

When compressors installed aboard a barge or salvage vessel are to be used in conjunction with raising a sunken vessel, care must be taken that the surrounding deck areas are adequately shored and stiffened to compensate for excessive vibration.

In conjunction with air compressors of large-rated capacities, large air tanks are most useful when available and where space permits. These large air tanks provide a reserve and act as a cushion to compensate for a variable demand of air.

Compressors will seldom be mounted on a partially sunken vessel. Care should always be taken to install compressors on barges adjoining the wreck. In the event of loss of the wreck, this precaution will prevent the loss of the expensive salvage compressors. Also as a precautionary measure, salvage compressors should be securely mounted to the decks and secured in such a manner that the air hose or fitting will part before the compressor is lost overboard.

The barge or vessel on which the compressors are secured should be moored a safe distance from the operating site, with sufficient maneuverability to avoid any collision with the sunken vessel during refloating operations.

In addition to de-watering compartments with air, the compressors may be used to advantage in operating air-driven submersible pumps, which are readily portable and prove invaluable in draining compartments. However, these pumps will sometimes be used in conjunction with de-watering the vessel by compressed air, when certain specified compartments are to be de-watered by using pumps. The same air supply may operate the pumps as well as de-water compartments.

The number of compressors necessary for a given salvage job and the time required to blow various compartments should be computed.

The time required to de-water a given compartment can be calculated as follows:

Compute the volume of the compartment and the number of compressors available and their efficiency, and use the following formula:

$$\text{Time (min.)} = \frac{\text{Volume} \times \left(\dfrac{\text{Depth}}{33} + 1\right)}{\text{Number of compressors} \times \text{Output} \times \text{Efficiency \%}}$$

By simple transposition, the number of compressors can also be determined from the above formula.

In large-scale salvage operations, sufficient numbers of stand-by compressors should be available for emergency use in the event of failure or breakdown of the operating compressors.

On small salvage jobs involving vessels of minor size, the 56- and 105-cubic-feet-per-minute air compressors may be used where large volumes of air are not required. These compressors have the advantage of being easier to handle than the 220-cubic-feet-per-minute compressor, although none of the three mentioned is readily portable.

After calculating the time required to de-water the compartments, a schedule should be drawn up to determine the total de-watering time necessary to float the vessel. This schedule should then be followed, and stability calculations should be determined for various critical periods of doubtful stability. These should be referred to constantly for assurance that the vessel is in a satisfactory condition of stability during all phases of the operation.

Once the de-watering operation has begun, additional leakage may be noted and traced by the appearance of water bubbles. These may be plugged or stopped by methods described on Page 151.

An indication that the sunken vessel is about to rise may be noted by the appearance of numerous bubbles on the surface of the water that approximate the outline of the sunken vessel. These are occasioned by the vessel breaking bottom suction. Once this suction is broken and the vessel begins to obtain positive buoyancy, it will rise very rapidly; and, upon breaking surface, preparations should be made to control the refloated vessel and prepare for tow.

No salvage operation may be considered complete until the vessel has, in effect, been salvaged. In de-watering by compressed air, the most critical phase of a salvage operation is from the moment the vessel begins to break ground until she breaks the surface of the water.

LIFTING

Lifting is generally used in combination with one or more types of salvage. Because of the stabilizing factor of lifting, it is frequently used in conjunction with compressed air; however, it has also been used where large or complete cofferdams are installed. The use of large cofferdams presents serious stability problems due to the free surface effect of the entrained water. Lifting has been accomplished by cranes, lifting vessels, small tugs, harbor and small craft, etc.

In some cases, lifting vessels have warped a sunken vessel inshore to ever decreasing depths to a point where it could be pumped, patched, and refloated.

Figures 101 and 102 illustrate the use of salvage cranes and pontoons in lifting a sunken French tug at Cherbourg, France, in 1944. The range of the tide was used to assist in the lift.

It must be remembered that lifting's basic advantage is in stability; however, weather and sea conditions adversely affect any lifting operation. To aid in lifting very small boats, chop a hole in the stern of the boat lying on the bottom and secure a line to the bow of the submerged boat. A strain is then taken on the bow line sufficient to lift the bow from the bottom. The lifting vessel then gets under way and commences towing the submerged vessel. The vessel will start along the bottom but will gradually rise and plane to the surface, where the flooded boat will de-water through the stern opening. This is effective only in small boat salvage; however, there must be

Fig. 101.   Use of salvage cranes and pontoons in lifting a sunken tug. (Official
U. S. Navy photo.)

sufficient lifting capacity on the towing vessel. This lifting capacity
can be augmented by a block and tackle handy-billy.

Lifting Vessels. Lifting craft generally take advantage of two factors: the lifting capacity of the winch power aboard the lifting vessel
and the lifting power made available by the range of tide.

The first requires only that the lifting vessel have sufficient power
to apply to the sunken vessel to commence refloating. In the second,

Fig. 102.   Use of salvage cranes and pontoons in lifting a sunken tug. (Official
U. S. Navy photo.)

the force of the tide is used to do the lifting, usually in gradual stages
while the vessel is moved inshore to ever decreasing depths. The procedure entails reeving slings under the vessel, securing them to the
lifting gear aboard the lifting vessel, then shortening up and removing all slack at a low tide. The incoming tide, combined with shifting
ballast aboard the lifting vessel, will provide the additional force

required to raise the vessel from the bottom. In this way the vessel is gradually "snaked" inshore to a position and depth where it can be repaired and refloated.

Lifting vessels are usually used in pairs, with one vessel secured on either side of a wreck. Heavy wire is used for slings, approximately 9 inches or less in circumference, depending on the size of the job. The slack is taken out of the wire at low tide. By trimming the vessel fore and aft, the slack may be removed from the slings so that the full effect of the tide may then be used for lifting.

Before any plans are made for a lifting operation in salvage work, a thorough survey of the wreck should be made to determine the capacity and number of lifting vessels required. After determining the amount of equipment available, the actual rigging of slings should commence. Messengers should be rove underneath the wreck. This job may be a simple matter of sweeping with a small craft, or it may be as complicated as necessitating two divers to work below while the sweep messenger is seesawed and maneuvered from the deck of the lifting craft. The first messenger passed underneath the hull is the most difficult, but it usually clears away any obstructions that may tend to foul the operation. After the messenger has been passed beneath the wreck, it is shackled into the lifting slings, which are then rove through and secured to the lifting wires on the crane or lifting vessel.

In the case of small vessels the size of tugs, fishing vessels, small craft, etc., a temporary lift may sometimes be made on the propeller shaft of the vessel. This lift should be only sufficient to pass a messenger beneath the hull. This temporary lift is then released, and the messenger is rove through, carrying the sling, and, after the installation of several slings, the lift is commenced. The lift should not commence, however, until several slings are, in fact, passed beneath the wreck, in order to adequately distribute the ensuing hull stresses, which may be set up during any lifting operation. A total loss can result from an otherwise successful lift because of the extensive damage sustained by the hull or superstructure during the lifting operation.

In the event that all other methods fail in sweeping a messenger beneath the wreck, tunneling may prove effective, providing the bottom is soft, muddy, sandy, etc. The tunnel is washed beneath the vessel, using a mixture of air and water. The lifting slings are passed through this tunnel.

With all the messengers placed and the lifting slings roved through, the lifting slings are then connected up to the hauling wires on the bow of the vessel; all slack is removed from the wires by shifting ballast and trimming by the stern during low water. The lift is then ready to commence on the next flooding tide. Once the bottom suction is broken, it may be possible to lift the sunken vessel farther with the salvage vessel's winches. The greatest holding power is in the bottom suction. In approaching to connect up to the messengers for a bow-lifting job, the lifting vessel should drop a stern anchor during the approach, bow first.

Another type of operation that usually requires two craft is the side lift. The operation for reeving the lifting slings is the same for bow lifting: flooding down the vessel at low tide, taking in the slack, pumping out, thus removing the slack in the wires. However, the slings are usually wrapped around the vessels in pairs, running from the starboard side of one vessel down beneath the wreck and on up to the port side of the sister vessel. The secondary wire is run down the starboard side of the sister vessel beneath the wreck to the port side of the adjacent vessel.

Cranes. Cranes used in ship salvage work can be classed in the general categories of land cranes or floating cranes.

The use of land cranes will generally be confined in ship salvage work to vessels sunk alongside a pier. The crane may be either a mobile crane or a rail track crane used for cargo handling. If not actually used for a salvage lifting operation, cranes are useful for innumerable rigging jobs preliminary to the salvage.

The floating crane in ship salvage operations is of secondary importance only to the pump. It is used either independently or in connection with pumping or air operations.

Floating equipment varies in tonnage from 3 to 300 tons, and, in some cases, larger cranes are available. The types of floating cranes are numerous.

Cranes are rigged for the job similar to lifting vessels.

Jacking. Jacks are used primarily in stranding cases where a large part of the vessel's shell structure is visible; however, jacks have been used successfully in small boat sinkings. The hydraulic jacks normally used in ship salvage work have a capacity of 60 to 100 tons.

The principal value of jacks in stranding cases is to minimize the ground reaction; they have the same effect as the unloading of cargo and removal of weights. Because of the downward thrust of jacks, they should never be used except where there is a hard foundation, such as found in rock and coral.

A method of rigging jacks to the side of a vessel is illustrated in Fig. 103. The usual method is to secure a 12″ x 12″ head timber below the sheer strake with 1¼″ bolts. A 7″ × 7″ angle iron is mounted to the bottom edge of the sheer strake, so that the head timber bears against one leg of the angle. The hydraulic jack is mounted on a 12″ × 12″ shore or 18″ diameter piling. The upper end of the piling is banded with steel bands to prevent splaying. The upper end of the jack bears against a steel plate fitted against the bottom of the head timber. The shoring or piling is mounted on wood mats, which should be a minimum of 8″ × 8″ timbers of sufficient dimensions to distribute the load over a wide area of the bottom.

First, the magnitude of the ground reaction is estimated, and a sufficient number of jacks, with a total capacity that exceeds the ground reaction, are secured to the sides of the vessel.

Beach gear is next planted to seaward for hauling the vessel. After the beach gear is rigged, a heavy strain is maintained on the wire pendants during a flooding tide. At a maximum high tide, jacking operations are commenced. As jacking continues, the ground reaction is gradually and continually reduced until the ship will eventually

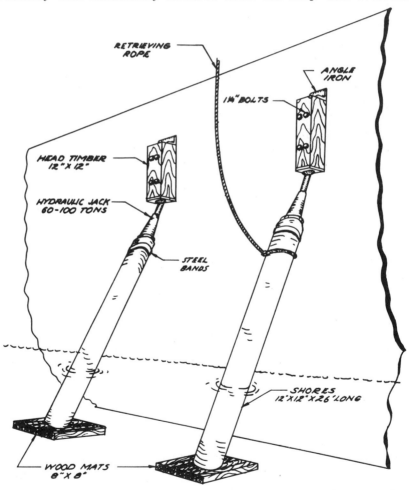

Fig. 103.   Jacking with hydraulic jacks.

begin to move in the direction of the pull of the beach gear, after which the pilings will trip. The pilings and jacks are reset, and jacking operations are commenced at the next high tide. Platforms must be rigged adjacent to each head timber so that each jack may be individually operated.

In the case of small sunken vessels, salvage may be effected by jacking, as illustrated in Fig. 104. Sufficient jacks are rigged on square-edged pilings laid between two barges in order to overcome the weight of the vessel to be lifted. Slings are placed under the sunken vessel and led to the jack blocks topside. All slack is taken out of the slings at a low tide, and jacking is commenced. The com-

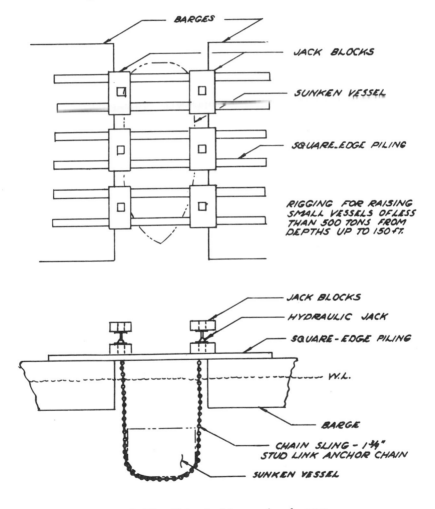

Fig. 104. Jacking, using barges.

bination of jacking and rising tide will lift the sunken vessel off the bottom, and it can be moved inshore to more shallow water, where the slings can be rerigged and the operation can be repeated during the following high tide. Successive operations of this type will eventually bring the vessel into shallow water, where it can be pumped dry. This type of salvage should not be considered for vessels weighing more than 500 tons.

Figure 105 shows a method of rigging the jacking block assembly. The U-toggle illustrated is inserted around a chain link after the hydraulic jacks have reached their maximum rise. This will hold the chain while the jacks are again lowered, when the U-toggle is reset and jacking operations are continued.

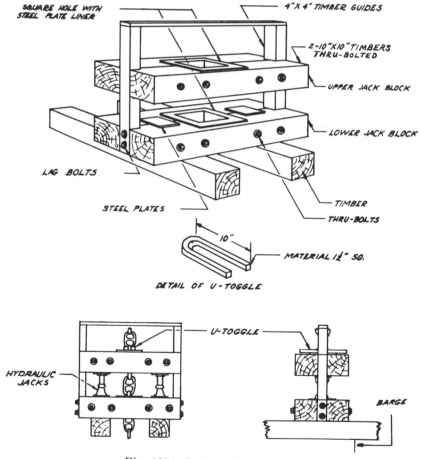

Fig. 105.   Jacking block assembly.

RESCUE (TOWING)

Rescue towing involves providing assistance to vessels in distress, either on the high seas, along coastal waters, or on inland waterways. Vessels become disabled and in need of assistance through any one of the following causes or combinations thereof:

1. Fire.
2. Machinery breakdown.
3. Storms and heavy weather.
4. Collision.
5. Shifting cargo and resultant damage.
6. Fractured tailshafts.
7. Loss of propeller.
8. Loss of rudder.
9. Striking a submerged object.

Successful rescue towing involves locating, connecting up, and taking in tow a vessel disabled from one or more of the foregoing causes. A rescue tow is not successful unless the distressed vessel is brought safely into port. The elementary problems involved in rescue towing are those of seamanship. The most difficult operation encountered is connecting up to the distressed vessel in a seaway. The secondary problem of towing a vessel is one that can be solved by the normal requisites of ocean towing.

Types of Tow. A *single tow* is what the name implies. It involves the towing vessel and the vessel being towed. The tow is generally in a column formation.

A *tandem tow* is a tow involving two vessels, in addition to the towing vessel. The vessels being towed may lie either in a column or abreast of each other.

Multiple tows involve one or two tow boats towing three or more vessels. The variations and hookups are many in this type of tow, two of them being the *straight-line column* tow and *Xmas tree*, or *Honolulu tow*, illustrated in Fig. 106.

Tugs. The tugs used for ocean towing vary in size from 200 HP and less for small jobs to 3,000 HP and more. The variety and types of ocean tugs are as varied almost in proportion to the number of tugs in operation. Standardization in types of tugs has been obtained only by large towboat companies, international salvage companies, and government services. However, it should be remembered when selecting a tug of particular size and horsepower for a specified towing project that a tug will develop approximately one-ton pull for every 100 HP available in the main unit. Generally speaking, for deep-water rescue towing, a tug of less than 1,000 HP should not be given serious consideration.

Tow Wire and Bridle. The average tow wire on a deep sea towing vessel is approximately 1,800 to 2,000 feet of 2-inch high-grade plow-steel wire rope. The longer the tow line and the heavier the gear in the make-up, the easier the towing will be.

Bridles are used in conjunction with towing wires to provide a better hookup to the vessel being towed. A bridle consists of two legs of heavy chain or two-inch high-grade plow-steel wire rope, with legs approximately 70 feet or more in length. One end of each leg is secured aboard the distressed vessel; the other ends of each leg are shackled into the towing wire. In addition to the bridles, back-up wires and preventers are sometimes secured to a point farther aft on the tow and connected to the bridles. The preventer will keep the bridle from falling overboard in the event that the bitts or cleats to which it is secured carry away.

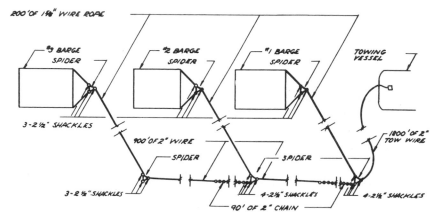

Fig. 106. "Xmas Tree" or Honolulu tow. Pins in the 2½-inch shackles should be free to rotate in the holes in spiders.

Towing Winches. Towing winches can be classified under the headings of automatic and nonautomatic.

The *automatic towing winch* can be set to a predetermined towing stress. When this stress is exceeded, the tow engine pays out wire, and, when the stress falls below a predetermined minimum, the towing winch automatically reels in tow wire. Theoretically, this is designed to provide a more easy-riding and following tow. Practically, however, it has been found that its use is limited to more or less ideal tows.

The *nonautomatic winch* is, as its name implies, a towing winch similar to any other type used for cargo or anchors, and it is dogged down when the predetermined scope of wire has been paid out on the tow. The winch does not operate from this point but is secured on the dogs. This type of winch is favored more by professional towboatmen because of its stationary operation under tow (inflexibility during tows underway).

Preparation for Tow. In preparing a vessel for tow, the bridle must be rigged aboard the tow, back-up wires and preventers should be installed, and the tow wire should be connected to the bridles. All shackles should be secured with split pins or wire keepers or both. A 30- to 90-fathom length of chain should be connected between the bridle and the tow hawser. This length of chain is most practicable if towing is to be done in fairly shallow water where there is to be a large catenary in the tow wire. The chain will better withstand chafing in the event of scraping the bottom. In the event that there is to be some anticipated maneuvering close inshore in strong currents and tides, a Liverpool bridle should be rigged aboard the towing vessel to enable the tug to maneuver more easily in strong currents, high winds, and tides. In addition, chafing gear should be provided for the bridles and where the tow wire passes over the stern, through chocks and around bitts, and over any obstruction that causes a sharp turn in the tow wire or bridles. This chafing gear can be made of Manila and canvas, sheet copper, or perhaps even of hardwood blocks shaped to the circumference of the wire. It is always best to bear in mind that when in doubt chafing gear should be installed, even though it may prove unnecessary in some cases.

In towing barges and small vessels, a wire rope bridle may be installed on the forward end of the tow. When the tow is heavier than a light barge, a chain bridle should be used, which is then connected to the towing hawser. When connecting up to a large vessel, the towing hawser can be secured to the anchor chains from which the anchors have been disconnected and stopped off. The anchor chain is then paid out to the desired scope, after which the chain stoppers are set up. The strain of towing is then taken by the chain stoppers.

Practical Towing. Practical towing, when it involves taking a vessel in tow from one port to another, presents no particular problem in connecting up and towing. Those problems normally encountered are overcome by good seamanship practices. However, practical towing, when involved in taking in tow a disabled vessel at sea, requires utmost skill and proficiency in the higher degrees of seamanship. Because of these requisites, reference here will be confined to the specific operation of taking in tow a vessel disabled at sea.

In good weather, the problem of passing a line and connecting up to a disabled vessel is a minor one. After connecting up, the tug takes the disabled vessel in a slow tow on a course paralleling the tow. When the slack is taken out of the tow wire, a course change can gradually be effected. In actual practice, the characteristics of the towing vessel, the conditions of weather and sea, and other influences that may add to the problem of ship handling are given much consideration by the tug handler. Because of this, the characteristics of each individual towing vessel must be known by the person who is to maneuver her.

In maneuvering a vessel alongside a disabled ship to initiate preparations for taking in tow, consideration must be given to the wind and sea conditions, which will affect the drift of the disabled vessel. It must be remembered that the lighter a vessel is the faster she will drift; consequently, the lighter vessel should be to windward of the heavier vessel when the task of running lines is started. Usually a disabled vessel will lie in a seaway with the wind abaft the beam. If there is any doubt of the rate of drift between the disabled vessel and the towboat, the towboat should lie stopped in a line parallel with the disabled vessel and the drift then observed. If the towboat is drifting faster than the disabled vessel, it should lie to windward of the disabled vessel and pass gear for rigging the tow. During the course of the tug's drift, care should be taken to ensure that it remains clear of the disabled vessel. If the seas are exceptionally rough, oil should be pumped overboard to calm the seas in the immediate vicinity of the towed ship.

Practical towing, more so than in any other salvage operation, requires a seaman's eye and an ability in seamanship that is above average; consequently, it is impossible to list all the requisites for a successful tow, although these basic rules should be remembered when involved in towing operations:

1. Do not rig a tow that cannot be released immediately.

2. Always use bolt-type shackles when connecting tow wires. Do not use screw-pin shackles.

3. Never allow a tow to commence to sea without a personal investigation of the bridle, towing pads, shackles, split-pin and wire keepers, chafing gear, back-up wires, securing of cargo, hull watertightness, bilge-pumping equipment, navigation lights, etc.

4. Never pass a tow wire to a stranded vessel without at least one anchor down.

5. Never use a badly kinked tow wire. Check the splicing of tow wire before all tows.

6. Do not tow in heavy seas using a short scope of wire.

7. Shift the position of the tow wire periodically, but never wait longer than twenty-four hours.

8. When turning, do not allow the tow to get forward of the beam.

9. All large turns should be made in increments of approximately 10 degrees.

10. Never make a sharp turn in shallow water with a large scope of wire out.

11. Stop the propellers whenever the tow wire parts.

12. Be prepared at all times to cast off a sinking tow.

13. When towing in heavy seas, adjust the length of the tow wire so that both tow and tug simultaneously reach the crest and trough of a wave.

CHAPTER VI

MISCELLANEOUS SALVAGE OPERATIONS, TECHNIQUES AND HAZARDS

THE LIVERPOOL BRIDLE

The Liverpool bridle is a tow line harness used by a towing vessel to maintain control over heading and position in relation to a stranded vessel, wreck, or tow, when wind, sea, and/or currents tend to set the towing vessel off its course. The bridle is most often used in stranding cases where currents, wind, tide, etc., tend to set the towing vessel in the direction of the set. The use of the bridle allows the towing vessel to direct its heading toward the set and maintain its relative position directly offshore from the wreck, thus preventing the towing vessel from drifting in the direction of the set while on a taut tow line. The principal hazard of pulling on a stranded vessel in a set without using a Liverpool bridle is that the towing vessel may also go aground. A standard towing bridle is illustrated in Fig. 107. Essentially, it is easy to rig. The tow wire is secured to bitts or cleats at a point just forward of the vessel's pivot point. The wire should be made fast along the main deck stringer plate on the weather, current, or windward side of the towing vessel. A heavy tackle is then secured from the after deck to the tow wire. By adjusting the length of this tackle, the ship's heading can be altered to veer into or away from the set. In this way, by taking in or paying out the tackle, compensation for the effects of adverse weather and current can be made to improve steering. For instance, by slacking off on the tackle and going ahead on the towing vessel's propellers, the vessel will head into the set; conversely, by hauling in on the tackle, the vessel's heading can be changed to alter away from the set for a more direct pull offshore. From this standard towing bridle, the Liverpool bridle was developed by Commander C. H. Holm, USNR, in 1944, and is illustrated in Figs. 108 and 109. This method was devised because of a need for quickly shifting the towing bridle in the event of changes in set resulting from variations of tide, current, or winds. The system requires a towing engine aboard the towing vessel. The main tow wire is kept on the towing engine. The Liverpool bridle is rigged from the bow and consists of two pendants: one each on the port and starboard sides.

The following gear is necessary for the make-up of the Liverpool bridle:

1. Two 1¼" wire rope pendants of sufficient length to extend from bitts located on the stringer plate forward of the pivot point of the ship to a point approximately 20 feet abaft the main deck after towing bitts. These pendants are run outboard of all main deck obstructions along the side of the vessel and are stopped off at convenient intervals. One pendant is used for a port set, and one pendant is used for a starboard set, as illustrated in Fig. 108. In one end of the pendant, an eye is spliced approximately two feet in diameter; in the other end, an eye with a thimble is spliced. The two-foot-in-diameter eye is laid around the forward bitts.

2. One towing clamp, carpenter, or boullivant stopper of sufficient size to fit the tow wire is connected to the thimble on the after end of the 1¼" pendant.

3. Two three-inch Manila line lazy jacks: one 50-foot length, one 100-foot length. Both lazy jacks have eye and thimble spliced in one end. A set of two each is used on both the port and starboard sides, the 50-foot length forward of the longer length.

To rig the bridle, the 1¼" pendants are secured to the bitts forward of the pivot point. The salvage vessel makes an approach to the wreck close aboard, passes the tow wire, and commences to pay out tow wire while proceeding offshore toward the set. When sufficient wire has been paid out, the bridle on the side of the vessel toward the set is then secured to the tow wire, using the boullivant stopper. The vessel's head is brought toward the direction of the set. The tow line is then paid out so that the tow line is off the vessel's side and the lazy jacks extend outboard. The heading of the ship can be controlled by reeving in or paying out the main tow wire, using the tow engine.

When the current, wind, or weather changes direction so that the set is now found to be on the opposite heading of the vessel, the bridle must be changed. The tow wire is brought in until the boullivant stopper is on deck. It is released, and the stopper of the bridle on the opposite side of the ship is then secured in its place. The tow wire is again paid out, and the opposite pendant then controls the vessel's heading, so that the towing vessel can readily be maneuvered into the current, wind, or weather.

In conjunction with the Liverpool bridle, additional pull can be exerted on the stranded vessel by the use of the bower anchors on the salvage vessel. After the main tow wire is secured aboard the wreck,

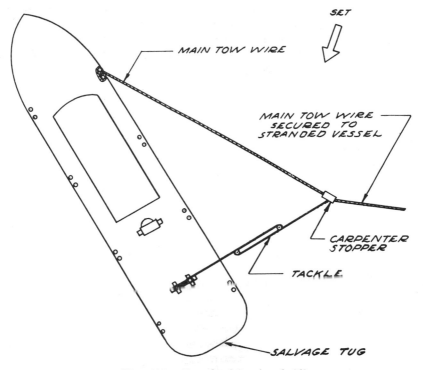

SET

MAIN TOW WIRE

MAIN TOW WIRE
SECURED TO
STRANDED VESSEL

CARPENTER
STOPPER

TACKLE

SALVAGE TUG

Fig. 107.   Standard towing bridle.

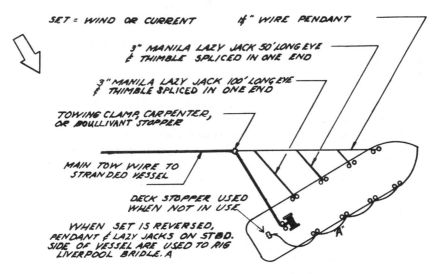

SET = WIND OR CURRENT   ¼" WIRE PENDANT

3" MANILA LAZY JACK 50' LONG EYE
& THIMBLE SPLICED IN ONE END

3" MANILA LAZY JACK 100' LONG EYE
& THIMBLE SPLICED IN ONE END

TOWING CLAMP, CARPENTER,
OR BOULLIVANT STOPPER

MAIN TOW WIRE TO
STRANDED VESSEL

DECK STOPPER USED
WHEN NOT IN USE

WHEN SET IS REVERSED,
PENDANT & LAZY JACKS ON STBD.
SIDE OF VESSEL ARE USED TO RIG
LIVERPOOL BRIDLE. A

A

Fig. 108.   Liverpool bridle.

it is paid out to almost maximum reach. The vessel is then steered into the set, and the anchor toward the set is dropped. The vessel then maneuvers to a point outshore and approximately 500 feet away from, and in line with, the first bow anchor, and the second bow anchor is dropped. The main tow wire is then taken in while both anchor cables

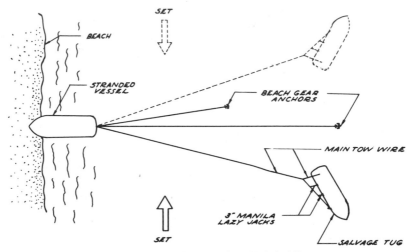

Fig. 109.   Using a Liverpool bridle.

are paid out until the vessel reaches a position where the bridles are to be rigged. In determining this position, care should be exercised to insure that the anchor cables have sufficient scope to provide adequate holding power. Then, by using the main engine and maintaining a strain on the bower anchors, an added advantage can be obtained in wrenching the vessel free.

RECOVERY OF BEACH GEAR ANCHOR

The following procedure may be used in order to effectively recover a beach gear anchor with a minimum of labor:

1. The salvage vessel approaches and lies to windward of the crown buoy. The forward boom is plumbed even with the rail, and a suitable block is shackled to the purchase hook of the boom. Another block is secured on deck as a means of fairleading the wire to the niggerhead of a winch.

2. The crown line is recovered after the crown buoy is brought aboard. The crown line is then rove through the purchase hook block, the fairlead block on deck, and led to the niggerhead on the winch. The boom purchase hook is then two-blocked, and the crown line is heaved in, using the winch, until the anchor is clear of the deck. The

boom is then swung inboard, and the anchor is lowered and secured to the deck. The 2¼″ chain is next brought aboard by several lifts, using the crown line.

3. When all the chain is aboard, a 5″ Manila messenger is passed outside the ship's rail from the fantail forward and bent on the 1⅝″ wire shackled to the 2¼″ chain. The wire would be stopped off and the chain unshackled. Then the 1⅝″ wire is cast off and the 5″ messenger is heaved around on the fantail capstan. The 1⅝″ pendants are thus hauled aboard over the fantail.

There are several other methods of retrieving the beach gear anchor; however, the foregoing procedure is recommended due to the ease of the operation. In the recovery and stowage of beach gear, the crew on the salved vessel usually handles the purchase blocks, wires, and stoppers, while the salvage vessel usually recovers the anchors, cables, and chains.

ANCHOR HAWK

The steel anchor hawk will vary in weight from approximately 200 pounds to 2,000 pounds, and it is used for recovering lost anchors, wire rope, chain, bridles, etc.

To use the anchor hawk, proceed as follows:

1. Stop off one bower anchor and unshackle the chain. Connect up the anchor hawk to the anchor chain.

2. Position the vessel on a heading perpendicular to the run of the lost object.

3. Lower the anchor hawk to the bottom and commence a run slowly ahead, paying out anchor cable to a length of approximately three times the depth of the water.

4. Secure the anchor chain with two parts of four-inch Manila. Disconnect the wildcat and take off the windlass brake. This will allow the chain to run out freely when the Manila parts.

5. Slowly steam ahead, being careful to insure that the anchor does not come clear of the bottom.

6. The anchor will drag along the bottom and catch on any obstruction. The parting of the four-inch Manila lashings will indicate that the hawk is hung up. The chain will then commence to run freely. At this point, the windlass operator should set the brake to maintain a light to moderate strain on the chain as the ship loses headway and is brought into position over the obstruction. In cases of chain and cable recovery, it is sometimes possible to heave aboard the chain and cable with the anchor hawk. In other cases of heavier objects, it is necessary to send a diver down and connect up retrieving wires, which are led to the niggerhead of the anchor windlass or to a forward winch. Figure 110 illustrates a typical anchor hawk.

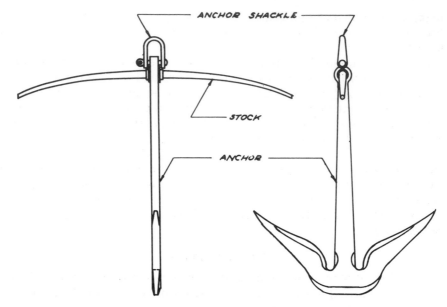

Fig. 110.   Typical anchor hawk.

THREE-POINT MOOR

There are numerous ways to set a three-point moor. The variations will depend upon the type of vessel being used to lay the moor and the size of the anchors carried aboard. Salvage vessels and tugs will usually use the two bower anchors and one 8,000-pound Eells anchor. The bower anchors will be dropped off the port and starboard bows, and the Eells anchor will be laid astern. General practice is to connect the Eells anchor to the main tow wire of the tug or salvage vessel. The main tow wire is led over the stern roller chocks, outside the rail and forward on the port or starboard quarter, to a point where the Eells anchor is hung over the rail from the after boom. The tow wire is then shackled into the Eells anchor. The Eells anchor is stopped at the rail, using a pelican hook, so that it may be cast off readily. A crown buoy and crown line should be used in conjunction with the Eells anchor to facilitate retrieving. Both the crown line and the crown buoy should be hung over the same side as the Eells anchor, ready for letting go.

The wreck should be marked with a buoy that is planted approximately above the position of the wreck and in the vicinity of the position where the salvage vessel is to moor.

Proceed across the wind at approximately three to five knots. When the buoy marker bears 315 relative at a distance of approximately 400 feet, the starboard anchor should be dropped. The salvage vessel continues on the same course, and, when the buoy is bearing approximately 225 relative at a distance of approximately 400 feet, the port anchor is dropped. The main engine is put full astern and the rudder hard left. The resultant maneuvers will change the ship's position to a point midway between both bower anchors and to the leeward of the wreck buoy. Maintain a moderate strain on the two bow anchors while backing down. The bow anchor cables, however, should be paid out as the vessel drops astern. When the 90-fathom shackles of the anchor chains are on deck, the vessel is in a position to drop the stern anchor. After dropping the stern anchor, the vessel moves forward, heaving in on the port and starboard anchor chains and paying out on the stern cable, until a point is reached in the vicinity of the desired position above the wreck. All slack should be taken out of the mooring cables, and they should be maintained taut in order to provide a tight moor, which is necessary for any salvage operation.

In order to recover the stern anchor, the bow anchor cables are paid out and the stern tow wire is taken in until the vessel reaches a relative position over the stern anchor. The crown buoy and crown wire are then retrieved, and the crown wire is passed through a snatch block on the purchase hook on the after boom. The crown wire is then led to the capstan on the towing engine and is hauled aboard. When the anchor is in sight, it is swung in over the deck, using the after boom, and the main tow wire is disconnected. The main tow wire is retrieved by heaving around on the main towing engine. After retrieving the stern anchor and tow wire, both bow anchors are recovered, using the anchor windlass.

Never commence diving, lifting, or any salvage operation while on a three-point moor, unless it is positively ascertained that the moor is secure. Constant bearings of points ashore should be taken by a man on watch on the bridge. The position should be continually checked in this manner and plotted on the navigation charts. Any variation in position during any check of bearings should warrant the temporary securing of any diving operations until such time as the bearings have been rechecked. Diving operations must not commence until it is established that the moor is, in fact, secure.

FOUR-POINT MOOR

A four-point moor is laid when a vessel is required to lay in a stationary position over a wreck for extended diving or salvage operations. A four-point moor is usually rigged with anchors approximately three times heavier than the regular bow anchors of the tug or salvage vessel. The extra weight in the anchors is necessary because the vessel is not free to swing on its anchors into the wind and sea. This places an additional strain on the mooring cables because there is more surface area of the vessel subjected to the effects of weather.

If a vessel is to anchor in depths up to 150 feet, 5,000-pound patent anchors are recommended. For depths beyond 150 feet, an increase in anchor weight should be approximately 1,000 pounds for every 50-foot increase in depth.

Vessels larger than ocean-going salvage tugs should be moored with heavier gear. Where additional holding power is required, secure two anchors to the same mooring cable.

Each mooring consists of the patent anchor, a length of approximately 15 fathoms of 1½" chain and 100 feet of 1⅜" 6 x 19 high-grade plow-steel wire rope, one 3-foot pendant and one 30-foot pendant of 1½" 6 x 19 high-grade plow-steel wire rope, and one mooring buoy with sufficient positive buoyancy to support the weight of the mooring wire.

One end of the 15-fathom shot of chain is connected to the patent anchor, and the other end is connected to the mooring wire with bending shackles. The short pendant and the lazy pendant are connected, using bending shackles, to a heart-shaped shackle on the bitter end of the mooring wire. The bitter end of the short pendant is secured to a log or can buoy. The bitter end of the lazy pendant has a large eye spliced into it, and it is lashed temporarily to a bail on the other end of the log or can buoy. When the vessel is ready to secure to the mooring, the eye splice of the lazy pendant is cut loose from the bail on the mooring buoy, and the ship's mooring hawser is connected up to the eye. Figure 111 illustrates the general make-up of the mooring.

The length of the wire rope connected to the 15-fathom shot of chain will vary in direct proportion to the depth of the water where the moor is laid. For depths over 100 feet, a length of 200 feet of wire rope should be used. For depths over 200 feet, a length of 300 feet of wire rope should be used.

The general arrangements of rigging aboard a vessel for setting a four-point moor are illustrated in Figs. 112 and 113.

The four mooring anchors are set out on the after deck of the tug or salvage vessel. All wires are led outside of the rail and forward to a point approximately amidship. The log buoys should be mounted on the ship's rail and held in place with small stuff or pelican hooks. The after boom is used to swing the anchors into position over the side for letting go. The mooring wire pendants may be temporarily lashed to the rail at several locations with one part of 16 thread, which will easily part under a strain after the anchor is laid and as the vessel moves ahead.

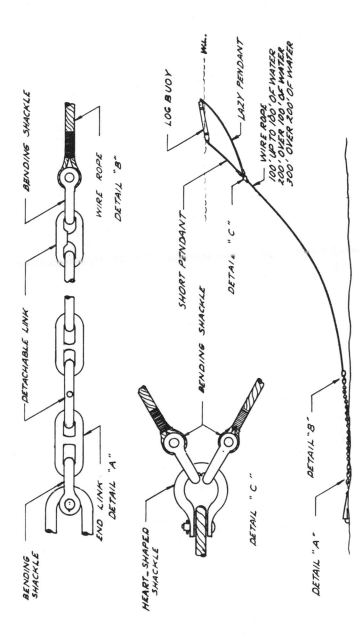

Fig. 111. Four-point mooring.

As each anchor is dropped, the boom is swung inboard, connected to another anchor, trimmed out over the side of the vessel ready for letting go. Two anchors are laid to port and two to starboard. Care should be exercised to insure that all chain, wires, and pendants are clear for running freely.

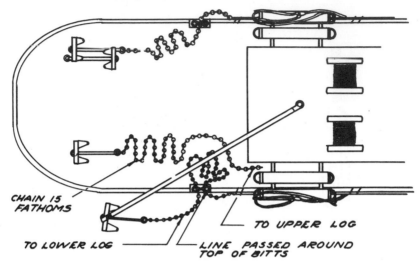

CHAIN 15 FATHOMS

TO LOWER LOG

TO UPPER LOG

LINE PASSED AROUND TOP OF BITTS

Fig. 112.   Four-point mooring. Note the position of chains with anchor for lower log buoy ready to drop.

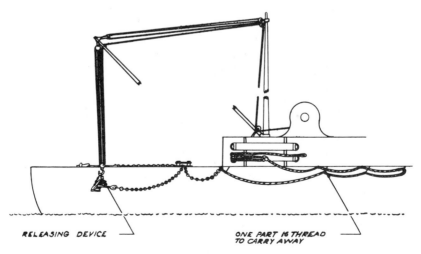

RELEASING DEVICE

ONE PART 16 THREAD TO CARRY AWAY

Fig. 113.   Four-point mooring. One log and anchor are ready to be dropped. Lower log is always dropped first.

Figure 114 illustrates a method of securing log buoys at the ship's side ready for letting go. The buoy lashing should extend outside all pendants and wires so that when the pelican hook is tripped the pendants and buoy will not foul.

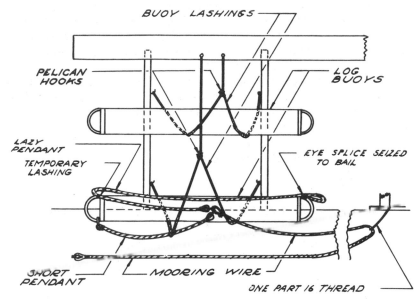

Fig. 114.   Four-point mooring showing detail of hookup. Lower log is ready to be dropped.

Laying a four-point moor is basically an exercise in seamanship. The wreck should first be exactly located and its position fixed on a navigation chart with bearings indicated from shore points. At the positions where each anchor is to be laid, bearings should also be indicated. A maneuvering pattern is then completed, as indicated in Fig. 115, during the course of which all four anchors are laid. While laying the moor, the vessel should proceed at the slowest rate of speed possible, and bearings should be checked constantly.

After the anchors are dropped, the salvage vessel approaches the first mooring buoy into the wind. The lashings securing the eye of the lazy pendant to the bail of. the buoy are cut, and the vessel's eight-inch Manila (110-fathom) hawser is connected to the eye. The hawser is paid out as the ship maneuvers across the set to the opposite, or fourth, buoy laid. Another hawser is connected in the same manner. The salvage vessel may now back down toward the two buoys astern. By slacking off and hauling in on the port and starboard bow mooring hawsers alternately, the ship can connect up the stern hawsers to the second and third buoys laid. The ship can be positioned accurately over the wreck by taking in and slacking off on the mooring lines as necessary. When the vessel is centered over the position of the wreck, all mooring lines should be hauled taut so that the mooring buoys are well submerged. The log or can buoys should be of such construction that they will not crush when submerged, and they must also be of a sufficient positive buoyancy to remain on the surface of the water in sight, supporting the wire pendants and chain when the vessel is not moored.

The dragging of one or more anchors while at a four-point moor may be easily detected by the resurfacing of one or more buoys, which would indicate that the opposite anchors of the moor are dragging and not holding the ground.

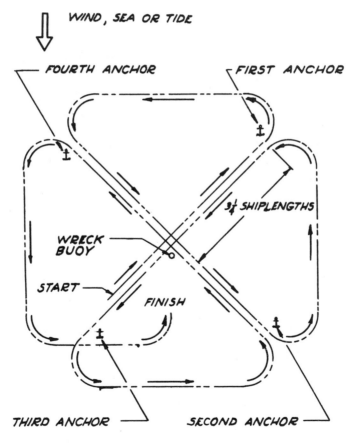

Fig. 115.   Chip method of laying mooring. Ghost lines indicate path.

When a vessel leaves a four-point moor the operation is reversed and the stern lines are cast off first. The lazy pendants must be re-secured to the bail of the buoy to facilitate retrieving when the vessel again moors.

The four-point moor should be used for securing floating cranes prior to any lifting operation.

The tug first plants the moor and then tows the crane to the scene. The tug maneuvers the crane into position at the first buoy, and the mooring hawser is connected up by a crew on the floating crane. The job of positioning a large crane in a seaway is difficult, at best, so the maneuverability of the tug will be restricted. To offset this lack of mobility of the tug, small boats may be used to tow the hawser to the mooring buoy. Once the second hawser is connected to the wire pendant by the small boat crew, some control can be maintained over the position of the crane by hauling and slacking the hawsers, using the deck winches or capstans. The stern hawsers are then secured to the remaining buoys.

HIGH LINE GEAR

A high line is an aerial carriage, suspended from elevated cables, used to transport materiel between ship and shore or ship and ship. The principle of operation is similar for both evolutions; consequently, we will apply this study to ship and shore transfer because it is more applicable to marine salvage operations.

Heavy weather and storms are the prime forces that cause vessels to ground in the absence of navigational errors. The heavy weather that causes a vessel to ground invariably kicks up heavy seas and pounding surf. These conditions cause the vessel to pound and wrack so badly that there is imminent danger of the vessel breaking up or turning turtle and becoming a total loss. The loss of the vessel can be rectified; however, there is usually a warranted concern for the lives of the seamen aboard, and every effort is made to remove them safely.

It can be seen that the conditions that caused the vessel to ground are the same that prevent the launching of lifeboats. There is no choice but for the seamen to remain with the wreck. Any venture into a turbulent sea is sure to spell disaster. As a result, the high line is used for rescue efforts.

After a vessel grounds and salvage efforts commence, heavy maté-riel and equipment must be transferred between the ship and shore. Salvage equipment must be placed safely aboard the vessel, and, should it be necessary to lighten the vessel, cargo must be transferred ashore with a minimum of damage and loss. Lifeboats and small boats generally are unsatisfactory for transfer of equipment because of the additional labor and time involved: first, in loading the boat;

then, in transporting the load; and, finally, in unloading on the beach
or possibly at a more distant pier. Loading heavy equipment into a
small boat, even under the best of conditions, is no mean task. With
a vessel stranded close inshore, the transferring of any equipment or
cargo to or from a small boat, pitching and rolling heavily in the swell
or surf, is dangerous to both personnel and boat. To offset these
problems, a high line is generally employed.

High Line. Figure 116 is a schematic drawing of a typical high line.
The cables are rigged between an A-frame ashore and one mast of the
stranded vessel. Line A in the illustration is the span wire on which
the carriage or traveling block moves. The shoreside end of the span

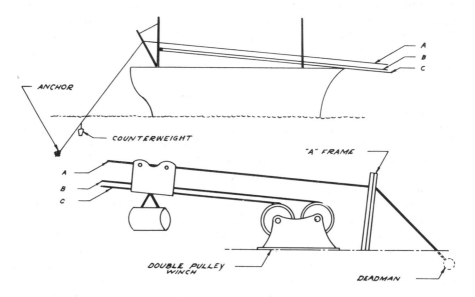

Fig. 116.   High line from stranded ship to beach.

wire is secured to a deadman and fairleaded through a block at the
top of the A-frame through the whip block of a boom on the stranded
vessel. The boom is topped to about 60 degrees, and the whip block
is two-blocked. The end of the span wire is fitted with a heavy patent
or Eells anchor, which is laid outshore from, and in line with, the
run of the cable.

In rigging the span wire, the anchor, with span wire connected, is
first dropped approximately 600 feet to seaward with a heavy counterweight attached to the span wire midway between the anchor and the
stranded vessel. The counterweight must be heavy enough to keep
all slack out of the span wire, as the vessel heaves or rolls while

aground. The weight should also be submerged to help dampen sudden surges. The whip block on the boom to be used is lowered to the deck, and the span wire is rove through the sheave and passed ashore, using a messenger, where it is rove through the sheave of a block at the top of the A-frame and fairleaded downward to a turnbuckle secured to a concrete deadman. The whip block is two-blocked, and all slack is taken out of the span wire.

Line B in the illustration is the overhaul wire, and line C is the whip. A snatch block is secured approximately mid-length on the boom to receive the bight of a wire whose ends are secured ashore to a tow-drum winch or to two separate air winches. All three cables pass through a carriage or traveling block.

A detailed arrangement of A-frame boom, counterweight, and anchor and carriage is illustrated in Fig. 117. In the illustration, air winches are used, as well as a temporary boom mounted in concrete foundations and concrete deadmen. However, the stranded vessel's own booms may be used unless they are completely demolished. On vessels fitted with steam reciprocating deck winches, they may be fitted for use with compressed air. The compressed air is obtained from an air hose floated out to the vessel from ashore. If the deck winches are electric-motor-driven, air winches, or heavy gasoline-engine-driven, winches must be mounted on the stranded vessel to provide power for topping the boom.

A typical traveling block or carriage is illustrated in Fig. 118. The carriage is fitted with pulleys for all cables and is supported on the span wire by the two top pulleys. The center overhaul wire is not free to pass through the carriage. The lower whip cable is rove under the pulley of a descending block in the center of the carriage. The descending block supports the load transported, and it is held in place during transfer by a trigger bolt. The trigger bolt mechanism is integral with the carriage and is spring loaded. The trigger bolt normally locks in the descending block and is held in place by the pressure of a spring. The block is released by pulling on a trip line secured to the trigger bolt, which overcomes the tension of the spring, causing the bolt to slip out of the trigger bolt hole of the descending block.

The operation of a high line is not complicated. The descending block is lowered by releasing the trigger bolt, using the trip line and slacking off on the whip line. When the descending block reaches the ground, a load is attached and secured, the whip line heaved around on a winch, which lifts the descending block and load clear of the ground. A pull on the trip line will hold back the trigger bolt until the descending block is home. It is then released, causing the spring to force the trigger into the bolt hole, locking the descending block.

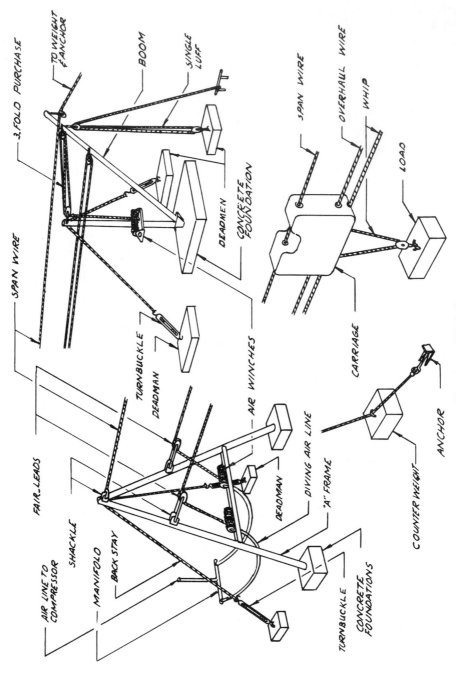

Fig. 117. High line gear.

With the descending block home and locked, the trip wire is aligned for a fairlead through the carriage and block pulleys for overhauling.

The overhaul wire is then slacked off while the whip wire is heaved around and the carriage is hauled over the span wire to the stranded vessel.

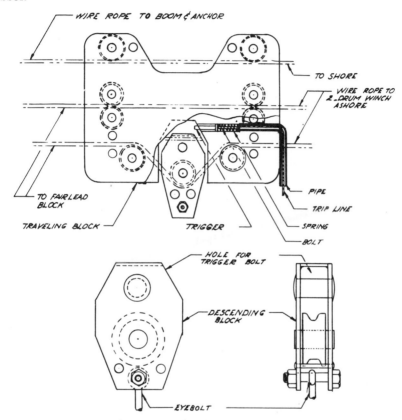

Fig. 118.   High line carriage.

When the load and carriage are over the deck of the stranded vessel, the trip line is pulled, releasing the descending block. The block is lowered by slacking off on the whip wire. In order to return the carriage, the procedure described above is reversed.

A simplified A-frame is illustrated in Fig. 119. Construction of this type is readily adaptable for use where great weights and large vessels are not involved. For small boat salvage or rescue, it can be quickly and inexpensively rigged. The deadman for the span wire is replaced by digging a deep trench and burying a long log transversely to the line of pull. The winch is mounted on a wood platform adjacent to the A-frame.

There are many types of high line and methods of rigging. Some lines are as simple as two single blocks strapped together and hauled by hand from the ship and shore alternately. Figure 120 shows a stranded vessel using a high line.

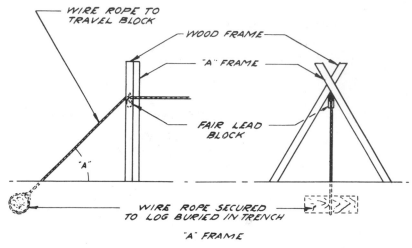

WIRE ROPE TO TRAVEL BLOCK

WOOD FRAME

"A" FRAME

FAIR LEAD BLOCK

"A"

WIRE ROPE SECURED TO LOG BURIED IN TRENCH

"A" FRAME

NOTE: ANGLE "A" NOT TO EXCEED 45°

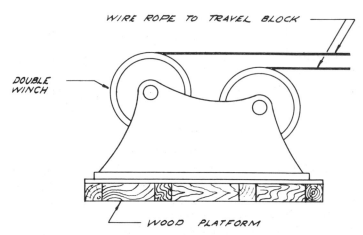

WIRE ROPE TO TRAVEL BLOCK

DOUBLE WINCH

WOOD PLATFORM

Fig. 119.   High line gear.

PROPELLER REMOVAL

Occasionally, in ship salvage work, it becomes necessary to remove the propeller of a stranded or sunken vessel.

The removal of a propeller from a small boat requires no great amount of work; however, a large vessel will require considerable

Fig. 120. High line rigged to stranded vessel.

rigging and time-consuming labor in order to remove the propeller. Figure 121 shows a detailed arrangement of the tapered tail shaft, nut, hub, fairwater, and method of securing the propeller to the tail shaft.

The propeller hub is fitted over the outboard, threaded, tapered end of the tail shaft and secured with a nut. A large tallow-filled fairwater cap is installed over the propeller nut and bolted to the propeller hub. The tallow prevents water from coming into contact with the tapered shaft threads or nuts. In order to remove the propeller, proceed as follows: Remove all stud nuts holding the fairwater cap to the propeller hub, except the top nut, which should not be removed. The fairwater cap is usually fitted with a plug for filling the fairwater with tallow. This plug is removed, and an eyebolt is inserted. A line is secured to the eyebolt, and a strain is maintained while the last top stud nut is removed. After the last stud nut is removed, the fairwater cap is lifted aboard the vessel, using the line secured to the eyebolt. It should be noted that the stud nuts are set in grooves

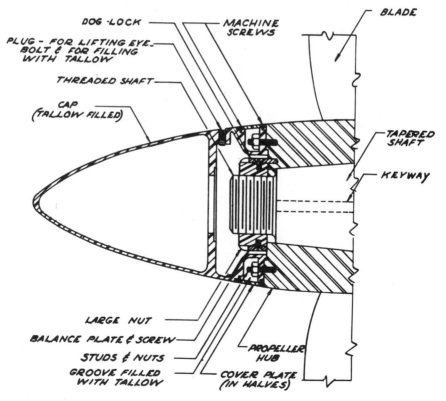

Fig. 121.   Method of securing propeller to shaft.

around the fairwater cap base. The grooves are usually filled with concrete. The propeller nut locking device is next removed. The propeller nut is now ready for backing off. The propeller nut wrench is next fitted to the propeller nut. The propeller wrench is rigged to a twofold chain-fall purchase, and a strain is taken, which usually loosens the nut. If the nut does not loosen, a force should be applied, using sledge hammers. The nut should then be backed off approximately halfway until the propeller is loosened. The propeller puller is fitted, and the propeller is backed off. After the propeller is loosened from the tapered shaft, the propeller nut should be removed all the way and taken on deck. A wire sling is fitted to an eyebolt inserted in the propeller hub. The propeller is rigged, as illustrated in Fig. 122, for removal and lifting aboard. The propeller and tail shaft are designed so that the tail shaft key will remain in the slot of the tail shaft when the propeller is removed. The backing-off wire, illustrated in Fig. 122, is fairleaded through a block, to enable a straight-line pull aft to a purchase on deck. This straight-line pull will prevent cocking the propeller and jamming it on the keyway.

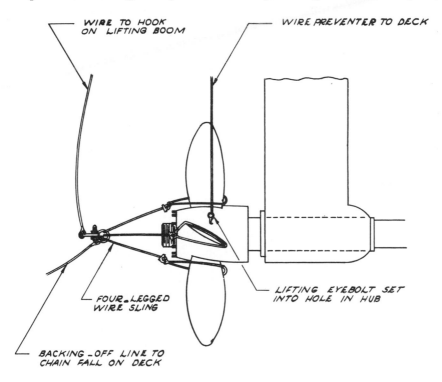

Fig. 122. Rigging for propeller removal.

The preventer wire to the deck should lead to a winch, and a slight strain is kept on the preventer wire while the propeller is being lifted off. After the propeller is completely free of the tail shaft, the preventer wire is slacked off, and the propeller is lifted to the deck from a wire leading to a boom on the upper deck. Many different methods are used to free the propeller nut and propeller. The exact method used will depend upon the experience of the people in charge and the particular type of operation preferred.

The sizes of the wires used in the rigging for the propeller will depend upon the weight of the propeller itself. Marlinspike Seamanship, Chapter IV, should be consulted for the proper size wire to be used for various weight propellers.

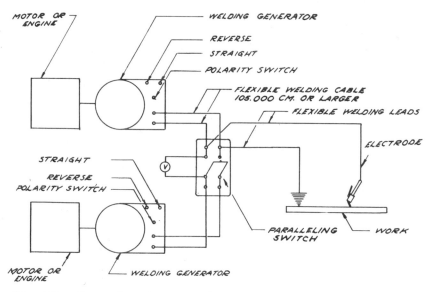

Fig. 123.   Connections for paralleling D.C. generator arc welding machine.

Basically, propeller removal is a problem in rigging, and careful consideration should be given to the planning and laying out of all wires, fairleads, blocks, and tackles.

Explosives have been used successfully from time to time for propeller removal, as well as for applying a force to the propeller nut wrench. Explosives should never be used, however, unless the salvage engineer has a thorough knowledge of their uses and applications, as serious damage can occur to the hull appendages and, possibly, to personnel.

Propeller removal on small boats requires less rigging than for large vessels and is a simple operation as compared with the foregoing method of removal of large ship propellers.

GAS HAZARDS

Gas is probably the most dangerous hazard encountered in ship salvage work. Whereas making a mistake in some phases of salvage can be rectified, a mistake where gas is involved can lead to loss of life. The entry of a man into a gaseous compartment that is not tested and proven gas-free is not a safe practice. The compartment must be certified safe prior to the admittance of any personnel.

Most gaseous compartments are dangerous, although they may have been open for ventilation for comparatively prolonged periods of time. The danger is even greater when they are open to other compartments that are not ventilated. Because toxic gases are usually heavier than air, the gas tends to flow to low points within a compartment much as water will flow; therefore, particular care must be taken to thoroughly ventilate low-lying areas of a compartment. It is not recommended that the safety of a compartment be judged solely by the presence or absence of low-lying gases, because some explosive gases that are commonly lighter than air may be trapped in the upper reaches of the compartment.

Most dangerous gases will readily dissolve in water. The amount that will dissolve will increase with an increase in the pressure of the water. Therefore, if the pressure on the water is released for some reason during the course of salvage, the dangerous gases will also be released. Consequently, care should be taken to insure that any water in a suspected compartment is pumped dry before anyone is permitted to enter the compartment.

In order to check whether gases may or may not be expected in a compartment, reference to the ship's manifest for the type of cargo carried should be made. The manifest will indicate the type, quantity, and location of all cargo aboard.

The following is a partial list of some of the materials carried aboard ships; however, it is not complete, so caution must be exercised to determine the nature and characteristics of each individual cargo.

Petroleum. Crudes may give off dangerous amounts of hydrogen sulphide, especially "sour" crudes, which may cause fires after air is admitted.

Bunker fuel usually will not give off inflammable vapors below the flash point temperature, which is over 150°.

Gasoline, naphthas, and light petroleum products present a serious explosion hazard.

Tankers with heavy internal tank scale are sometimes dangerous. After a tank has been vented and cleaned, the rust and scale may retain products that will later vaporize and pass into the tank atmosphere. The resultant mixture can be explosive.

The heat produced by welding on a fuel tank bulkhead may raise the temperature of the fuel and result in a serious explosion hazard.

Coal. Coal presents a fire hazard from spontaneous combustion. A coal bunker fire may give off carbon monoxide.

Cereal Products. Grain, sugar, molasses, starch, flour, and other cereal products in air when mixed with water will ferment, producing carbon dioxide. In the complete absence of air, they may give off a combustible gas-methane, in addition to carbon dioxide. The fermentation in air causes an atmosphere that is irritating to the eyes and unbreathable.

Animal Products. Hides, meat, fish, hair, wool, silk, etc., when mixed with water, will ferment and give off hydrogen sulphide and carbon dioxide.

Vegetable and Cellulose Fibers. Cotton, linen, rayon, paper, rope, and wood may ferment in absence of air and presence of high temperatures above 100° F. The presence of straw and sewage will favor fermentation. The danger from these products is less than with cereal products. However, the compartment or hold containing such materials must be tested before entering.

Following are the gases and the materials from which they are produced:

Hydrogen sulphide (H_2S) can usually be detected by a strong odor of rotten eggs. The usual test to detect the presence of the gas is to wet a piece of white paper with a solution of palladium chloride. The paper will turn gray or black in the presence of hydrogen sulphide. Hydrogen sulphide is usually present on shipboard where animal and organic materials, such as hides, meats, fish, and hair, are stowed in a decaying condition. The slow burning of wool, silk, hides, and hair will also produce hydrogen sulphide. Sewage produces large amounts of this gas.

The presence of hydrogen sulphide in the atmosphere will turn white lead to a brown or black color. Failing all else, small cans of white lead can be placed in suspect compartments during prolonged salvage operations, and the change of color can be noted. These samples should be placed in the lowest points in a compartment, as the gas, being heavy, will seek the lowest level.

Dioxide (O) is usually produced by decaying vegetable matter, smoldering coal, paper, and carbohydrates.

Hydrogen (H) is produced by storage batteries, acid action on steel, and fermentation.

Carbon monoxide (CO) is produced by smoldering wood, paper, coal, hides, and film. Generally speaking, this gas is produced by combustion and fire. It cannot be detected by smell, sight, or feel. It is a gas that is not as toxic as hydrogen sulphide; therefore, the hydrogen sulphide test may be used to determine its presence.

CL is produced by batteries and electrolytic action on salt water. *NH* is produced by burned wool or silk and is present in certain types of refrigerators.

Gases generally found in salvage work are classed under the following headings:

EXPLOSIVE	TOXIC	OXYGEN DEFICIENT
Crude oil	Carbon tetrachloride (154)	Rusting or oxidation of iron
Fuel oil	Sulphur dioxide (64)	Drying of paint
Exhaust gases	Hydrogen chloride (36. 5)	Fire
Gasoline (56)	Hydrogen sulphide (34)	Bacterial action
Alcohol (46)	Chlorine (71)	Fire extinguishers
Acetylene (26)	(02) (28)	Refrigerants
CO (28)		Carbon dioxide
Ammonia (18)		
Methane (16)		

The figures in parentheses following the gases, in the foregoing lists, indicate their molecular weight. Air has a molecular weight of 28. It will be noted that most explosive gases are lighter than air and most toxic gases are heavier than air.

All compartments in a vessel must be tested. The recommended order in testing for gases is: (1) explosive, (2) oxygen deficient, (3) toxic. Explosive gases being the most feared on shipboard, their presence should be detected as quickly as possible.

The most general means used today to detect explosive gases is the Davis Electrical Meter. In this meter, the gas is pumped through the instrument, using a hand pump or bulb, and passed over an electrical resistance. If an explosive gas is present, the resistance will be affected by the rise in temperature caused by the gas burning, and this change can be read on the millimeter. Two other methods, which are not in general use today for detecting explosives, are the flame safety lamp and the Burrel Indicator. Because they use a flame as a means of detection, there is a constant hazard of explosion, which may be caused by the meters themselves.

In the use of the flame safety lamp, the lamp is lowered slowly into a compartment, and one of the following three reactions may be observed if there is an explosive mixture in the atmosphere:

1. The flame pops slightly and goes out: explosive mixture present.

2. The flame flares up brightly: there is a lean mixture of explosive gas.

3. The flame flares up and goes out: there is a rich mixture present.

In the presence of an oxygen-deficient atmosphere, the flame will extinguish very rapidly. The gases causing an oxygen-deficient atmosphere are usually heavy and will seek the bottom of holds, tanks, or compartments; therefore, it is imperative that the test include all levels of these areas.

Oxygen deficiency, depending upon the amount or per cent of deficiency, may result in fatalities.

The results of oxygen deficiencies at various percentages are indicated in the following table:

PERCENTAGE OF OXYGEN IN AIR	EFFECT ON LIFE	EFFECT ON LAMP FLAME
None	Death	No flame
0-6%	Collapse in six to eight minutes	No flame
6-10%	Eventual collapse, but recovery with prompt treatment	No flame
10-16%	Dangerous, but usually not fatal	No flame
16-18%	Lowered efficiency, but usually no collapse	Dim flame
18-21%	Safe to work in	Moderate flame
21%	Normal air	Bright flame

The concentrations and effects of carbon monoxide and hydrogen sulphide are indicated in the following table:

PERCENTAGE OF GAS IN AIR	CARBON MONOXIDE	HYDROGEN SULPHIDE
0.4	Fatal in less than one hour	Rapidly fatal
0.2	Dangerous	Rapidly fatal
0.1	Not dangerous in less than one hour	Rapidly fatal
0.5	No effect after one hour	Dangerous in one-half hour
0.01	Bearable	Slightly harmful
0.005	No effect	Slight symptoms

To cope effectively with any of the foregoing gases, an oxygen mask is used.

VENTILATION

Ventilation is a process whereby air is caused to circulate through a room, compartment, hold, or enclosed space, so as to simultaneously replace foul air or gas.

Ventilation may be effected by natural draft, forced-draft fans, and exhaust blowers. Time is an important factor in ship salvage work, and confined shipboard spaces are not readily ventilated; consequently, ventilation through natural draft need not be considered.

Because toxic gases are usually heavier than air and access to most holds and compartments is from above, forced-draft fans will not prove so successful as exhaust blowers.

The flexible suction ducts of the exhaust blowers are run to the lowest point in the hold or other enclosed compartment, drawing the gases out. The gases should discharge to leeward through ducts at a location where they cannot re-enter the hull.

Example 1: Foul Air. Assume we have a hold 40' x 60' x 50'. The blower available is rated at 2,000 cubic feet per minute. How long will it take to ventilate the hold?

$$V = L \times B \times D$$

Volume $= 40' \times 60' \times 50'$

$$V = 120,000 \text{ cubic feet}$$

$$\text{Time} = \frac{2 \times \text{Volume}}{\text{Blower Capacity}}$$

$$T = \frac{2 \times 120,000}{2,000} = 120 \text{ Minutes}$$

Note: The "2" used to multiply the volume in the formula is a safety factor. The multiplier "2" allows for variables such as efficiency of the blower, mixing of gas and air, and duct resistance; therefore, it will take approximately two hours to ventilate the hold using the one blower.

Example 2: Toxic Gas. Where toxic gases are present, considerably more ventilation is required. The concentration of hydrogen sulphide (H_2S) must be kept below .01 per cent. The rate of generation of hydrogen sulphide is rather slow. If 0.20 cubic feet per minute of H_2S is generated and we must keep the concentration at 0.005 per cent, what blower capacity will be required? The problem is to determine in how much air we must dilute 0.20 cubic feet per minute of H_2S to obtain a concentration of 0.005 per cent:

$$\frac{0.20}{X} = \frac{0.005}{100}$$

$$\frac{X}{0.20} = \frac{100}{0.005}$$

$$X = \frac{100 \times 0.20}{0.005}$$

$$X = \frac{20}{0.005} = 4,000 \text{ cubic feet per minute}$$

Therefore, it will take a blower capacity of 4,000 cubic feet per minute to maintain a concentration of H_2S at 0.005 per cent.

Example 3: Explosive Gas. Explosive gases do not require the ventilation necessary for most toxic gases. Generally, it is believed explosive gases need only to be kept below a concentration of 0.5 per cent. To remove one cubic foot of explosive gas to maintain a concentration of 0.5 per cent, how much air will be needed?

$$\frac{1}{X} = \frac{.5}{100}$$

$$X = \frac{100}{.5} = 200 \text{ cubic feet of air}$$

Therefore, 200 cubic feet of air must be moved to maintain a concentration below 0.5 per cent. This is approximately ten times that necessary for carbon dioxide and approximately 1/50 that necessary for hydrogen sulphide.

SAFETY PRECAUTIONS

Gases in ship salvage work are generated from many materials. A complete study of the hazards due to gases and vapors in salvage operation is not possible here; but if salvage men realize from this writing the potential sources of danger from gas, which are latent hazards in most salvage operations, it will have served its purpose.

Cutting or **Welding** above or below water should never be attempted until it has been *positively* and is *periodically* established that there are no explosive mixtures present in the compartment where work is to be done and in adjacent compartments.

Canvas patches are susceptible to disintegration due to fermentation of cotton and other vegetable fibers.

Toxic gases held in suspension in water under pressure will be released when the pressure on the water is removed; therefore, limber holes should not be cut in a bulkhead to drain water in an adjacent flooded compartment or hold, unless oxygen masks are worn.

No closed space can be considered safe. Before any work can be accomplished in a compartment, it should be thoroughly ventilated and proven gas-free. The tests should be continued at regular intervals as long as the compartment is being worked.

Oxygen breathing apparatus must be donned before entering any compartment. A line should also be secured around the upper torso of a man entering a compartment so that if he collapses in a gaseous compartment he may be pulled out without exposing rescuers to the same hazard.

Chemicals. Never work in a hold in which the existence of chemicals is known without consulting a chemist.

Explosives. Never work in a vessel known to contain explosives without a thorough knowledge of the uses of explosives. Deteriorating explosives generate dangerous gases.

CUTTING AND WELDING

SURFACE OXYACETYLENE CUTTING

Surface oxygen and acetylene equipment consists of the following items:

1. Oxygen and acetylene cylinders.
2. Acetylene and oxygen regulators.
3. Oxygen and acetylene hoses.
4. Cutting torch.
5. Various sized cutting tips.
6. Goggles with clear lens, covered by shade lenses.
7. Torch igniter.
8. Protective clothing and gloves. The protective clothing is usually limited to a leather apron worn over regular work clothes.

Procedures to be followed in setting up the cutting equipment are:

1. Remove the cylinder valve protective caps and crack both the oxygen and acetylene cylinder valves to blow out the cylinder outlets. This should remove any dirt that may be lodged in the cylinder valve and prevent it from entering and clogging the regulator.

2. Connect the regulators to the cylinders.

3. Connect the oxygen and acetylene hoses to the regulators. Oxygen hose connections have right-hand threads, and acetylene hoses have left-hand threads. In addition, the acetylene hose usually has small grooves pressed or cut around all fittings. These fittings prevent the inadvertent interchange of both hoses. In many instances, the oxygen hose is colored green, while the acetylene hose is red.

4. New hoses are dusted internally with talc, so they should be blown out with compressed air before being used. If no compressed air is available, then blowing out with respective gases is advisable.

5. Connect the cutting torch with the proper size tip to the hoses.

6. Back off the regulator adjusting screw; that is, it should be turned counterclockwise, before opening the cylinder valves. When the regulator adjusting screw is backed off, the high-pressure side is closed off from the low-pressure side of the two-stage regulator. This procedure is advisable before admitting the high-pressure gas of the cylinder to the regulator in order to prevent damage to the rubber seat of the regulator. If the rubber seat is damaged, it may result in what is known as a "creeping" regulator. Damage to the rubber seat will also occur if the oxygen and acetylene bottles are jarred or rolled during transporting with the regulator adjusting screw screwed in (turned clockwise). Constant vibration will cause snapping of the seat and may result in damage.

7. Crack the oxygen cylinder valve and open slowly until pressure gradually builds up on the gauge. After pressure is built up, open the valve wide; then open the acetylene cylinder valve 3/4 to one turn.

8. Finally, adjust the working pressure on the regulators. The pressure used will be determined by the thickness of the plate to be cut, the size of the tip, and the experience of the operator.

The following chart will indicate the pressure values to be used for surface cutting:

TIP SIZE	OXYGEN PRESSURE	ACETYLENE PRESSURE	THICKNESS OF STEEL
No. 1	15-30 lbs.	3 lbs.	1/8" to 3/4"
No. 2	15-50 lbs.	5 lbs.	1/4" to 2"
No. 3	20-60 lbs.	5 lbs.	1/2" to 4"
No. 4	30-60 lbs.	5 lbs.	2" to 6"

As noted above, the exact pressure used will depend upon the experience of the operator.

The oxygen and acetylene pressures should be adjusted by the following methods:

1. Open up the acetylene inlet valve a couple of turns and screw in the regulator adjusting screw in a clockwise direction until the desired pressure is indicated on the gauge. Close the acetylene valve.

2. Open the oxygen valve and screw in the regulator adjusting screw in a clockwise direction until the desired working pressure is indicated on the gauge. Close the oxygen valve.

To ignite the torch, open up the acetylene valve about one turn and ignite the acetylene at the burner tip with a spark igniter. Then adjust the flame so that it appears to be about $\frac{1}{16}''$ to $\frac{1}{8}''$ away from the end of the tip. Open the oxygen valve and adjust the amount of oxygen for neutral combustion. Four small, distinct cones will appear at the end of the tip. If too much oxygen is used, the cones will be reduced in size. A feather will appear if there is not enough oxygen or too much acetylene.

Cutting Operations. To start a cut, place the tip of the cutting torch at the edge of the plate and allow the plate to build up to an ignition temperature, cherry red in color. Sparks emitting from the torch will also indicate a proper ignition temperature. The oxygen jet valve is then squeezed open, and the cut is started. The tip of the cutting torch should be kept approximately $\frac{3}{16}''$ to $\frac{1}{4}''$ above the plate during the cut. The advance along the plate should be slow and even. After the cut is completed, the torch is secured by closing first the acetylene and then the oxygen valves.

The cutting action obtained by an oxyacetylene cutting torch is basically a chemical process. The jet of oxygen, when directed against the red-hot plate of steel, causes the iron and oxygen to react chemically almost instantaneously. The resultant heat produces iron oxide, which melts and is blown away by the oxygen jet pressure. The process is similar to that which occurs in rusting, except that in oxyacetylene cutting the process is concentrated and speeded up thousands of times.

UNDERWATER OXYACETYLENE CUTTING

Compressed acetylene over 15 pounds per square inch becomes unstable, causing a breakdown of its chemical components, carbon and hydrogen. This instability of acetylene under pressure may cause it to explode; consequently, it should never be used, under any circumstances, at a pressure over 15 pounds per square inch. Because of this maximum operating pressure factor, acetylene cannot be used for underwater cutting beyond a depth of twenty feet.

UNDERWATER OXYHYDROGEN CUTTING

The underwater cutting equipment consists of the following:

1. Torches: The following commercial torches are available: Airco, Monarch, Victor, and KG.

2. Cylinders: An equal number of hydrogen and oxygen cylinders, with sufficient oxygen and hydrogen pigtails. Oxygen fittings have right-hand threads and hydrogen fittings have left-hand threads.

3. Regulators: One two-stage oxygen and hydrogen reducing valve.

4. Hose: One 100-foot length of twin hose for oxygen-hydrogen; one 100-foot length of green hose for air.

The procedures to be followed in setting up the cutting equipment are:

1. Attach the hydrogen regulator to the manifold on the oxygen-hydrogen cylinders.

2. The copper pigtail should be connected at one end to the oxygen manifold and at the other end to the inlet of a heating tank. The oxygen regulator should be connected on the shut-off valve on the tank.

3. All three lengths of hose should be properly attached to their respective sources of supply and then connected up to the cutting torch. The oxygen and hydrogen cylinder valves are cracked, and pressure is applied to the regulators as described in the foregoing procedures for oxyacetylene cutting. After the valves have been opened fully and the pressure has been regulated to the desired pressure on the gauges, the unit is ready for cutting operations.

Cutting Operations. Complete details cannot be given on how to use the underwater oxyhydrogen cutting torch, as experience in using the equipment is necessary in order to cut successfully.

To light the torch topside, crack the hydrogen valve and open approximately ½ to ⅔ of a turn. Ignite the hydrogen with the friction-type lighter. Increase the hydrogen flow slightly and open the oxygen needle valve. The flame can then be adjusted.

Adjust the preheat flame so that the flame appears colorless. The compressed air valve should be opened to a previously predetermined setting. The setting should have been determined by placing the torch under water and opening the air valve until a bubble approximately 3″ long extended from the end of the torch tip.

The torch is then passed to the diver in the water. A correctly adjusted flame will not extinguish. The diver, in preparing to cut, should compensate for the increased underwater pressure by making final adjustments on the pressures.

To light the torch under water, open up the hydrogen needle valve and adjust until a bubble of hydrogen about 2¼″ long appears at the end of the torch tip. Remember the setting and close the valve. Set the oxygen in the same manner. Then set the air valve for a bubble approximately 3 inches long. Next, open the hydrogen and oxygen valves to the original settings and bring the igniter to the tip of the torch and squeeze the igniter. The torch should now be ignited.

For actual cutting, place the tip of the torch above the edge of the work to be cut. Upon the occurrence of sparks, squeeze down on the oxygen jet valve. Cutting will now commence. Draw the torch along the line of cut slowly and evenly.

If the preheating flames do not heat the metal rapidly, readjust the oxygen and hydrogen alternately until a proper flame is obtained. The torch should be held approximately ⅛″ above the metal to be cut, and the metal should show a cherry-red color before the oxygen jet valve is squeezed.

The surface of all metals to be cut should be comparatively free of all rust, scale, heavy coats of paint, etc., which will prevent the preheating flame from reaching the metal and consequently tend to dissipate much of the heat of the flame.

When securing the torch under water, the hydrogen should be turned off first.

Experienced divers can usually tell by the sound of the flame under water when the torch flame is properly set and when the metal is actually being pierced after turning on the oxygen.

Tip sizes are also an important consideration in underwater cutting operations. It is equally possible to use a large cutting tip ineffectively as to use a too small cutting tip ineffectively.

The following chart indicates the approximate operating pressures to be used for this type of underwater cutting torch.

The hydrogen pressure will vary from 20 pounds for No. 1 tip, 25 pounds for No. 2 tip, to 30 pounds for No. 3 tip. The pressure should be increased approximately one-half pound for every foot the diver descends. If more than one section of 100-foot length of hose is used, the pressures should be increased accordingly.

DEPTH BELOW WATERLINE (FEET)	AIR PRESSURE (POUNDS)	UP TO 1" NO. 1 TIP	UP TO 2" NO. 2 TIP	UP TO 3" NO. 3 TIP
		Oxygen (In Pounds per Square Inch)		
10	20	50	60	70
20	25	55	65	75
30	30	59	69	79
40	35	63	75	84
50	42	66	80	90
60	48	71	84	94
70	55	76	87	98
80	62	82	95	104
90	70	85	98	108
100	75	89	103	115

ARC-OXYGEN UNDERWATER CUTTING

The arc-oxygen method of underwater cutting is similar in operation to surface electric welding, except that the electrode is tubular and hollow. After an arc is struck under water, the oxygen jet valve is squeezed, and a jet of oxygen is discharged through the center of the tubular electrode and against the metal to be cut. The arc or spark ignites the oxygen, and the metal is cut through oxidation. The cutting is most effective against steel.

Two types of steel tubular electrodes are widely used: the type CP electrode, manufactured by the Metal and Thermit Corporation, and the Cutend V electrode, manufactured by the Arcos Corporation. The type CP electrode has a pink coating; the Cutend V has a gray coating.

There are several other types of covered steel tubular electrodes available commercially.

Operation. For underwater arc cutting, a welding machine having a capacity of 300 amperes is recommended. In the event it becomes necessary to parallel two D.C. welding machines, the following steps should be taken:

1. Install a double pole, single throw, unfused safety switch on the welding leads.

2. Set both machines on straight polarity.

3. Each machine should be set so that under a load each will carry half the load.

4. Adjust the voltages on both operating machines so that they are equal. This is necessary to prevent reversing polarity on one machine.

5. Connect jumpers from the machine to a paralleling switch.

6. Install a voltmeter at the parallel switch. With the parallel switch open, start both machines and equalize the voltage as pre-

viously described. Next, close the parallel switch. The voltmeter should now register zero volts, and the ammeters on the welding generators should register zero current.

7. The generators are not properly paralleled if there is a voltage reading or if the ammeters read over the 25 amps. In this event, the paralleling switch should be opened, the circuits and voltages rechecked, and paralleling procedures started again.

8. With the machines properly paralleled, connect the grounding lead to the work, pass an insulated electrode holder to the diver and cut in the line switch when notified by the diver.

9. The work of cutting now commences.

Note: A line switch is always installed after the parallel switch and before the flexible welding leads. The diver will always control when the line switch is to be closed or opened, by verbal orders or prearranged signals.

Figure 123 illustrates the connections for paralleling two D.C. generator arc welding machines.

METALLIC-ARC UNDERWATER CUTTING

Metallic-arc cutting is a method of underwater cutting that can be used when oxygen is not available. Of course, the thickness of metal that can be cut is limited, but the method is most effective when used on steel less than $\frac{1}{4}$-inch thick and for cutting nonferrous metals.

Standard welding electrodes are used. The electrodes are covered. The cutting technique requires that the electrode be dragged across the work, for it is the heat of the electric arc that melts the metal. The metal does not oxidize as it does when using oxygen.

Operation. For underwater metallic-arc cutting, welding machine of at least 400 amperes' capacity is recommended. In the event it becomes necessary to parallel two D.C. welding machines for increased power output, follow the procedure described above under Arc-Oxygen Underwater Cutting.

For 300 amperes, use $\frac{3}{16}''$ electrodes, and, for 400 amperes, use $\frac{1}{4}''$ electrodes.

The same type of electrode holder used in air may be used for underwater work, provided it is thoroughly and completely insulated. This is a difficult process, and a doubtful electrode holder should not be used under water if the operator is uncertain whether it is properly insulated.

UNDERWATER WELDING

Because of advances in recent years in underwater welding, 50 per cent of the strength of surface welds can be attained under water. The equipment used for underwater welding consists of the following:

1. Electrode holder: A special type of holder that is insulated completely and thoroughly. When a commercial underwater welding holder is not available, a surface welding electrode holder may be used, provided it is well insulated and taped.

2. Electrode: The standard electrode to be used should be approximately $\frac{5}{32}''$ or $\frac{3}{16}''$ diameter. The electrodes should be dipped in waterproofing solution of a commercial type prior to use in water.

3. Waterproofing solution: Any of the following may be used for electrode waterproofing:

a. "Ucilon"—Manufactured by the United Chromium Corporation, New York City.

b. "Selac"—Manufactured by the Duralac Chemical Corporation, Newark, New Jersey.

c. A celluloid and acetone solution made up of approximately one-half pound of celluloid to one gallon of acetone.

Welding Techniques. For horizontal and vertical fillet welds, a $\frac{3}{16}''$ electrode is recommended; however, when welding to thin or light material, a $\frac{5}{32}''$ electrode will be used with greater success. The self-consuming technique is used when welding under water. Before any type of welding is commenced, the surface of the work must be adequately prepared to receive the weld. All rust, scale, paint, and marine growth must be removed. It is practically useless to start welding on a fouled surface.

Welding Operations. The following procedure may be used for underwater welding:

1. With the welding machine on, or with two machines running parallel and the safety switch open, the diver descends to the job.

2. The surface of the metal to be welded is thoroughly cleaned and brushed by the diver, using wire brushes, scrapers, or even pneumatic tools where necessary.

3. Set the current on the welding generator to approximately 30 per cent above the normal current used for topside welding.

4. The diver then places the electrode against the work and calls for "switch on." The safety switch topside is closed by his tender. The circuit should now be completed, causing an arc to strike immediately.

5. During the welding process, an angle of approximately 30 degrees plus or minus 15 degrees should be maintained between the electrode and the surface of the work. The electrode should be held against the work with sufficient pressure to allow the electrode to consume itself.

6. After the electrode is completely consumed, the diver calls for "switch off." The safety switch is immediately opened by the tender, and the diver changes electrodes. After a change of electrodes, the diver may again call for "switch on."

The techniques for underwater welding are basically the same as those used for surface welding, and improvement is only gained after much practice. However, the need for underwater welding practice is not as great as for surface welding.

Welding Machines. For underwater welding, a welding machine of at least 300 amperes' capacity is recommended. In the event it becomes necessary to parallel two D.C. welding machines for increased power output, follow the procedure described above under Arc-Oxygen Underwater Cutting.

If a 200 or 300 ampere welding generator is not available, the 300 ampere A.C. transformer may be used; however, use of the A.C. transformer requires additional safety precautions because of the greater danger of electric shock.

The safety switch should be installed in the welding circuit. The switch should never be opened or closed except on orders from the diver. In securing the ground lead, the diver should clamp the lead as close as possible to the work in the vicinity of the welding.

In any underwater cutting or welding operation involving the use of welding machines, the diver should be fully insulated from the work, the torch, and from the water itself; consequently, a deep sea diving dress is used. At no time should the diver get between the electrode and the ground, nor should he allow any part of his body to come into contact with any part of the grounded work.

Safety. Underwater welding is extremely dangerous due to the explosion hazard. Underwater welding will produce up to 70 per cent hydrogen, and, unless this gas is vented from the compartment where work is being done, there is a grave possibility that the collected gases may explode, resulting in fatalities or disaster.

No underwater welding or cutting operation should be commenced without the supervision of a thoroughly experienced diver who has a complete knowledge of underwater welding and cutting.

GLOSSARY

Abaft. Aft; toward the stern of; to the rear.

Abeam. At right angles to the keel; abreast.

Aces. Lengths of steel rod shaped at the end into hooks which are used to pile and stow the anchor chain in the chain locker.

After perpendicular. The vertical line intersecting the load waterline at the after end of the sternpost.

Air holes. Small holes cut into longitudinals and floors of confined compartments in order to permit venting while pumping the compartment.

Amidships. A term used to define the center section of a vessel as opposed to its bow and stern ends.

Anchor. A cast steel or heavy iron shaped implement fitted with tapered flukes which engage the ground. The vessel is connected to the anchor with a length of chain cable or wire rope, and as a result the vessel remains stationary in the water.

Aperture. The space provided for the propeller between the stern frame and the sternpost, bounded at the bottom by the skeg and at the top by the oxter plates.

Appendages. Those fittings and structures which extend beyond the outline of the hull; that is, bilge keels, rudder, rudderpost, strainers, struts, skeg, etc.

Arch piece. The upper curved section of the stern frame in way of the aperture oxter plates at the junction of the propeller post and the sternpost.

Astern. 1. To the rear or abaft of an imaginary transverse line drawn at the stern of a vessel.

2. The movement of a vessel backwards.

3. The direction the main engine is turning as opposed to ahead.

Barge. A craft of steel or wood construction used to transport cargo over water. A true barge is nonself-propelled.

Bar keel. A solid heavy wrought iron bar of rectangular cross section used in older ships.

Bearding. The line of intersection at the junction of the butts of plates and the stem of sternpost.

Bending slab. Heavy, rectangular or square, cast iron latticed blocks over 2 in. thick on which shapes may be bent.

Bight. The middle part of a rope forming a loop.

Bilge. The lowest portion of a vessel inside the hull.

Bilge keel. Longitudinal steel plates fitted externally along the bilge strake to decrease rolling of the vessel; commonly called *rolling chocks*.

Bitter end. The inboard end of any line, cable, anchor chain or pendant. The end opposite to the anchor end.

Bitts. A heavy steel casting used to lead and secure mooring or towing hawsers to a dock or tug. Usually constructed of two short vertical cylindrical capped hollow posts fitted to a base plate which distributes the load to the deck plating. The base plate is drilled for attaching to the deck with bolts.

Block. The combination of frame and pulley, or sheave, bounded and secured by a strap and pins, and mounted with a hook and becket which is used to gain advantage or fair-lead in the make-up of lines attached to a load.

Bottom, outer. The outer shell bottom plating of a double-bottom vessel, the inner bottom being the tank tops.

Bower. An anchor carried in the hawse pipe at the bow of a vessel.

Brace. A diagonal transverse or longitudial shape or structural member used to strengthen, stiffen and distribute the load between structures.

Brackets. Small pieces of plate, usually triangular in shape, used to join beams to frames, frames to floors, etc.

Breast hooks. Horizontal steel plates installed internally at the bow to stiffen the bow plating against *panting*.

Broach. To veer with the set; a stranded vessel lying broadside to the shore as a result of the effects of winds, seas, or currents.

Buoy. A stationary floating object moored to the bottom with an anchor and cable.

Camber. The transverse curvative of any deck.

Chafing gear. Material, such as canvas, wood, or soft metal, installed on wire or fibre rope in way of sharp corners or contact with other surfaces in order to minimize the effects of rubbing and wearing.

Chamfer. The angle of the joint formed by cutting a bevel into the faces of two adjoining wood surfaces.

Coaming. The vertical plating fitted around the periphery of a hatch opening.

Coefficient of friction. The friction loss due to the contact of a vessel's bottom with various types of ground: that is, sand, mud, coral, rock, etc.

Cofferdam. A watertight structure temporarily installed on a submerged vessel to obtain freeboard in order to pump out the water and raise the vessel.

Collar. A plate doubler fitted around a pipe at its penetration through a bulkhead or deck in order to make for a watertight joint.

Counter. The section of the ship which extends abaft of the sternpost and overhangs the aperture and rudder.

Dead rise. The amount of vertical rise of the bottom from the keel to the turn of the bilge, also called the *rise of floor*.

Deadwood. The portion of the hull in way of the sternpost and the keel. There is no internal space in way of the deadwood.

Deck beam. A horizontal transverse shape connecting the port and starboard shell frames. The deck plating is secured on top of the deck beams.

Deck girder. Horizontal, longitudinal shape or deep plate built-up structural, attached beneath the deck beams to distribute the load on deck to the stanchions.

Deck stringer plate. The heavier outboard strake of main deck plating which is connected to the gunwale bar and the sheer strake.

Deep frame. A special frame of greater width than the normal frame through which side stringers pass and which provide added transverse strength.

Devil's claw. A hook-shaped clamp, forked to engage a link of anchor chain and hold the anchor and chain while the wildcat of the anchor windlass is disengaged.

Dished plates. The shape of the flat plate keel when it is slightly flanged upward where it joins the garboard strakes.

Dolly bar. A curved offset holding-on hammer used to back up a rivet being driven in an inaccessible space.

Dolphin. A cluster of numerous piles driven adjacent to each other and bound together with wire rope, clamps, and through bolts which is used to fend and warp vessels docking.

Double bottom. A vessel fitted with bottom tanks extending from the bottom plating to approximately 4 ft. high to the inner bottom plating or tank top is said to have a double bottom.

Doubler. A steel plate of small dimensions used to reinforce openings in the hull for additional strength, or to repair small holes or cracks.

Drag. A vessel is said to have drag when it is trimmed by the stern.

Drain holes. Small holes drilled in way of the bottom of longitudinals and floors to facilitate the draining of liquids when pumping.

Eyebolt. A piece of solid stock threaded at one end and bent back upon itself to form a loop on the other end and shaped to receive the pin of a shackle.

Falls. The rope which makes up the tackle rove through the sheaves of a block.

Flat plate keel. A fabricated steel keel built up from three members: the flat plate or dished keel, the center vertical keel or keelson and the rider plate.

Floor plates. Usually diamond plate, fitted above the floors to facilitate traversing internal bottom areas.

Fluke. The tapered prong of an anchor at the palm, which holds the ground.

Foot valve. A clapper valve installed on the lower end of a vertical suction pipe in order to permit the flow of liquid in one direction only. It prevents the liquid from flowing downward and thus aids the pump in maintaining suction.

Forefoot. That part of the lower end of the stem which is connected to the keel.

Frames. Vertical structural shapes, extending from the floors in way of the margin plate to the junction of the deck stringer plate and sheer strake. Frames determine the shape of the hull. The shell plating is attached to the frames.

Framing, Isherwood System. A longitudinal system of framing having numerous continuous longitudinals, stringers and girders, and fewer widely spaced deep frames or web frames, commonly used in tanker construction.

Freeboard. The distance between the surface of the water and the main deck. It is the measurement of the reserve buoyancy of a vessel.

Freeing ports. Openings in the lower ends of bulwarks at the deck to allow for quick drainage of water and thus freeing the deck of the weight of seas. Sometimes fitted with swing check gates and gaskets to allow for the passage of water in one direction only— overboard.

Furnaced plate. A plate which requires heating in order to shape and fashion it to unusual curvature.

Garboard strake. The first longitudinal strake of plating secured to the dished keel. It is usually heavier plate than the adjacent bottom plating and is identified as "A" strake.

Gross tonnage. A volumetric measurement of the internal capacity of a vessel, assuming 100 cu. ft. to equal 1 ton.

Grounding. A vessel's bottom touching ground voluntarily or involuntarily, or a vessel resting on the bottom as a result of tide changes, currents, etc., but, in any instance, the vessel is capable of refloating itself.

Ground tackle. The combination of planted anchor and cable.

Gudgeon. A projection of the rudder post fitted with a bushing in order to receive the pintle of the rudder blade.

Gunwale bar. A structural shape, usually angle bar, used to tie together the deck stringer plate and the sheer strake.

Guys. Wire or manila rope falls and pendants used to maintain lateral position of booms, davits, spars, masts, etc.

Hawser. A hemp or Manila rope of large circumference, or a wire rope of large diameter, used for mooring or towing.

Hogging. 1. The tendency of a vessel to arch amidship, that is, to lower at both ends and simultaneously rise amidship as a result of loading, or working in seas.
2. The practice of hauling a patch to a ship's side using lines which extend below the patch and beneath the hull.

Intercostal. An internal structural shape, either longitudinal or transverse, which is cut to allow the passage of a continuous member at right angles to the run of the intercostal.

Joggling. The offsetting of the edge of a plate or structural by knuckling to allow a fair outline in way of lapped joints.

Jumping the line. The practice of a tugboat coming up taut suddenly on a slack tow hawser using full power.

Knuckle. A change in direction of plating, framing, or hull structure usually within a short radius.

Lightening holes. Large holes cut or punched in a floor, or deep web frame, in order to reduce the weight of the member without sacrificing strength.

Limber holes. Small holes cut or drilled in the lower ends of floors and longitudinals to permit the passage of water for drainage.

Main deck. The principal strength deck in the vessel and the upper flange of the hull girder. The main deck is usually an exposed deck and consequently is sometimes called the *weather deck.*

Margin plank. The notched, wood deck plank extending around the outboard edge of the main deck of a vessel to which the deck planks are fitted. In costly yacht construction, the margin plank is unnotched and continuous.

Margin plate. The outboard diagonal plate which connects the inner bottom plating to the shell plating at the turn of the bilge. The margin plate is the outer limit of the double-bottom tank.

Messenger. A convenient line of small diameter used to pass a line of larger diameter.

Net tonnage. A volumetric measurement of the internal capacity of a vessel, assuming 100 cu. ft. to equal 1 ton. The measurement excludes the crew quarters and machinery spaces. It is the measurement of the passenger- and cargo-carrying capacity of a vessel.

Nose plate.   The vertical shaped and furnaced rounded plate fitted around the forward face of the stem which joins the forward edges of the port and starboard strakes and provides a stem fairwater to permit easy entrance of the bow.

Oakum.   Strands of hemp or jute impregnated with pine tar, used for caulking the seams and butts of planking of wood vessels to make for a watertight joint.

Oxter plates.   Plates attached to the stern frame forming the counter in way of the rudderpost.

Padeye.   The combination of a circle of steel stock secured to a doubler plate which is attached to a deck, bulkhead, overhead, or structural. It is used to secure blocks, stoppers, rigging, deck cargo, straps, etc. The doubler serves to distribute the load over a greater area.

Panting.   The tendancy of the bow plating to move in and out as a result of the water pressure differential caused by a vessel pitching in a seaway.

Peak tanks; fore and after.   Large compartments located at the bow and stern of a vessel for the storage of water or ballast. Peak tanks are fitted with piping for the transfer of water. The trim of the vessel can be changed by transferring water from one tank to the other.

Pelican hook.   A quick-release hinged hook used where speed in disconnecting is a prime requisite.

Pintles.   Vertical pins attached to rudders which fit into gudgeons on the rudderpost about which the rudder pivots.

Pitch, propeller.   The distance the blade of a propeller will advance during one complete revolution.

Planking.   The wood covering of a hull and decks. Planking is secured to frames, floors, and beams.

Plumb line.   A weight bob and line used to measure vertical dimensions and horizontal deflection.

Pontoon.   A portable steel tank or fabric balloon used to displace water and provide positive buoyancy. The lifting capacity of a pontoon is equal to the weight of the volume of water displaced.

Rabbet.   A step in the edge of a material to receive an adjoining material and make for a fair surface. The stem is rabbeted to receive the shell plating.

Rake.   An inclination from the vertical of a mast, stem, stack etc., usually in a fore and aft direction. A term also applied to the bow and/or stern compartments of certain barges.

Ram plates.   Vertical plates installed in way of the inner bow spaces to prevent "panting" of the bow plating. Usually fitted in conjunction with breasthooks.

Rider plate. The horizontal centerline plate fitted on top of the center vertical keelson and installed as a reinforcement in the total keel construction. The plate is generally extra heavy.

Rigging. The guys, standing and running Manila and wire ropes used to support and operate the movable parts of masts, booms, and king posts of a vessel.

Rise of floor. Commonly called the *dead rise*, it is the distance that the bottom of a vessel rises determined from a measurement between the keel and the turn of the bilge.

Rolling chocks. Longitudinal steel plates fitted externally along the bilge strake in order to decrease transverse rolling of a vessel; it is sometimes called the *bilge keel*.

Sagging. The tendancy of a vessel to sag in the middle; that is, to be supported at both ends and simultaneously to lower amidship as a result of loading or of running in a seaway.

Saloon. The officer's dining room on a merchantman.

Scantlings. The dimensions of shapes, plating, etc., used in the construction of vessels.

Sea chest. A structure fitted to the internal shell plating below the waterline to which valves and pipes are attached for supplying water to condensers and engines, sanitary water, etc. The structure is usually box-shaped and fitted with external strainers.

Set. The direction in motion of a current, wind, or sea, or a combination thereof.

Shapes. Rolled steel bars of various cross sections used for framing, stiffening and connecting plating.

Sheer strake. The uppermost side shell row of plates secured longitudinally to the gunwale bar.

Skeg. The lower extension of the stern frame of a vessel that extends aft of the sternpost and is used to support the rudderpost. It confines the lower limit of the aperture.

Snatch block. A block which can be opened at one end to receive the bight of a rope.

Soft patch. A temporary repair to a crack or hole in a plate. The small steel patch is secured with bolts and made tight with a gasket and sealing compound.

Sound. The practice of measuring depth with a line and weight.

Spar. A length of wood or steel of circular cross section serving as a mast, boom, or yard.

Splice. A method of joining two ropes together or of forming a loop in a line by bending back the line onto itself. The splice is made by unlaying the strands and interweaving to form a permanent connection.

Stem. The bow frame casting at the extreme forward end of a ship to which the Number 1 plates of all strakes are attached. The nose plating is fitted around the forward end of the stem.

Stiffener.   Any shape used to provide rigidity and strength to the plating of a bulkhead. The shapes most commonly used for stiffeners are: the angle bar, tee bar, flat bar, zee bar, and bulb angle bar.

Strake.   A continuous row of plating from the bow to the stern, identified by letters, beginning with "A" strake which is the garboard strake and continuing outward and upward to the sheer strake. The letter "I" is not used to identify a strake and it is always omitted.

Stranding.   A grounded vessel incapable of freeing itself unassisted is stranded.

Stringer.   1. Longitudinal side shell internal stiffeners.
2. Diagonal side frames to which the treads and handrails of ladders are attached.
3. The outboard plating of any deck.

Superstructure.   A bridge, pilothouse, cabin, mast, or similar structure built above the main deck.

Tackle.   A term applied to the combination of falls and blocks used to gain advantage in power, or for fairlead.

Tank top.   The plating, sometimes called the inner bottom, which confines the upper limits of a double-bottom tank.

Template.   A pattern shaped to the dimensions and form of a piece of work that is to be fabricated. Information such as sizes of laps, thickness of plate, location of rivet holes, type of weld, etc., is indicated on the template.

Tooker patch.   A hinged circular watertight patch constructed in halves for installation over portholes.

Trim.   To adjust the fore and aft drafts by transferring cargo or ballast longitudinally within a vessel.

Tripping bracket.   Small plates or flat bars attached at right angles to floors, keelsons, girders and beams at intervals along their length as a reinforcement to prevent racking.

Tumblehome.   The gradual narrowing of a vessel's beam from the water line to the top of the sheer strake.

Visor.   The small inclined canvas or metal awning extending around the pilothouse over the portholes or windows to reduce sun glare.

Whaler.   A length of heavy timber or steel structural shape to which planks are fastened to form a bulkhead or cofferdam. Sometimes used to temporarily shore or stiffen bulkheads or decks.

Wrenching.   To alternately pull in opposite directions on the outshore end of a stranded vessel in an attempt to wrench the vessel free of the ground.

Appendix

REPORTS AND RECORDS

The successful planning of any salvage operation requires the accumulation of detailed information which is readily available for quick reference. To best meet the foregoing requirement, the information should be recorded in the form of records, reports, and survey data sheets.

Salvage ventures are as unique as the techniques of the salvage engineers; therefore, no two plans will be alike. Although the plans will be different, certain basic information should be accumulated and recorded. This Appendix contains some of the suggested records which may be kept. Regardless of the final form adopted by the salvage engineer, the basic information recorded here should be ascertained. The author would vary the details of the information suggested, depending upon the size and scope of the operation.

SOUNDING RECORD

S. S. _____   DATE _____
OFF. NO. _____   TIME _____
GROSS TONS _____
DATE OF STRANDING _____

	PORT					BOW	STARBOARD				
	50'	40'	30'	20'	10'	:	10'	20'	30'	40'	50'
0'						:					
20'						:					
40'						:					
60'						:					
80'						:					
100'						:					
120'						:					
140'						:					
160'						:					
180'						:					
200'						:					
220'						:					
240'						:					
260'						:					
280'						:					
300'						:					

TIDE: High ____ A. M.   Low ____ A. M.
           ____ P. M.   ____ P. M.

TYPE OF BOTTOM: Sand __ , Mud __ , Coral __ , Rock __ .

NOTES:
1. Check actual soundings against tide tables.
2. Use separate record sheets for each set of sounding, or record a high and low in each box.
3. Indicate on record location of outshore extremity of stranded vessel and deep water.

WEATHER RECORDINGS

S. S. _____ LOCATION:

OFF. NO. _____ LONG. _____

GROSS TONS _____ LAT. _____

DATE OF CASUALTY _____

Time	Date	Sky	Wind Direction	Wind Velocity	Temperature Wet	Dry	Barometric Pressure	Sea Temp.
0000								
0400								
0800								
1200								
1600								
2000								
2400								
0000								
0400								
0800								
1200								
1600								
2000								
2400								

WEATHER BUREAU REPORTS:

24 HOUR FORECAST _____

LONG RANGE FORECAST _____

STRANDING

TOP SIDE SURVEY

DATE OF SURVEY_____   TYPE_____
VESSEL NAME _____   GROSS TONS_____
OFF. NO._____   FLAG_____
OWNER _____

LOCATION_____
DATE OF CASUALTY_____   START OF SALVAGE_____
BUILT BY_____, AT_____, DATE_____
CONSTRUCTED OF WOOD_____, STEEL_____
DISPLACEMENT_____
LENGTH_____ BEAM_____   DEPTH_____

EXAMINED
YES   NO
_____

DECK LOG_____
ENGINE LOG_____
CURVES OF FORM _____
SHIP'S PLANS_____
CARGO MANIFEST_____

TIDE TABLES:
    DEPTH AT TIME OF STRANDING_____
    MAXIMUM HIGH TIDES_____

WEATHER:
    WIND VELOCITY AT TIME OF STRANDING_____
    EXPECTED WEATHER_____

CURRENT:
    DIRECTION_____ SEAS _____
    SPEED_____ SURF_____

TYPE OF GROUND: _____ COEFF. OF FRICT._____

DEGREE OF LIST: _____ TO PORT - STARBOARD_____

DRAFTS:	FWD	AFT	MEAN
BEFORE STRANDING	_____	_____	_____
AFTER STRANDING	_____	_____	_____
CHANGE IN DRAFT	_____	_____	_____

CHANGE IN MEAN DRAFT - INCHES_____
TONS PER INCH IMMERSION_____
GROUND REACTION (tons aground)_____

SALVAGE PLAN

STRANDING

1. TONS AGROUND _____
2. TONS REMOVED _____
3. TONS PULL, BEACH GEAR _____
4. TONS PULL, TUGS _____

STRANDED
VESSEL

N

W   •   E

S

COMPASS ROSE

NOTES:
1. Draw in outline of stranded vessel.
2. Draw shoreline in relation to stranded vessel.
3. Indicate the direction on compass rose.
4. Indicate direction and force of any set.
5. Fill in tons, for 1, 2, 3 and 4.
6. 2, 3 and 4 should cancel out 1
7. Plot the beach gear anchors and indicate bearings for range markers.

EQUIPMENT AVAILABLE:

PUMPS:	TYPE	NUMBER	SIZE	CAPACITY (Tons/Hr)

WINCHES: ELECTRIC _____, STEAM _____.
POWER SUPPLY: A. C. _____, D. C. _____, VOLT. _____, CYCLE _____.
AIR COMPRESSORS: NUMBER _____, C. F. M. _____, PRESSURE _____.
BOILERS: TYPE _____, Lbs/Hr _____, PRESSURE _____.
PORTABLE MACHINERY.

	CARGO	BALLAST
No. 1 HOLD		
No. 2 HOLD		
No. 3 HOLD		
No. 4 HOLD		
No. 5 HOLD		
No. 6 HOLD		
No. 7 HOLD		

FUEL OIL & FRESH WATER:

LOCATION	AMOUNT(tons)
F. O.	
F. O.	
F. O.	
F. O.	
F. W.	
F. W.	

WEIGHT REMOVAL:

ESTIMATED CARGO REMOVAL (Tons) _____

    "   FUEL   "   "   _____

    "   WATER   "   "   _____

    "   BALLAST "   "   _____

    "   TOPSIDE "   "   _____

    "   TOTAL   "   "   _____

*   "   TONS AGROUND AFTER REMOVALS _____ PULL

NUMBER OF SETS OF BEACH GEAR _____ , _____ TONS _____

    "   " TUGS   _____ , _____ TONS _____

TOTAL PULL DEVELOPED _____ ** TONS _____

(** MUST EQUAL OR EXCEED *.)

CONDITION OF HULL

DAMAGE:	Location	Nature	Extent	Flooded? Capacity (tons)
				#2 Deep Tk
Example 1.	Fr. 66, P.	Hole	2' x 3'	Flooded 80 Tons
Example 2.	#5 Hold, S.	Hole	4' x 5'	Partially Flooded 300 Tons
Example 3.	Main Deck #3 Hold, P.	Crack	10' x 0''	

BULKHEADS:

DECKS:

INTERNALS:

	A TONS	B DAYS, HOURS.
TONS CARGO TO BE REMOVED, ESTIMATED TIME REQUIRED		
TONS LIQUID TO BE PUMPED, ESTIMATED TIME REQUIRED		
LAYING BEACH GEAR		
PATCHING		

MAXIMUM TIME LISTED IN COLUMN "B"

TIME OF MAXIMUM HIGH TIDE: _____

Month   Day   Year

DESCRIPTION OF PROPOSED SALVAGE (Detail):

SALVAGE LOG:

DIVING RECORD

S.S. _____ DIVER'S NAME _____

OFF. NO. _____ RIG:

GROSS TONS _____   DEEP SEA _____

DATE OF CASUALTY _____   SHALLOW WATER _____

    SCUBA _____

DATE	DEPTH OF DIVE	TIME ON BOTTOM	OFF BOTTOM	DIVING TIME	(C - Complete) (I - Incomplete) TYPE JOB (Brief)
_____	_____	_____	_____	_____	_____
_____	_____	_____	_____	_____	_____
_____	_____	_____	_____	_____	_____
_____	_____	_____	_____	_____	_____
_____	_____	_____	_____	_____	_____
_____	_____	_____	_____	_____	_____
_____	_____	_____	_____	_____	_____
_____	_____	_____	_____	_____	_____
_____	_____	_____	_____	_____	_____

LOCATION:

        LONG. _____

        LAT. _____

TYPE OF BOTTOM _____

DIRECTION OF CURRENT _____

SPEED OF CURRENT _____

CLOSURE LOG

S. S._____

OFF. NO._____

GROSS TONS_____

OPENING		CLOSED, PATCHED, OR PLUGGED	DATE	BY WHOM
TYPE	LOCATION			

NOTES:
1. List all hull openings; sea chests, portholes, etc.
2. List all internal openings; doors, hatches, etc.
3. Record method used to close openings, etc.

Index

INDEX